Praise for *Slava!*

"A much-needed publication, opening doors for the English-speaking diaspora and enthusiasts of Slavic culture, especially those interested in exploring South Slavic heritage and traditions. Anna's scope of research includes both the neo-Pagan traditions of Rodnovery (Native Faith) and the old syncretic Dual-Faith practices of the South Slavic common folk, offering a unique synthesis of lore and practices accessible to modern Polytheists, Pagans, and witches alike. The author's care to interview local Rodnovery groups in several countries, as well as meticulous sourcing of information, is commendable. Complete with examples of historical spoken charms, family recipes for traditional dishes, and contemporary rituals and exercises, *Slava!* is a homely, cozy, and accessible guide into South Slavic-inspired practice."

—JOANNA TARNAWSKA, author of *Polish Folk Magic*

"Within these pages, you will encounter tree and plant wisdom, spells, ancestor veneration and considerations, environmental stewardship connections, rites directly from Slavic tradition and those created by the author, deities, fairy-lore, useful tools, and more. This Polytheistic, earth-centered, and, at times, Otherworldly tome looks at the past to pave a road to a lively and meaningful Slavic magick practice of now and the forevermore."

—PRIESTESS STEPHANIE ROSE BIRD, author of *Sticks, Stones, Roots & Bones*

"Anna Urošević Applegate's book begins with an exploration of the native, Pagan origins of the Slavic faith, and goes on to examine how this later became coupled with Christianity to survive as a Dual-Faith Tradition. Urošević Applegate includes rituals, prayers, and even recipes to provide a truly immersive experience for anyone who would like to learn more about the cultural traditions of Eastern and Central Europe."

—ALARIC ALBERTSSON, author of *Wyrdworking*

"Urošević Applegate, priestess and Serbian American witch, invites readers to experience the mythic depths of Slavic faith, ancient and new. Magical stories from the author's own past and family tradition/history enrich her substantial scholarship with immediacy and depth, showing how strong and *fresh* the living current of Slavic devotion runs—right here, right now, in this 21st-century time of need.... A comprehensive reference and inspiration both, this book glows in its depictions of Slavic rituals and sacred space, and of the divinities and earthly powers in the Slavic world of the sacred. As a syncretic priestess, Anna brings insight from several traditions (as well as Serbian sources unavailable to the general English-speaking public) into her illumination of Slavic faith. She presents us with many beautiful rituals and suggestions for devotional practice, not neglecting the importance of simple prayer. *Slava!* entices all who are curious—for knowledge, for connection, for beauty—to be drawn deeper into the rich tapestry of Slavic cultures and, if so called, to make it their own."

—PAUL B. RUCKER, visionary artist at paulruckerart.com

"A masterful work of ancestral reclamation, demonstrating how folkloric heritage can be woven into a meaningful and beautiful spiritual practice. Equal parts scholarly survey and intimate memoir, this book guides readers through the rich world of Slavic folkways with clarity and care. By and by, *Slava!* is a profoundly resonant book that contributes much to the growing body of literature on contemporary folk practice and the reawakening of ancestral identity."

—KELDEN, author of *The Crooked Path*

"A richly researched and exquisitely written book that fulfills such an important need, not just from a Pagan perspective, but from a cultural, historical, and sociological one. Right from the first word, I found my heart fully enchanted. Reading even just the acknowledgement and dedication brought me to tears. The deep love which Urošević Applegate brings to her lived experience alongside her breathtakingly vast historical and cultural knowledge has resulted in a brilliantly crafted, important work. A wealth of practical exercises, journal prompts, and traditional practices allows a welcoming pathway into engagement. Urošević Applegate has brilliantly captured just how fluid the influence of belief and practice can be. Even if one had little interest in Pagan practice, this book serves as an important record of historical and cultural patterns and influence. For those who are interested in Pagan literature, but find the current array overly weighted to recognizable themes and topics, *Slava!* is an engrossing read that offers a perspective both familiar and yet rivetingly new."

—TIFFANY LAZIC, registered psychotherapist and author of *Psychopomps and the Soul*

"Urošević Applegate reveals the magical treasures of the Slavic Pagans.... She weaves together Slavic history, Cunning practices, and her own family traditions into a book that feels like it's being read to you by the village witch."

—CHRIS ALLAUN, author of *Whispers from the Coven*

"Urošević Applegate's work is priceless for any seeker wanting to understand the process of assimilation, syncretism, and survival of Pagan deities and spirits within the Church.... *Slava!* is much more than a book about the spirituality of the Slavs; it is a reunion of the author with her roots."

—NESS BOSCH, Priestess, Iberian Shamaness, and author of *Sacred Bones, Magic Bones*

"*Slava!* invites readers of both Slavic and non-Slav background to learn about the nitty-gritty of the traditions and beliefs of a huge area of Europe. More importantly, Urošević Applegate speaks directly and repeatedly to the question of Dual-Faith, a question many readers from many backgrounds are tackling for themselves."

—BENJAMIN STIMPSON, author of *Ancestral Whispers*

"One of the most important books to come out of contemporary Polytheism today.... This book is essential for anyone interested in the potent call of gods that predated Christianity by millennia."

—GALINA KRASSKOVA, PhD candidate, Theology, Fordham University; author of *A Modern Guide to Heathenry*

SLAVA!

SLAVIC PAGANISM AND DUAL-FAITH FOLK WAYS

First Edition
First Printing, 2026

Book design by Rordan Brasington
Cover art by Nataša Ilinčić
Cover design by Kevin R. Brown
Interior illustrations
Nataša Ilinčić: 38, 55, 109, 121, 131, 135, 143
Llewellyn Art Department: 57, 71, 123

Library of Congress Cataloging-in-Publication Data (Pending)
ISBN: 978-0-7387-8067-2

Llewellyn Publications
A Division of Llewellyn Worldwide Ltd.
2143 Wooddale Drive
Woodbury, MN 55125-2989
www.llewellyn.com

Printed in the United States of America

GPSR Representation:
UPI-2M PLUS d.o.o., Medulićeva 20, 10000 Zagreb, Croatia
matt.parsons@upi2mbooks.hr

Other Books by Anna Urošević Applegate

In Praise of the Lady of Power:
An English-Language Booklet of Prayers Dedicated to La Santa Muerte
(Nemetona Press, 2024)

Disclaimer

The information regarding plants and herbs included in this book is based on historical record, folklore, and the author's own experience in devotional ritual use and spellcraft. Any magical, medicinal, or ritual use of these plants is at the sole discretion and responsibility of the reader. Readers are responsible for educating themselves on proper plant identification, safe harvesting and handling, recommended dosages, and contraindications, which are beyond the scope of this book. The author and publisher therefore take no responsibility, legal or otherwise, for any misuse of these plants resulting from poor judgment or misinformation on the part of the reader.

The Slavic Native Faith organization websites and individual practitioner's/musical groups' websites, social media handles, and other contact information listed in this work are current at publication time, but the publisher cannot guarantee that any site will continue to be maintained.

Acknowledgments

I am deeply grateful to Elysia Gallo at Llewellyn Worldwide, who approached me at the 2024 Paganicon, asking me if I would consider writing a book. I also owe huge thanks to her colleagues Bill Krause, Shira Atakpu, Sami Sherratt, Alison Aten, Markus Ironwood, and everyone else on the book midwife team who helped birth this book into the world. I am in awe of the *divno* cover design and artwork by Nataša Ilinčić. *Hvala na svemu!*/Thank you for everything!

I express my heartfelt gratitude to the amazing Fio Gede Parma for their incredible words in the foreword as well as for the vital work they are doing in rewilding witchcraft in our communities around the globe. *Onward, Beloved!*

I also want to express my deepest thanks to my mother, Milanka; my first cousin, Neli; my awesome nephew, Aleksandr; and my American Heathen, witch, and Druid friends Richie, Shanel, Galina, and Katie Jo for their abiding encouragement and support. My wonderful Polish friend from high school, Renata, kindly translated my interview questions into Polish so I could reach out to Slavic Native Faith folks in that country. I am also grateful to the "Polish Folk Witch," Joanna Tarnawska, for her input on folk observances of *Dziady*.

I am indebted to Dr. Smiljana Đorđević-Belić, faculty member of Folkloristics Department at the Institut za Književnost i Umetnost [Institute of Literature and Arts], Beograd, Serbia, for her permission to reprint a healing charm recorded in 2006 by ethnologists in the field studying modern-day *bajalice,* or Cunning Women.

As for the groups and individual Rodnovers in eastern Europe who were a delight to contact and ultimately befriend, I want to especially thank Croatian artist Dražen Markotić Vega of Su'Vid, Polish musician and artist Maryo Hnoss of Volhv Ridnovir, and Serbian Rodnover Dušan Božić of Lug Velesa for their kindness and cooperation as I worked on my research. *Slava našim bogovima! Glory to our native gods!*

Dedication

For the dead: I dedicate this book to the memory of my father, Uroš; to my brother, Marko; to my uncles, Milan and Mirko; to my aunts, Dobrinka, Dušanka, and Vera; to my Deda Miloš and my Deda Bogoljub; and to my Nana Milojka and Nana Natalija. Outside of immediate family, I dedicate this book to the memory of a dear family friend, Baba Živka Vulović (1911–2008), and to two friends from Serbia who towered in the Slavic Native Faith movement and whom I miss dearly: sculptor Jovan Petronijević (1956–2025) and *vračar* and author Radomir Ristić (1973–2020). *Večnaja Pamjat.*

For the living: I fervently dedicate *Slava!* toward the cause of peace and unity among all Slavs worldwide. мир свима!/*Mir svima*!

CONTENTS

PART III
THE WORK
(Посао)

Exercises

"The gods live in the land, in the blood and in the heart and soul of the people. Change any of these things, and our experience of the gods will change."

—Christopher Penczak, *Feast of the Morrighan*, 56

Foreword

When I was eighteen and recently initiated into the Coven of the Wildwood, I met a young Slavic witch. She began attending our open rituals at the time. She was Czech and her family consciously followed peasant-Pagan practices that they'd brought with them to so-called Australia. She was raised with herbal magic, cartomancy, knowledge of the spirits and magic, and a working understanding of the folklore of her culture. She told me once that if I travelled to the edge of the forest, turned away, hung upside down and looked between my legs—that I might behold an ancient forest god. This made quite the impression on me, and I may have performed this ritual several times.

When Anna asked me to write a foreword to this book on Slavic deities, folklore, magic, and ritual, I wondered, why? I admit, I know next to nothing about this topic, though I do know and trust Anna and I am honored to have been asked. As I began to read this book, I quickly realized that the witchcraft and folk ways I practice in my life share much in common with what is revealed and discussed in this book. It also dawned on me that we share a particular perspective on culture and magic that is neither endorsed nor desired by the oppressive and controlling dominant paradigm of imperialism and capitalism.

Anna and I both grew up in families with members of multiple generations who practice magic and spirit work, in countries that are created by colonization with assimilationist agendas. We both retain enduring links to our parent cultures. I was raised with a syncretic and unique form of Hinduism born of the island of Bali, connected to several living and dead family members who were known spirit workers, seers, and healers. Anna was raised with a Serbian Christian Orthodoxy drenched in the continuing and ever-adapting customs and magical knowledge of her ancestors, of the people of those Slavic lands. Read on and you will discover much richness simply by listening and paying attention to Anna's reflections and stories of her own family and the magic and lore that was transmitted in daily domestic action, as well as in more mythic storytelling.

I come to this book a witch initiated in four traditions of the Craft, traditions that are largely anchored in syncretism, dual- or even tri-faith, and the sheer stubborn evolution and versatility of folk magic and witch story that arises from the cataclysms of the past few hundred years and beyond. I come to this book a priestess who is sworn to Great Spirits who are known to be Greek, Celtic, and Hindu, depending on which way you look. And yet I see my Old Faith and the precious knowings of those old and ever-renewing ways reflected powerfully in these pages.

I first met Anna at an intensive I led in Chicago. I have since spent powerfully ecstatic time with Anna at other magical workshops and workings. I have witnessed—each time—a priestess of precise power, intense focus, passionate knowledge, and a depth of dedication who impresses me to no end. Anna is also so many kinds of magic, initiate many times over, and somehow all of it can exist within the largeness of her being that is supported by the blessing of many ancestors, gods, and spirits.

The power and gift of *Slava!* is its precious intimacy. We are invited into the heart and hearth of Anna and her people, with profound insights of neighboring Slavic cultures and communities. Through fierce scholarship, integrated magical prowess and practice, and a sheer enthusiastic desire to share the bounty of Slavic lore, mythos, and history, we become not just acquainted, but touched by these forces and these ancient and revived ways.

Each spell, ritual, prayer, and offering in this book hums with a virtue gathered mindfully and humbly by Anna. At her fingertips and through her delightful, poetic, and enriching writing, we are anointed by the sacred oil, we bend our foreheads down to praise Mother Earth, we wrap our brows in the leaves of the birch and the willow, and we recall the strength and vivacity of the witches and cunning folk of Slavic cultures. If you are of Slavic culture or descent and desire a connection to your inheritance, here is one. If you are—like me—not at all Slavic but feel called to these gods or desirous of respectfully engaging the practices of your beloveds with deeper appreciation, here is a book that opens the way fruitfully.

As I write this, Ukraine is still being invaded by Russia and many Slavic countries exist in socioeconomic precarity and political turmoil. We are all connected and not one of us is free until we all are free, to paraphrase words spoken by the civil and women's rights activist Fannie Lou Hamer. This book is a salve in these times of unrest and upheaval, and the magic and insight contained in these pages may help you—the reader—to make sense of your place in the world, in time, and in your relationships with the spirits and capacity to create change in this world.

In what is transmitted in these pages, Anna has successfully invoked a Slavic spirit that feels primordial and present in this modern age. A necessary and profound resistance to the forces of domination, hatred, and greed. In focusing on something specific—as always—we end up feeling something far more cosmic, universal, connective. The gods and spirits we meet in *Slava!* never died. They bear the ancient cunning of many of our ancestral deities, the Old Powers of this earth. They know how to transform and adopt new faces in new times and places. They change their names if they need to, but their prayers and rituals in the world barely shifted. We continue to draw from the spring, turn with the sun, rejoice in and bear witness to the feasts of the year, and give credence and room to the darker, underworldly forces that shape so much of who we are. By Wolf, Serpent, and Bear, we are led to a treasure trove of magic that links us in with the life force, gathering us home again. May we be strengthened in these times to be evermore fiercely loving, welcoming, artful, and humble as beings of this Great Earth.

Fio Gede Parma

In the unceded, stolen, Sovereign Lands of the Gadigal and Wangal Peoples

April 2025

Introduction

As a child, I felt profoundly embarrassed by my Serbian heritage. My parents emigrated to the United States in 1967 and 1968, respectively (my father arriving first to pave the way for my mother), from the Serbian republic of the country then known as Yugoslavia. They chose to settle in Chicago, Illinois, which has the largest Serbian population of any city in the world outside of Serbia itself.[1]

My folks raised my brother Marko and me to be bilingual, speaking Serbian in the home; frankly, I detested the sound of my parents' Slavic language. It didn't have the musicality, I thought, that I heard in the lilting notes of the Colombian Spanish, the Athenian Greek, the Sicilian Italian, or even the Seoul-ful Korean spoken by my neighboring fellow first-generation American friends and playmates in the Chicago apartment building where I grew up. Serbian didn't sound

1. Pacyga, "Slavic Chicago."

pretty, *period*. I wanted to speak English 24-7. My *Tata* smilingly denied my requests.

Besides the language, other things about my ethnicity bothered me. The cuisine, heavy with a variety of grilled meats and a ubiquitous red pepper–based spread called *ajvar,* which I *loathed*; there was also way too much onion and garlic permeating every dish. Mark would joke that at least vampires would be kept at bay! In terms of religion, I wished we belonged to an "American" denomination and not the Serbian Orthodox Church, replete with its Julian liturgical calendar that never overlapped with any Gregorian calendar holidays or saints' feast days taught to me and my classmates in our Catholic school catechism.

"Why is your Christmas Eve on January 6?" my Irish American and Filipino American classmates would ask me, their little button noses wrinkled with mild distaste. "That's so weird! Everybody knows Jesus was born on December 25!" I didn't have an adequate answer for them. I just wanted to see a hole open in the tile floors of my homeroom—a gaping chasm that I could disappear into forever, traces of my Serbian identity rendered null and void, a place where I'd be able to change my last name to something that sounded "American," not a last name that non-Slavic folks struggled to pronounce.

"Someday, you're going to not just appreciate, but really *treasure* your *roots*!" my mother would emphatically tell me. "Give thanks to God that you're not like *these Americans*, people who have no understanding of culture at all, of who they really are, where they come from—people who have no connection to their ancestral language or their *roots*! Without roots, these people have nothing to anchor them; they drift aimlessly in life, looking for meaning in all the wrong things. That is not you! And that is not Marko. You have *roots*! You may not see it now, but someday, God willing, you will see the wisdom of what I'm telling you. Be proud of who you are," she'd say, exasperated that she even needed to issue this reminder to me.

The antidote to my ethnic self-loathing, of course, according to her and my father's reasoning, was to immerse me (Mark also) even more in all aspects of Serbian culture, and that entailed making good use of our passports to spend weeks at a time in Serbia. When school would let out for the summer, my family would divide our three months' worth of vacation time between staying with relatives on my father's side of the family in the central-eastern town of Gornji Milanovac and with my mother's parents in the central-western Serbian town of Užice in the Old Growth Forest–dominated Zlatibor District, home of the Tara National Park. We would also go on holiday along the Dalmatian coastline of Croatia, staying at villas on the Adriatic Sea, as well as spend a few days in Mostar, Bosnia-Herzegovina, and in Budva, Montenegro.

If there was one thing that started to catch my eye in all these distinct locales spread across the six republics within Yugoslavia, it was directly witnessing everyday people's folk religious observances, folk magical beliefs and practices, and superstitions galore. My scientifically educated mother, a highly regarded civil engineer in both Serbia and Chicago, didn't like the time I spent with my father's family due to what she called their "primitive" beliefs.

My uncle Mirko could foretell a change in the weather based on which way the sheep in the pen were facing. Mirko's sister, my aunt Vera, kept a severed viper's head in a linen bag lined with straw on the same eastern-wall shelf that housed her home's blessed icons of Orthodox saints. And my own father told me that when he served as a midwife at the birth of a lamb or calf, the skull of a wolf would be brought into the barn, the jaws of the skull opened, and the head of the newborn animal would be placed in the space of the mouth in the hopes that the animal would (a) grow strong and healthy, and (b) never fall prey to the wolves that frequented the hills above the farmstead. Vera loved to embroider but never on a Friday; to do so on that day of the week would invite horrible disaster, even death.

My eyes widened upon learning each new taboo among the hundreds of taboos that seemed to govern the lives of my father's family. Invariably, I'd report my findings to my mother. "You can't expect to be in civil society when you're surrounded by uneducated people who believe in primitive things," my mother would sigh and say. "But this is your father's family and you're respectful and helpful, which is good," she'd say as she wiped my sweat-soaked bangs to the side of my forehead.

"I really like it here, Mama," I pleaded, my hands folded in prayer. "Can I spend the whole summer here with *Tata* and you and Mark go be with *your* Mama and Tata?"

"No, *Ankica.* In two weeks' time you'll be with my mother and brother and your cousins Nena, Tsola, Neli, and Milica. No more baseball shirts and dirty coveralls! Your cousins are *ladies* and when you're with them, you're going to be a lady, too!" my mother prophesied with sheer Virgo determinism.

I couldn't bear the thought of being forced to wear dresses. But at least at my Nana's house in Užice, I'd have plum orchards to run around in, and cute little lizards sunning themselves on the white stucco walls of my grandparents' cozy house to catch by their tails and try to bring indoors, if only to scare my reptile-phobic Nana for even just a few seconds.

On a more serious note, even as a nine-year-old I noticed the battle lines of sorts being drawn in my mother's head, the tribalism at work: My mother and Mark and her family were on the "city folk" side, urbane and disdainful of the sights and especially the smells of rural Serbian life; across the dividing line stood "primitive" Tata and I and his parents, siblings, and nephews. We were wilder, somehow less holy. *Vipers' heads and wolf skulls and icons, oh my!* I started to feel something stir inside me, besides an inkling of cultural pride. I would eventually come to recognize it as a budding sensibility of my innate predisposition toward all things witchcraft related.

In mid-July of 1987, when I was thirteen, Mark (then seventeen), my female first cousins, and I were given a chaperone-free day pass from Užice to explore Tara National Park and Mount Zlatibor.[2] I remember feeling strong inner pulsations of déjà vu throbbing throughout my body-mind as we hiked along well-marked trails. I kept looking over my shoulder at the slopes of Mount Zlatibor that we'd just descended. Despite the intense summer heat, I broke out into a clammy, cold sweat. The path ahead continued downward at a relatively steep decline amid a landscape of an intensely green forest of fir and pine trees, with white birch trees adding a smatter-

2. Its name means "Golden Pine Mountain" due to the beloved beauty of its pine trees *(zlata,* "gold").

ing of pale contrast here and there. The green seemed to shimmer in the late afternoon sun.

I had the overwhelming notion that I'd been at this location before, even though that was impossible. Every step I took seemed charged with some type of electricity, physical or spiritual. I also very much felt like my brother, cousins, and I were being watched by one or more Numinous Powers. This was five years before I officially "came out of the broom closet" to my parents and when I would start carrying things on my person like spiritual protection sprays or amulets like hagstones. So at the time I tried to telepathically "speak" to whoever was there at Tara National Park and announce that *my* intentions as an interloper, at least, were nothing but respectful.

I kept my strange sensations to myself that day. It wasn't until a bizarre dream I had a month later—which would repeat itself exactly *twenty years* later—that I connected the Slavic mythological dots of Zlatibor together. Even as an uninformed kid, though, I knew I was connecting with the powerful energies of place in an extrasensory kind of way. The Zlatibor area and places like it throughout the Slavic world are places where the gods of my ancestors were actively worshiped, and where the current resurrection of that worship is growing and coming out of hiding despite the vociferous denunciations of the Serbian Orthodox Church.

That summer of 1987 experience, coupled with my own innate curiosity about the folk magic I was watching transpire before my very eyes during service on certain "days of power" (to quote my mother) in the Serbian Orthodox Christian liturgical year as well as magic practiced in the home, propelled me headlong into the joyful quest that has captivated and enchanted my heart to this day. It's the quest of discovering, uncovering, sharing, and translating into lived daily spiritual practice the world of contemporary Slavic Paganism and magic.

Meet the Slavs

Slavic languages—grouped into Western, Southern, and Eastern blocs—emerged from what was likely a single language in use until the late ninth century CE; these languages compose the largest branch of the

Indo-European (IE) linguistic family tree.[3] That IE linguistic dominance seems fitting when you realize that the vast geographic territory composed of Slavic nations in Europe—stretching from south-central Europe to the far northeast, bordering east Asia—completely dwarfs Western Europe.[4]

The Slavic peoples are divided into three main groups: Western Slavs include the nations of Poland, the Czech Republic, and Slovakia. Southern Slavs include Bulgaria and the former Yugoslav republics-turned-independent nations of Croatia, Slovenia, Serbia, Bosnia-Herzegovina, Montenegro, and North Macedonia.[5] East Slavs include the nations of Ukraine, Belarus, and Russia.[6] Of course, there are large Slavic Diasporas across the planet: in addition to the Slavic countries listed above, Slavic peoples inhabit many countries in Western Europe, the United Kingdom, Scandinavia, the Baltic nations, central and east Asia, North America, and Australia.

Linguistic affinity alone is not enough to create ethnic identity, however, so in the case of the Slavic peoples, as with any ethnic group, one has to look for signs of a common ideology, perhaps reflected as "a matter of myths and symbols, memories and values"; a shared history; the evidence of distinctive material culture (the archaeological record); an association with a specific territory; and a sense of solidarity.[7] Any ethnicity reflects a particular group's human experiences of "conferring meaning on their cultural, spatial, and temporal properties of their interaction and shared experiences."[8]

As the subsequent chapters explain, there was remarkable uniformity of religious belief and social structure in the world of the pre-Christian Slavs, no matter which part of Europe's vast landmass they came to settle from the fifth century CE onward in their centuries-long migration period from their ancestral homeland in the marshes of what is now far southwest

---

3. Gimbutas, *The Slavs*, 19.
4. Russia's southern border faces Mongolia, China, the Korean peninsula, and Japan; Johnson, *Slavic Sorcery*, 5.
5. It is called this to distinguish itself from Greece's northernmost Peloponnesian territory, which is also called Macedonia.
6. Ivakhiv, "The Revival of Ukrainian Native Faith," 211.
7. Barford, *The Early Slavs*, 29.
8. Barford, *The Early Slavs*, 29.

Ukraine.[9] Regardless of any neighboring cultures—Celts, Romans, Teutons, and Turkic peoples; Huns, Scythians, and Sarmatians; Byzantines, Balts, and Scandinavians—that may have exerted cultural and linguistic influences on them, the early Slavs' religiosity stemmed from a Polytheistic and animistic worldview that teemed with gods and spirits—beings of the Otherworld, the natural world, and the human world, including the venerated ancestors of one's family or clan.[10]

In the wake of the historical event known as the Great Schism of 1054 CE, which divided Christianity into geographically demarcated western and eastern spheres of influence via the Roman Catholic and Eastern Orthodox Churches, respectively, the protracted Christianization process the Slavic peoples experienced took on a far different flavor depending on whether the mediating influence was Catholicism or Eastern Orthodoxy. The historical and anthropological records show that Slavic lands Christianized by the Eastern Orthodox Church retained elements of Slavic Paganism to a far greater degree than the lands Christianized by Catholicism.[11] That definitely tracks with my lived experience as a first-generation Serbian American raised in the Eastern Orthodox Church but whose formal education from first grade to twelfth grade was shaped by Roman Catholicism.

Both Christian denominations would bring literacy to the Slavs but would also totally control the narratives regarding the Slavs in the process. Slavic temples and "idols" were described in writing by the very people who destroyed them. A chilling example is given by the medieval Christian Danish historian Saxo Grammaticus in volume XIV of his *Gesta Danorum (History of the Danes)*, written in the year 1208 to praise Denmark's King Valdemar II for his destruction of the West Slavic Vendii tribe's temple, known as Arkona, which was dedicated to Svetovid, the Slavic god of divination and war.[12] Valdemar's slaughter of the temple clergy and theft of all temple treasures in the late twelfth century CE on the island of Rügen in the Baltic Sea is lauded as a victory for Saxo Grammaticus and his Christian

9. Dvornik, *The Slavs*, 47.

10. Gimbutas, *The Slavs*, 135.

11. Ivanits, *Russian Folk Belief*, 4.

12. Gimbutas, *The Slavs*, 152.

compatriots, not just politically but spiritually in terms of the god of Abrahamic monotheism righteously asserting its superiority over the "false" gods of the Slavs.

Given the paucity of direct written sources overall, the study of Slavic pre-Christian beliefs and practices is largely a work of reconstruction, piecing together information gleaned from written records, from similar beliefs outlined in Indo-European and Indo-Iranian mythological sources, from surveying the fruits of archaeology in Slavic lands, to the legacy of surviving folklore, or, "the oral epics, songs, tales, enduring customs and superstitions" of the Slavs.[13]

Reconstructing the Paganism of the Slavs for Today, for *All* Peoples

At the time of writing this book, a quarter century into this new millennium, I'm tremendously excited to see the development—in my parents' birth country, in neighboring Eastern European countries, and here in North America—of a movement aimed at reviving the Polytheistic, earth-centered, and Otherworld-inspired religious beliefs and practices of the pre-Christian Slavs and adapting them for the use of *all peoples* today.

Why turn to the past? As a Slavic woman raised to place my faith in the traces of these beliefs and practices, there is a conviction that my ancestors' wisdom is worth preserving for *all of us* in these by turns marvelous and harrowing times we find ourselves in as human beings facing an uncertain future on an increasingly fragile planet. These Slavic traditions can offer "a secure foundation and an enduring wellspring of inspiration for a profusion of vibrant Pagan movements."[14]

For modern Polytheists like me who are of Slavic heritage, there may be a component of wanting to preserve and pass along this element of ethnicity by engaging in this sacred work of reclamation and reinterpretation of the Slavic Pagan past. I do genuinely believe that my ancestors of blood, especially immediate family members such as my father and brother, are guiding, even *compelling* me to do this work. For others, especially folks

13. Gimbutas, *The Slavs,* 151.

14. Strimska, "Modern Paganism in World Cultures," 2–3.

for whom the issue of preserving a Slavic ethnic identity is not relevant, the study, interpretation, and adaptation of Slavic beliefs and practices can shed new insights into or ways of approaching their own established Pagan or witchcraft practices.

I have several Polytheist students in my teaching temple who are people of color. A few have approached me within the past five years, announcing that they perceive the gods and goddesses of my ancestors—Veles in particular—to be "knocking on the head," as one woman put it, and they're coming to me to respectfully ask how they might respond to these invitations for contact in a culturally appropriate way. One huge aim of mine with this book is to help them and anyone else interested in establishing a mutually satisfying devotional relationship with Slavic deities to do so. And to do so joyfully, with a heart chakra–expanding attitude that I like to think accompanies the mental state of what Zen Buddhists call "Beginner's Mind."

There are, sadly, factions of modern Slavic Pagans within the Native Faith resurgence in former Communist countries that politically align themselves with extreme right-wing parties in their given countries and tie the pre-Christian beliefs of their ancestors to a rabid nationalism. They reject Christianity as a Middle Eastern import (these groups appallingly skew anti-Semitic) and uphold an exclusivist mentality that maintains that the worship of Slavic gods should be for peoples of Slavic heritage *only*. I wholly disavow such thinking and believe it has *no place* in a world that is increasingly becoming interconnected *because it has to* if the human race is to survive at all. Certainly, the ideas presented herein and the groups and individuals I've interviewed as part of my research for this book are not associated in the least with such ethnic chauvinist–fueled types of Rodnovery.

Thankfully, *Rodnovery*, like the term *Paganism* itself, is a bit of an umbrella term. It covers a variety of groups, from revivalists of pre-Christian Slavic Polytheistic and animistic practices that are rooted in the particularities of landscape to more broadly Pagan or Pagan-inspired groups and even groups that promote a fusion of Slavic beliefs with more established/commodified, Westernized forms of New Age practices (e.g., UFOlogy and "pyramid power" cultists and tour groups operating in Bosnia-Herzegovina, New Age healer-shamans in Russia, etc.).[15]

Part I begins with an overview of Slavic Native Faith today and presents the cosmology, deities, and spirits central to Slavic Paganism past and present. Part II chronicles the impact of Christianization and the continuance of Pagan beliefs and practices under a Christian veneer in folk Orthodoxy, a syncretism known as Dual-Faith. Part III guides the reader in adapting the lore for devotional practices today, from altars and ancestor work to complete rituals. The appendices include a glossary with pronunciation guides to deity names and key Serbian terms, a smattering of my family's recipes for Serbian foods well suited as ritual offerings, and a vital resource guide of organizations and individuals in the Slavic Native Faith communities within Serbia, Croatia, Poland, and the United States.

With the passage of time, I am happy to declare that I agree with what my mother said to me in my childhood all those years ago, when I wished to hide from my Serbian ethnicity: The day has come of me not just *appreciating,* but truly *treasuring* my roots. I believe this book is a testament to that attitude of pride in my ethnicity as well as to a Pan-Slavic spirit of cultural celebration and ambassadorship. I hope that the readers of this book will agree.

Slava!/Glory!

Anna Urošević Applegate
Chicago, Illinois
April 2025

15. Ivakhiv, "The Revival of Ukrainian Native Faith," 223.

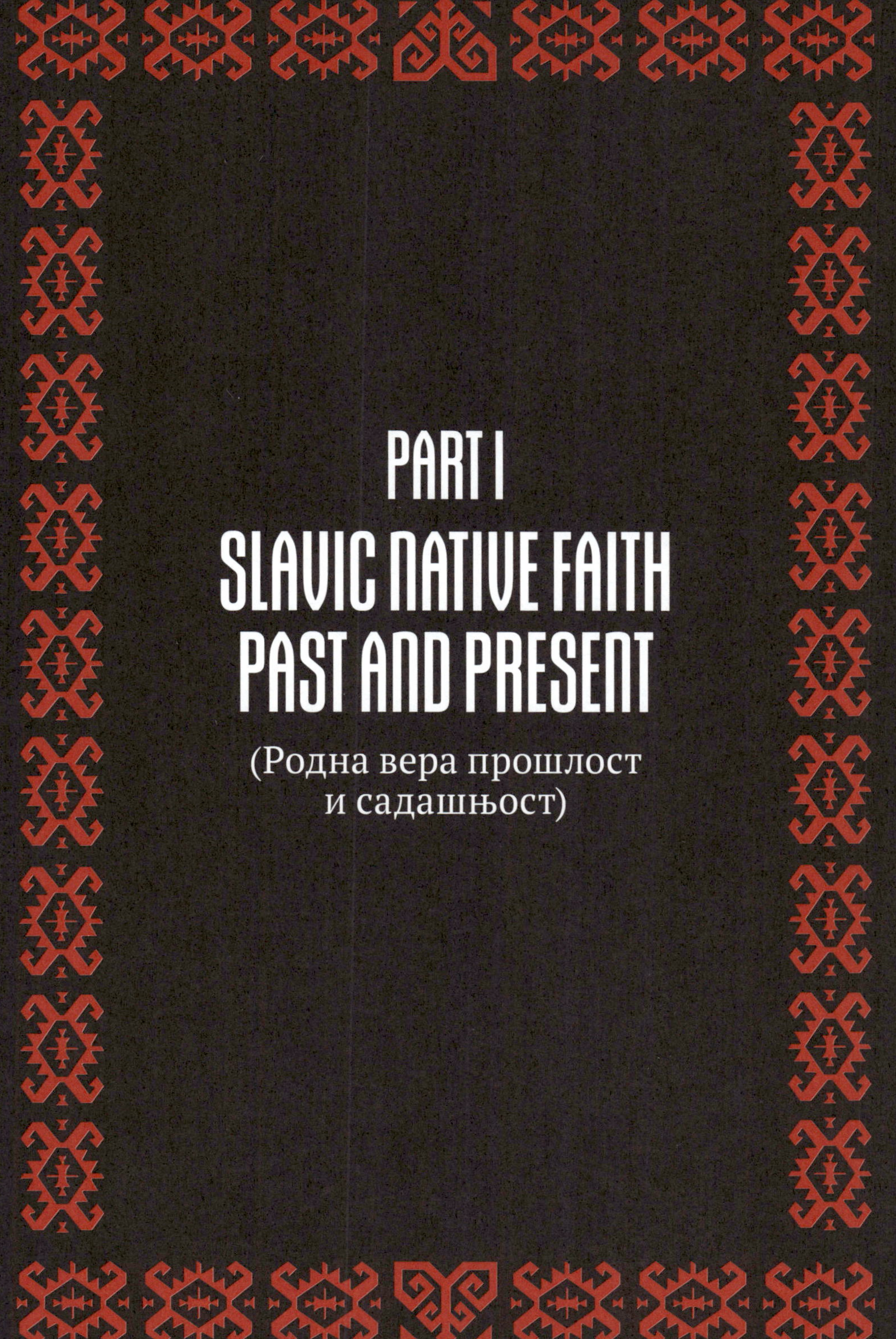

PART I
SLAVIC NATIVE FAITH PAST AND PRESENT

(Родна вера прошлост
и садашњост)

CHAPTER 1
An Overview of Slavic Native Faith

Since the fall of the Soviet Union in 1991, religious movements dedicated to reviving, reinterpreting, and adapting for modern societies the Polytheistic, earth-centered religions of the pre-Christian Slavic peoples have been growing across Eastern Europe and North America. These movements are grouped under the religious umbrella terms *Slavic Native Faith* or *Rodnovery* in English, derived from the Common Slavic root terms *rod,* meaning "kinfolk," "clan," "ancestral origin"; and *vera,* "faith," "belief." Languages derived from the three Slavic groups—West, South, and East Slavs—have their own variations on the name: Polish *Rodzimowierstwo*, Czech and Slovak *Rodná Víra*, Croatian *Rodnovjerje*, Serbian *Rodnoverje* (родноверје), Ukrainian *Ridnovira* (рiдновира) or *Ridnovirstvo* (рiдновiрство), Russian *Rodnovérije* (родноверие), and so forth.

Unlike other modern religions, such as Wicca, which may eclectically draw its theological strands from a variety of sources and cultural influences, Rodnovery places an emphasis on spiritual traditions that are *indigenously Slavic* and that were at the very least disrupted, if not forcibly suppressed, by the introduction of Christianity into Slavic lands from the sixth to eleventh centuries CE.[16] If they're being honest with themselves and others, Slavic Native Faith adherents *aren't* making claims that what they believe and practice is directly passed down in some unbroken chain from their Slavic forebears since time immemorial (if they do claim such things, *run*). Rather, as with modern-day Heathenry or Celtic/Druid or Hellenic Polytheistic faiths also gaining ground in the Western world today, Slavic Native Faith is a Reconstructionist attempt at *reimagining and rebuilding* religious traditions from the remnants of the past, in this case the pre-Christian Slavic past. The legacies of that shared past survive in the languages, the landscapes, and the vibrant living folk traditions of the Slavic peoples.

A Profusion of Practices Anchored by Core Tenets

It would not do Slavic Native Faith justice to think of it as a monolithic entity. It "encompasses various beliefs and rituals, yet it remains unbound by any single tradition," explains the American-based Rodnover fellowship Perun Mountain.[17] There is no overseeing religious body or authority figure. Individuals and groups alike operate autonomously. "I think that the biggest misconception about Slavic Native Faith is that there's a single, clear path to follow," writes ArgonNights, moderator of the American-based Rodnovery forum on Reddit. "In reality, there are many different paths and even more names for the same gods, spirits, rituals ... depending on whether you are a Southern Slav or an Eastern Slav."[18]

16. This is the abbreviation for Common Era, in reference to the world's current calendar system, replacing the Christ-centric AD as a year notation.

17. Perun Mountain, *Discovering Rodnovery*, 8.

18. ArgonNights, reply to "What are some of the biggest misconceptions that people tend to have about Slavic Paganism?"

However, whether Rodnovers belong to groups (open or closed) or practice solely in private as a family unit or as a solitary person, there are generally agreed-upon tenets or core beliefs that form the basis of their religious worldview. These tenets are what largely separate Slavic Native Faith from other kinds of Neopaganism that have been flourishing in the Western world since the cultural revolution of the late 1960s.

Honoring the wisdom and the legacy of ancestral traditions rooted in/arising from native Slavic land. Slavic Native Faith aims to honor the wisdom of the forebears of the Slavic peoples—traditions and rituals practiced by folks within a specific Slavic culture whose spiritual essence is mediated by the land itself and the people's ties to that land and how it provided them with their understanding of who they are. The land can be thought of as "the most sacred manifestation of a timeless reality," the gateway to accessing Otherworldly powers of deities and ancestors through time-honored practices within a given Slavic culture that have achieved prominent cultural significance over many generations.[19]

A religion centered on contemporary Polytheism, Animism, and Ancestor Reverence. Belief in the literal, objectively real existences of gods and a plethora of spirits—including the spirits of one's family dead as well as teeming classes of nature spirits—is fundamental to Slavic Native Faith.[20] Religious worship, not magical work, is the main objective of ritual. The notion is that gods/spirits and humans are bound by rules of reciprocity and take turns in the host-guest relationship and the resulting bestowal and receipt of blessings; the core value of hospitality fuels this relationship dynamic. "The pantheon of Slavic gods and goddesses is not a static collection of ancient stories and myths but a living, dynamic tapestry of faith. It continues to evolve and resonate with the Slavic people, adapting to the changing times while preserving the essence of their cultural heritage," explains Perun Mountain.[21]

The gods are not reducible to empty personifications of the forces of nature. Nor are they internalized to represent psychological abstractions.

19. Artisson, *The Witching Way of the Hollow Hill*, 15.

20. Perun Mountain, *Discovering Rodnovery*, 96.

21. Perun Mountain, *Discovering Rodnovery,* 23.

They are living forces at work in the world, beings of agency with distinct personalities who are instrumental to upholding cosmic processes and who are believed to take a keen interest in the goings-on of this earthly realm, as well as shape and influence the lives of the devotees who call upon them. *"Svi su potrebni, zbog toga i postoje* [They are all necessary, that's why they exist]," says Dražen Markotić Vega, a Croatian Rodnover, artist, and front man of the Slavic Pagan folk band Su'Vid.[22] One's ancestral Slavic homeland and the land where one lives currently throughout the Slavic Diaspora are the touchpoints for accessing these Holy Powers.

A profound call to ecological stewardship. Nature's inherent sanctity requires humans to serve as consciously aware, proactive stewards of finite resources and increasingly fragile ecosystems—ones such as the Bialowieza Forest that straddles the border between Poland and Belarus; it is Europe's last lowland Old Growth Forest, home to the nearly extinct European bison *(Bison bonasus).*[23] The Slavic worldview holds that humans and nature are engaged in a relationship of symbiosis, where each party is dependent upon and responsible for the others' well-being.[24] Maintaining a harmonious relationship with the natural world is a moral imperative. It is therefore not surprising that many adherents of Slavic Native Faith also choose to commit themselves to environmental causes.

Attuning to the cycles of nature finds revelation in communal rituals that are chiefly conducted outdoors and are Pan-Slavic in cultural expression. These rituals, which may reflect cultural and even regional variations within a Slavic culture, nevertheless illustrate profound cohesiveness in symbology and ritual action from one Slavic country to another. That's because they're reflective of a calendar that is rooted in the cycles of the seasons and the agrarian fertility cycle, which are part of the shared Slavic experience centuries after Christianization, whether the latter occurred via the Roman Catholic or the Eastern Orthodox Church.

---

22. Dražen Markotić Vega, interview with the author, October 30, 2024. The English translation is the author's own.
23. Hance, "Stuff of Fairy Tales."
24. Perun Mountain, *Discovering Rodnovery,* 12.

Let's say a hypothetical celebrant participates in a *Kupalo* or *Ivandan* ritual, whose energies are aligned with the Summer Solstice. Whether that celebrant happens to be in the Dinaric Alps of Croatia or in a forest clearing outside of Novgorod, northwest Russia, chances are extremely high that circle dances around a bonfire and bathing in a local body of water are going to ensue because those are universally Slavic ritual actions for that Native Faith holiday.

The following are the main holidays or sacred feast days that are celebrated by modern Slavic Native Faith believers. Many of the holidays that are deity specific (as opposed to seasonal markers like the equinoxes and solstices) have had their dates determined by reclaiming for the god or goddess the feast day subsequently assigned to the Christian saint whose cult was meant to supplant the deity's. Some Rodnovers use the modern Gregorian calendar while some in countries where the Orthodox Church became dominant use the Julian calendar (which runs about thirteen days "behind" the Gregorian). Others, like me, celebrate both dates and honor the deity twice! Table 1 notes these dates.

Table 1. Slavic Native Faith Celebrations

Seasonal Festival	Deity/Deities Honored	Gregorian Calendar Date	Julian Calendar Date
New Year's Day		January 1	January 14
Božić	Dažbog, Svarožić	December 24–25	January 6–7
Gromnica	Perun	February 2	February 16
Noć Velesa/Veles's Night	Veles	February 11	February 25
Babinden	Baba Marta	March 1	March 1

Seasonal Festival	Deity/Deities Honored	Gregorian Calendar Date	Julian Calendar Date
Spring Equinox/ *Velikdan/Jare* Święto/*Jare Gody*	Moist Mother Earth, Vesna, Živa	Date of astronomical event	Date of astronomical event
Vrbica	Doda, Lazarica	Saturday before Catholic Palm Sunday	Saturday before Orthodox Palm Sunday
Earth Day	Moist Mother Earth	April 22	April 22
Jariljdan	Jarilo/Yarilo/Jurej	April 23	May 6
Vidovdan	Day of Svetovid	June 15	June 28
Summer Solstice	Dažbog, Svarog, Perun, Jarilo	Date of astronomical event	Date of astronomical event
Kupalo/Kupala Noć/Ivandan/Kres	Mara/Jarilo/ Mokoš/ Water Spirits such as the *Rusalki*	June 23 (eve) and 24 (day)	July 6 (eve) and 7 (day)
Perun's Day	Perun	July 20	August 2
Mokoša's Day	Mokoša	August 15	August 29
Harvest/*Swięto Plonów*	Jarilo, Mokoša, Ancestors, *Polevoi*, *Ovinnik*, *Domovoi*	September 23	First full moon after Ivandan
Autumn Equinox/ *Plodovi/Siewna*	Mokoša, Mara	Date of astronomical event	Date of astronomical event

Seasonal Festival	Deity/Deities Honored	Gregorian Calendar Date	Julian Calendar Date
Dziady/Zadušnice	Ancestors, Veles, Mara	Movable date: second dark moon after Autumn Equinox (Rodnovery); November 1 or 2 (Dual-Faith, folk Catholicism)[25]	Saturday before November 8 (Dual-Faith, folk Orthodoxy)
Noć Velesa/Veles's Night	Veles	October 31	Saturday before November 8
Winter Solstice	Dažbog, Triglav, Mara	Date of astronomical event	Date of astronomical event
Koleda/Koliada/ Szczodre Gody/ Svečki	Ancestors, Svarog, Svarožić, Dažbog, Triglav, Veles	December 24 through January 3	January 6 through 18

These seasonal rituals are held outdoors whenever possible by Rodnovers because it is known, historically, that the pre-Christian Slavs worshiped their gods atop hills, in the clearings of wooded groves, and by sacred springs and other bodies of water—places of Otherworldly power consistent with the beliefs of other Indo-European societies.[26] In the home, thriving cults to one's ancestral spirits and the spirits of the home/farmstead, which likely shared a common origin, have survived for centuries after Christianization well into the present day.

25. Joanna Tarnawska, personal communication with the author, August 22, 2025.

26. Gimbutas, *The Slavs,* 151.

A holistic worldview that unites family, kin, Slavic nations, all Slavs, and ultimately all humans with All That Is. The concept of *Rod* at the root of *Rodnovery* is both the name of a creator god as well as the Common Slavic term for "kin," "ancestry." As a divine essence, however, Rod is profoundly far-reaching.

The interconnectedness implied in Rod embodies not just the sense of the unity within a family unit and its biological kin or even a sense of Pan-Slavism, but a macrocosmic and profound sense of unity with Ultimate Reality. Rod forms the very basis of natural law, "an all-encompassing energy from which everything emerges and to which everything returns."[27]

In my personal meditations on Rod as a concept, I find it as a "me-we" phenomenon. Through Rod I reach back into the past and reconnect with my Serbian ancestral traditions. But the essence of Rod permeates the present and inspires my daily lived Slavic Polytheistic practices and my sense of connection not just with the natural world and my gods but with other Slavic peoples, with whom I partake of a collective identity and shared cultural heritage. Rod also extends into the future, into a world of humanity united and dedicated to preserving the planet for future generations.

This holistic concept of Rod finds expression in a phrase I like to use ritually as "the Circle of *Rodu*." The gods and humans. Living humans and our beloved dead. People and animals/the natural world. The three levels of the Slavic World Tree. The past, present, and future. All That Ever Was, Is, and Will Be. These are all yoked together, in my thinking and lived experiences, in the Circle of Rodu. Rod is far, far more than just having shared DNA. For me, Slavic Native Faith reaches its fullest potential when it embraces this broad and cosmic understanding of what Rod can truly mean.

A worldview that emphasizes personal integrity and other virtues. Slavic Native Faith espouses personal liberty as well as a sense of obligation to serve and contribute to the well-being of the greater community. Taking full responsibility for one's actions is paramount, especially since it's believed that one's ancestors and the gods are always taking note of how a believer behaves. Be true to your word. Work hard. Care for the land. Pro-

27. Perun Mountain, *Discovering Rodnovery,* 48.

tect your family. Act with honor. Be hospitable and generous. Love the gods with all of who you are and practice your faith: Pray and do devotionals.

These simple, straightforward precepts are proving to be immensely attractive to potential Native Faith followers, especially in Eastern Europe, as these principles are viewed as being in sharp contrast to both the ethos that guided the Soviet Union in the recent past and the hollow consumerist promises of happiness and the ethnicity-nullifying forces currently perceived as dangerously flowing in from the postmodern West.[28]

Present-Day Native Faith Groups

Throughout Eastern Europe in particular, Slavic Native Faith groups have been vying for—and gaining—national recognition within their respective countries as officially recognized religious organizations going as far back as the late 1980s, but the movements really began to accelerate in the mid-1990s.

In Poland, the Native Polish Church (*Rodzimy Kościół Polski*) was registered by its cofounders Lech Emfazy Stefański and Kazimierz Mazur on March 24, 1995.[29] Overall, the country is currently estimated to have between five thousand and eight thousand *Rodzimowiercy* actively practicing in registered groups (bear in mind 87 percent of the people in Poland identify as Roman Catholic).[30]

Ukraine has also served—since the mid-1960s, in fact—as the home to a diverse array of groups that fall under the proverbial *Ridnovira* big top, from *Yazychnyks* (the term applied to those who practice pre-Christian Polytheism and animism) to the highly organized RUNVira (the acronym for Native Ukrainian National Faith) movement, which is actually a hybrid of monotheism and panentheism. The pre-Christian god Dažhboh is the one honored, and he is seen as the cosmic principle underlying the phenomena of our visible world. RUNVira is centered around the writings of its charismatic founder, Lev Sylenko (1921–2008).

28. Ivakhiv, "The Revival of Ukrainian Native Faith," 235.

29. Slowianska Polonia, "Poles Promoting Slavic Culture."

30. Sobolewski, "Roots Revival."

It's challenging to obtain reliable figures on the number of Ukrainians involved in one form of *Ridnovirstvo* or another: Sociologists' estimates run the gamut anywhere from ten thousand people to roughly eighty thousand people. The country has been evidencing a much broader interest in topics related to Paganism and the revival of publicly performed folk traditions in Kyiv and elsewhere associated with seasonal festivals and markers in the agricultural year. "Interest in folk magic is widespread, even among practicing Christians, and the line between occultism, magic, parapsychology, and religion is much more blurred than it is in many Western countries," explains Ukrainian Native Faith scholar and believer Adrian Ivakhiv.[31]

Looking at South Slavic countries and my own ethnic heritage in particular, as of the time of this book's publication, there are at least three robust Slavic Native Faith fellowships in the former Yugoslavia: one in Slovenia, *Društvo Slovenski Staroverci,* or the Association of Old Believers, whose members include the Polytheist group that goes by the name Veles; one in Serbia, *Lug Velesa,* or the Valley of Veles, which is centered in the north of the country and puts out educational and beautifully produced Serbian-language (with subtitles) videos on YouTube regarding the pantheon of the Slavic gods and related content; and one major association in Croatia, *Savez Hrvatskih Rodnovjeraca,* or the Federation of Croatian Rodnovers.

One of the groups registered with this latter association is *Udruga Perunova Svetinja,* which, with the backing of Croatia's Ministry of Culture, reestablished a public sanctuary to the sky/thunder god Perun at a hilltop site (also called Perun) where such a sanctuary to the god historically once stood: *Perun na Učki,* on Croatia's Istrian peninsula. This sanctuary's official dedication, complete with a beautifully carved nine-foot-tall *kipa,* or god-pole, of Perun, occurred on July 2, 2013—just one day after Croatia was inducted into the European Union.[32]

These Native Faith associations in the former Yugoslavia frequently interact with and support one another's events. Similarly in Ukraine, sociologists have noted the interaction between different Ridnovira

31. Ivakhiv, "The Revival of Ukrainian Native Faith," 223–224.

32. Svarica, "*Postavlanje Kipa Perunu.*"

groups, leading to a cross-fertilization of ideas and "substantial porosity of membership between at least four different groups."[33]

In the United States, my own native city of Chicago, Illinois, is home to a Slavic Native Faith group called *Słowiańska Polonia,* which serves the Polish Diaspora community. That a Slavic Native Faith group would be located in Chicago is no coincidence: The United States' third-largest city happens to be home to the largest Polish population outside of Poland (~800,000 people) and the largest Serbian population outside of Serbia (~350,000 people), and it is also home to the second-largest Ukrainian American population in the United States (~100,000 people).[34]

Communities that are essentially tiny religious minorities in their respective countries should turn to each other and rally for support, especially when there's a shared heritage in question. As the daughter of Serbian parents who hailed from what was once Yugoslavia, "the Land of the Southern Slavs," I love seeing the Slovenian, Croatian, and Serbian Native Faith groups simultaneously supporting one another while also serving as cultural ambassadors of their own countries. This is all the more poignant and necessary given the recent traumatic history of secessionist wars and years of being uneasy neighbors with each other due to political tensions.

More importantly, these South Slavic Native Faith groups are busy denouncing nationalism, which has sadly become a deeply disturbing political shadow that has unquestionably accompanied the emergence of Slavic Native Faith groups in various countries, especially in East Slavic countries.[35] It is to this dark subject that we now turn.

The Perversion of Slavic Native Faith by Eastern European Fascists

Sadly, not unlike *völkisch* (folkish) Heathenry, which is rooted in racism, anti-Semitism, and ethnocentrism, some Rodnover organizations—chiefly in Russia and Ukraine—have allied themselves with extreme right-wing

33. Ivakhiv, "The Revival of Ukrainian Native Faith," 231.

34. Pacyga, "Slavic Chicago."

35. The Federation of Croatian Rodnovers has a great statement on their website, which can be translated into English (https://rodnovjerje.com.hr/index.php/hrvatsko-rodnovjerje/).

political factions that openly espouse not only a rabid ethnochauvinism and xenophobia, but white supremacist ideologies as well, especially anti-Semitism. Halyna Lozko—Ukrainian philologist, folklorist, and university lecturer in comparative religions—currently serves as the leader of *Pravoslavia,* the first *Yazychnytstvo* (Slavic Polytheist) group to be recognized in her country. Deplorably, she routinely espouses anti-Semitic rhetoric; in fact, her prayer manual, *Pravoslav,* includes a list of "Pagan Commandments" that include an exhortation to avoid involvement with Jews.[36] In other writings, she warns that "monotheistic ideas are the fruit of Judaic religions which aim for global world domination."[37]

A pronounced antipathy toward globalism, fear of loss of cultural identity, and the marked alienation of people in modern urban society fuel the xenophobia and exclusionary mindsets of these bad actors in certain Slavic Native Faith groups. But it gets worse. And I cannot wrap my mind around it at all.

As the granddaughter of a WWII soldier (my father's father) who was taken as a prisoner of war and tortured by the Nazis during their occupation of Yugoslavia (1941–1945), I am truly horrified and bewildered by the brazen neo-Nazi element present within some of these Slavic groups. There they are, fighting right now in the Russo-Ukrainian War that is still tragically raging at the time of this book's writing, openly carrying the universally condemned swastika flag of the Third Reich into battle alongside their Ukrainian national flag. The "they" I am referring to in this instance is the notorious Azov Battalion, which is part of Ukraine's national guard. It has been known for espousing neo-Nazi ideology and for recruiting neo-Nazis (including fighters from the United States) into its ranks for many years. The US-based nonprofit organization known as the Southern Poverty Law Center, which monitors white supremacist groups worldwide, has frequently reported on the doings of the Azov Battalion and, disturbingly, its incorporation of Pagan imagery into its aesthetics. (The Azov Battal-

36. Ivakhiv, "The Revival of Ukrainian Native Faith," 234.

37. Ivakhiv, "The Revival of Ukrainian Native Faith," 229.

ion, incidentally, has been tied to the training and radicalizing of US-based white supremacist organizations.)[38]

The most frequently co-opted Slavic Native Faith symbol is the *kolovrat* (коловрат), an enclosed wheel with eight spokes that terminate in little arms. It's a wholly modern symbol for the Slavic Native Faith movement that is meant to symbolize the spinning sun and thus the cyclicity of time. While the majority of Rodnovers who wear it do so as an outward display of their faith—one that would be recognized by other believers across the Slavic Native Faith Diaspora just as a crucifix on a chain worn by a Catholic would be recognized by Catholic Christians worldwide—they do very much run the risk of the symbol being wrongly perceived as a swastika and themselves as advocates of extreme right-wing, fascistic, or neo-Nazi political leanings. For those reasons alone, I would not openly wear a kolovrat pendant on a necklace here in the United States where, shamefully, anti-Semitic hate crimes have risen 150 percent since 2019.[39]

The question that anyone seeking to join a Slavic Native Faith group needs to ask is whether the presumed "natural" relationship between the Slavic peoples and their lands automatically excludes the possibility of non-Slavic folks from having a legitimate place in those lands. After all, every Slavic country has its share of ethnic and religious minorities who often can legitimately claim an ancestral connection to that land that dates back several centuries, so on what basis can people be excluded if they are, in fact, indigenous to that land?

Fortunately, the individuals and groups in Europe that I interviewed as part of my research for this book advocate for Slavic Native Faith to be an inclusive religion, adapting to the times. As the front man for the Croatian Native Faith folk band Su'Vid explains, "There is no strict rule as to who should respect old Slavic customs. Today, everything is available to people; it is only important that something is truly respected, and knowledge and conviction will come with time and learning."[40]

---

38. Hayden, "Disinfo Covers for White Supremacy After Buffalo Attack."

39. Federal Bureau of Investigation, "Hate Crime in the United States Incident Analysis."

40. Dražen Markotić Vega, interview with the author, October 30, 2024. The translation into English is the author's own.

Overcoming Other Challenges in the Twenty-First Century

Issues of overlapping with extreme right-wing political factions aside, Slavic Native Faith believers in Europe also have other challenges to overcome. One is "the inherent difficulty in reconstructing an ancient faith with limited historical resources."[41] We certainly have gaps in understanding as to how the pre-Christian Slavs carried out their religious practices.

One possible remedy comes in the form of what North American and Western European Polytheistic communities have termed Unverified Personal Gnosis, or UPG: some form of understanding of the divine that has arisen from personal experience, intuition, or perceived direct contact with the gods. UPG has come to be accepted as a subjective source of spiritual authority on daily praxis for the modern-day devotee of a god whose cult, say, has been rendered obscure by Christianization. In the context of zero to little surviving texts or archaeological findings or ethnographic data, UPG can help eliminate the gaps in known religious knowledge.

My personal stance on this matter is this saying: "Doing the work will teach you how to do the work." Often, I find that people who are new to Slavic Polytheism will have decision paralysis, effectively stopping their practices before they even get started. They have noble intentions—they don't want to "do something wrong" and offend the deity or spirit they are hoping to establish a relationship with—but a preoccupation with replicating historical conditions down to the exact minutiae can lead to just giving up. The most important factors I see in getting started are having an open heart and mind.

Another challenge faced by Slavic Native Faith in the twenty-first century is posed by Christianity, the dominant religion in every Slavic country today, whether spearheaded by Roman Catholicism or Eastern Orthodoxy. Generally conservative in outlook in their respective Slavic nations, Catholics and Eastern Orthodox Christians look upon any "Pagan" religion with alarm and hostility. The situation of Hellenic Pagans in Greece, whose religion was only officially recognized by the Greek government in 2017 but

41. Perun Mountain, *Discovering Rodnovery,* 107.

who continue to experience religious hate crimes and vandalism of their public temples, offers close parallels.[42] Even with secularized media outlets, reporting on Slavic Native Faith tends to be dismissive at best if not ridiculed or subjected to Christian excoriations.

Last, in its efforts to build genuine communities and foster networks between them, Slavic Native Faith adherents—especially in English-dominant countries—have been steadily turning for the past decade or so to social media platforms. While sites such as Tumblr, Reddit, and Facebook can facilitate the discussion of topics of interest to Rodnovers and share content, post notices of local events, and the like, there's no way for newcomers in particular to effectively sort out purveyors of helpful knowledge from the traffickers of fakelore and misinformation. And the recruiters for right-wing hate groups are out there in cyberspace as well, so it's more critical than ever for people turning to the Web to exercise critical thinking skills.

Exercise
Exploring Slavic Lore—A Journaling Prompt

It's a good idea to have a journal and reflect on the chapters of this book as you work your way through the content and rituals. Some questions to consider for your first journal entry include the following:

- If you're reading this as a person in the United States or another country in the English-speaking world, does putting an ethnic-specific label on your spiritual practices matter to you? Why or why not?
- If you are of Slavic heritage, what has brought you to this threshold?
- What is your current spiritual practice like, and what do you hope to find in this book that you can possibly incorporate into your practices?
- What is your level of familiarity with the Slavic gods?

Let's learn about the gods in the next chapter. *Slava!*

42. Souli, "Greece's Old Gods Are Ready for Your Sacrifice."

CHAPTER 2
The Slavic Gods

With its notions of fixed, typically henotheistic, groupings of deities, the term *pantheon* can be a problematic one when it comes to surveying the goddesses and gods of Slavic mythology. The ancient Slavs, Polytheistic and animistic, were highly tribalistic, and their deities were primarily localized ones, meaning that the gods could have numbered into the tens of thousands, if not more. This makes a tally of the deities composing the Slavic "pantheon" in its entirety impossible.[43] Another major complication stems from the fact that when Slavic mythology was recorded at all, it was recorded by Paganism's detractors: Christian clerics writing at the behest of heads of nascent states/empires. They certainly championed biases, which we as modern readers must learn to detect and sift through.

43. Dvornik, *The Slavs,* 51.

The task has fallen to religious historians, comparative religious scholars, linguists, ethnologists, and, yes, even to modern-day Slavic Native Faith adherents and other practicing Pagans to reconstruct Slavic pre-Christian religion and mythology based on the archaeological, linguistic, and toponymical evidence. Other research-based tools at our disposal include making comparisons to wider Indo-European/-Iranian and Baltic mythic constructs as well as documenting the "modifications" of Slavic mythology in surviving folklore, literature, and national customs.[44]

Prince Vladimir's Curated Tenth-Century Pantheon of the Kievan Rus'

Most people's starting point for learning about the gods of the Slavs is the brief catalog of deities highlighted as cultic focal points within Prince Vladimir's short-lived, state-based Polytheism (980–988 CE). We learn a few names with little else by way of detail from this perfunctory passage in the Russian *Primary Chronicle,* which was first compiled in approximately 1111 CE.[45] "And Vladimir began to rule Kiev alone, and he set up idols on a hill outside the palace court—a wooden figure of Perun, and his head was of silver and his mouth was of gold; Khors, and Dažbog, and Stribog, and Simargl, and Mokosh—and he and his people made sacrifice to the idols."[46]

Elsewhere in the *Chronicle* we learn that also in the year 980, Vladimir's uncle, Dobrynya, moved to Novgorod and set up "an idol of Perun" above the river Volkhov for the townsfolk to worship.[47] Intriguingly, however, we learn that Perun (Перун) and the god Veles (Велес)—whose statue was not erected on the hilltop in the company of the other "idols" outside Vladimir's palace in Kiev but was instead relegated to the valley town of Podil below, outside the merchants' quarters—were established in their worship in Kievan Rus' well before the year 980.[48] Prince Sviatoslav, son of the Christian princess Olga, made a commercial treaty with emissaries of the

44. Gimbutas, *The Slavs,* 151.
45. Gimbutas, *The Slavs,* 156.
46. Gimbutas, *The Slavs,* 156.
47. Gimbutas, *The Slavs,* 156.
48. Ivakhiv, "The Revival of Ukrainian Native Faith," 214.

Byzantine Empire in 971 CE that was ratified on oaths sworn to both Perun and Veles. After laying down their shields, weapons, and gold, all parties agreed that oath-breakers would evoke Veles's curse of death by disease/ plague (yellowing of the skin is mentioned) and Perun's curse of a shameful death at the hands of the oath-breakers' own weapons.[49]

The fact that Perun's "idol" outside Vladimir's palace is the only one to have had precious metals laid over its wooden base is a testament to the god's cultic preeminence not just among the East Slavs, but likely among all Slavs. Historians going as far back as Procopius in the sixth century have speculated that Perun, god of war and therefore patron of military leaders—as well as a storm god whose life-giving rains were fundamental to successful agriculture—must be the "supreme god" of the Slavs. "He has the same function as the Vedic Parjanya and his existence and worship can be traced among other Indo-European peoples," explains historian Francis Dvornik.[50]

The West Slavs called him Pron and Perom; the Polabian Slavs referred to the day of the week we know as Thursday as *Perundan.*[51] Polish people referred to thunder and lightning as *piorum.* Indeed, the root of the god's name comes from the Proto-Indo-European **per-*, **perk-*, or **perg-,* meaning "to strike."[52] Among the Southern Slavs, an extensive toponymy bears witness to cultic sites dedicated to Perun (e.g., *Perunovna Planina* [Perun's Mountain] in Bosnia-Herzegovina, *Perunovo Brdo* [Perun's Hill] outside Podstrana, Croatia; *Parunovac,* Serbia; *Pernik,* Bulgaria).[53] Bull sacrifices to Perun in the months of July and August, when his life-giving rains were most needed to ensure a fruitful harvest, managed to endure well into the twentieth century in rural North Macedonia![54] "He is definitely a very old god and common to all the Slavs," declared the famous Lithuanian archeologist Marija Gimbutas.[55] Perun's epithet of *Gromovnik,* "the Thunderer," as

49. Gimbutas, *The Slavs,* 157.
50. Dvornik, *The Slavs,* 48–49.
51. The Polabian Slavs are the Vendii tribe, as named by the Franks of the Carolingian Empire. They've since been anglicized as "Wends."
52. Gimbutas, *The Slavs,* 165.
53. Gimbutas, *The Slavs,* 165.
54. Gajić, словенска митологија *[Slovenska Mitologija],* 41.
55. Gimbutas, *The Slavs,* 165.

well as many folk beliefs related to his cult, was transferred after Christianization to the cult of Saint Elijah/Sveti Ilija.

The god Veles had oaths sworn to him alongside Perun in the tenth century during the ratification of treaties with Byzantium, but the god's statue was conspicuously absent from the roster of the "official" Kievan pantheon displayed outside Prince Vladimir's palace. It was not the elite warrior class but the classes of merchants and pastoral farmers that Veles championed: with one of his epithets being *skotnii bog,* or "cattle god" in the East Slavic tongues, and given the association throughout Europe with heads of cattle as a highly desired form of riches, Veles was more than likely mentioned in these treaties to secure favorable trading conditions for the Rus' and to help build the empire's wealth.[56] Recall that Veles's statue was erected down the valley in Podil, where the merchants' quarters were situated, their trading ships moored on the Pochaina River.[57]

This spatial/geographic opposition between the two gods is quite telling, whether it was consciously intended by Vladimir or not. Perun was accorded a place of literal high prominence and Veles a low one. This heights-versus-depths opposition with its implied mythic antagonism tells us a great deal about Slavic cosmology.

It is fleshed out iconographically as a grand picture of the cosmic World Tree (*Drvo Svijeta* in Croatian) at the center of the universe. This tree has Perun in eagle form perched in its branches (the Realm of *Prav,* or Divine Law) while Veles, in horned serpent or black dragon form, lies coiled at the roots, gateways to the Underworld (known as *Nav,* Abode of the Ancestors). The battle between the celestial versus the chthonic power creates thunderstorm conditions in the tree's middle realm of earth (called *Yav,* the Visible Realm), the domain of living people.[58] Could this mythic struggle between these two gods serve as a dimly heard ancient echo depicting the contentious shift, after the last Ice Age, from hunter-gatherer and pastoral societies (Veles represents both) to agricultural ones (as Perun's blessings ensured abundant crops)?

56. Warner, *Russian Myths,* 10.

57. Warner, *Russian Myths,* 15.

58. Ivakhiv, "The Revival of Ukrainian Native Faith," 230.

Incidentally, if this World Tree cosmology brings the Norse Yggdrasil to mind, it shouldn't be much of a surprise: after all, Scandinavian Vikings (Varangians) helped form the nation-state of the Rus' in the ninth century CE, so a cross-fertilization of spiritual ideas would only be natural between the two cultures.[59]

Linguistic analysis sheds light on Veles's, or Volos's, many mythic functions and cultic animal associations. We know that the Russian term *volosiny,* assigned to the constellation we know as the Pleiades, was likely named after Volos/Veles and was associated with the prehistoric bear cult, suggesting a fusion of ancestor and cultic animal reverence that dates all the way from the Paleolithic.[60] The position of the Pleiades in the heavens may have signaled to the East Slavs when to begin their annual bear hunt, which Veles presided over.[61] In this context, it is speculated that Veles's earliest role is that of a Master of Animals/Lord of the Forest, guide and guardian of the souls of animals hunted for their food and their skins.[62] That would put him in some kind of hierarchical relationship with the Slavic spirit beings of the forests.

From the archaeological record and from toponymy, we know that the worship of Veles, "who dwells in the underworld in the shape of a black snake," was prevalent in all Slavic lands prior to the coming of Christianity. His origins are quite old.[63]

A complex Lord of the Underworld and Master of Magic responsible for all earthly wealth, for the health and fertility of humans and livestock, Veles is often depicted as a robust, bearded older man sporting horns on his head and carrying a shepherd's crook; or he may be depicted as a bull- or ram-horned serpent. "He was a popular folk deity, shamanistic in nature," wrote the late Serbian sorcerer Radomir Ristić, who continued: "Veles is the protector of cattle, wildlife, music, magic, trickery, and health. He is

59. Gilchrist, *Russian Magic*, 15.
60. Cvetković, *Slavic Traditions & Mythology*, 414.
61. Gilchrist, *Russian Magic*, 76–77.
62. Ivanits, *Russian Folk Belief*, 17.
63. Ristić, *Witchcraft and Sorcery of the Balkans*, 73.

also known for his generosity and magical powers... He fought his battles in the form of a black dragon, a snake, or a bull."[64]

Veles also has close parallels with Baltic and Indian gods. In Latvian mythology, Vels is a god of the Underworld and guardian of cattle.[65] In Lithuanian folklore, Velinas is a one-eyed ancestral god and giver of prophecy; like the Teutonic Wodan or Odin, he leads a troop of the dead to course through the skies in their Wild Hunt raids.[66] In the Lithuanian language today, *velinas* means "devil" and *vėlė* is "spirit of the dead."[67] These etymologies also conjure associations with the Vedic deity Varuna, or Varuna Asura as he is mentioned in the *Rig Veda*—the god of oaths who upholds cosmic order by binding his enemies with spells.[68]

As with Perun, toponymy also reveals the cultic influence of Veles, particularly among the South Slavs. The most apparent one is the city of Veles in North Macedonia. Also in Macedonia lies the city of Velestovo. Neighboring Serbia has Velesnica; in Bosnia-Herzegovina, there's the town of Velešići; and Croatia has Volosko. The Czech mountain of Velež is thought to be named after Veles as well. In East Slavic lands, the northwestern Russian city of Volosovo depicts the god Volos on its coat of arms and informs the reader that the god was worshiped in its vicinity.[69] Historically, the Russian cities of Novgorod and Rostov were strong cultic centers of Volos's worship, and after Christianization churches dedicated to Saint Blasius/Blaise *(Vlas* or *Vlah* in Slavonic) were built on Veles's cultic sites. In Orthodox Christianity, Saint Vlas is the guardian of cattle.[70]

The next four deities rattled off in the Russian *Primary Chronicle* as composing Prince Vladimir's courtly pantheon in Kievan Rus' are likely not indigenously Slavic but point to the centuries of cultural influence from the Slavs' Iranian-speaking tribal neighbors of the Sarmatians and the Scythi-

64. Ristić, *Balkan Traditional Witchcraft,* 189.

65. Gimbutas, *The Slavs,* 167.

66. Johnson, *Slavic Sorcery,* 90.

67. Gimbutas, *The Slavs,* 167.

68. Gimbutas, *The Slavs,* 167.

69. Volosovo Gorod, "Volosovo Gorod."

70. Gimbutas, *The Slavs,* 168.

ans.[71] We know that the Pagan Slavs were avid sun worshipers and the name of the solar god Khors (Хорс) is derived from the Iranian Khursīd, the sun god.[72] In cultures the world over, solar deities are identified with the symbols of wheels and circles to connote cyclicity, and *Khors* is likely the root of the Ukrainian and Russian style of ancient circle dances known as *khorovody* (in Serbian we call those dances *kolo,* our word for "wheel"). Even after Christianization, sun worship continued among the Slavs, as the numerous folk practices and spells detailed later in the book describe; to this day in Serbian culture, the dead are buried facing east and the icons of one's family protector-saint need to be hung on the east wall.

Solar attributes also belong to the god known as Dažbog/Dajbog (Дажбог/Дајбог), whose name can be traced to the Persian Baga.[73] In Common Slavic, *Dažbog* literally translates to "the god who gives," from the root verb *dati* (to give) combined with the noun that means "god" but also "wealth": *bogû.* However, Dažbog also has chthonic connotations, not just solar ones. As we saw with Veles's complexity as a god of the dead who is also god of cattle/livestock and wealth, the patron of merchants, the Pagan Slavic understanding of the Underworld viewed it as the Otherworldly origin point for material blessings to flow into this world.[74] The plants humans depend on for food for themselves and for their livestock emerge from the dark, rich earth—from the chthonic realm of the ancestors and the gods who shepherd their souls. Minerals, ore, and metals—so fundamental to the development of human civilizations—also became available to the hands of human beings as gifts from the gods of the chthonic realm. Hence some scholars and even some Rodnovers today see Dažbog as an aspect of Veles, not as a separate god.[75]

While curiously not included in Vladimir's pantheon of the Kievan Rus', the god Svarog (Сварог) is credited as the creator of fire, both in terms of the celestial source of light as well as the gift of controlled fire to humanity. In the twelfth-century Russian translation of a Greek text known as the

71. Dvornik, *The Slavs,* 48.
72. Gimbutas, *The Slavs,* 164.
73. Dvornik, *The Slavs,* 48.
74. Johnson, *Slavic Sorcery*, 185.
75. Ristić, *Balkan Traditional Witchcraft*, 187.

Malalas Chronicle, Svarog is equated with the Greek blacksmith god, Hephaistos. Svarog's name is more than likely related to the Indic terms *svargas*, "radiant sky," and *svarati*, "gleaming."[76] Another epithet for Dažbog that clearly shows his relationship to Svarog is Svarožić (Сварожић), a diminutive that means "Little Svarog" as in "Svarog Junior," i.e., the Son of Svarog. The South Slavic term today for "Christmas" is *Božić*, a diminutive that literally translates to "the Little God." Since Christmas was grafted onto Winter Solstice observations to help convert the Pagans, and since Winter Solstice the world over is a time to commemorate the birth or rebirth of the sun, the god honored at that time of year is likely "Little Svarog," or Svarožić.

It isn't in the *Primary Chronicle* but in a Russian epic poem composed about a hundred years later called *The Tale of Igor's Campaign* where we learn any characteristics at all about the god Stribog (Стрибог): "These winds, the grandsons of Stribog, blow as arrows/from the sea onto the brave warriors of Igor."[77] Aside from this scant source, there have been attempts to reconstruct Stribog's functions from the etymology of his name, which, aside from the Iranian-derived suffix of *-bog* for "god" as well as for "wealth, riches," leaves us with little clarity. Some scholars interpret *stri-* as derived from the Common Slavic root *srei,* meaning "to flow."[78] Others maintain it stems from the Common Slavic *sterti,* "to stretch out, widen, scatter."

These speculations coupled with Dažbog/Dajbog as the "Giving God" have helped some scholars and Slavic Native Faith practitioners conclude that Stribog is the god who disperses things, for good or ill.[79] They may be blessings, from health to the seeds of plants, or they may be disasters, such as the gale-force winds that battered Prince Igor's troops in the poem excerpt—or even diseases. Despite this negative connotation, among Slavic Pagans today, Stribog can be called upon to send spells on the winds; in current folk beliefs, the breath of Stribog is thought to usher in the goddess

76. Gimbutas, *The Slavs,* 162.

77. Anonymous, *The Tale of Igor's Campaign*, stanza XVI, lines 1–2.

78. Gimbutas, *The Slavs,* 164.

79. Cvetković, *Slavic Traditions & Mythology*, 504.

Mara (Мара) at the onset of winter and the goddess Vesna (Весна) at the onset of spring.[80] This aligns his power with that of the sun in terms of rotating the cycles of the seasons.

The last male deity cited in Vladimir's pantheon of the Kievan Rus' is our only zoomorphic-presenting one: Simargl (Симаргл), a griffin that can be best described as a winged wolf. This being is definitely a direct cultural borrowing from the Sarmatians: Simargl derives from the Persian Simurg, a creature described in Zoroastrian texts as "the wisest being in the world because it has seen the destruction and creation of the world three times," explains contemporary Serbian Native Faith adherent and author Stefan Cvetković.[81] The griffin is thought to perch atop the Tree of Life and act as its guardian, making it cognate with the more familiar Pan-Slavic motif of the eagle—animal form of Perun *par excellence*—who sits in the tree and repels attacks from the serpent or dragon coiled at the base, i.e., Veles.

The final deity named in Vladimir's pantheon is the only female one, and hers is among the most primordial of cults among the Pagan Slavs: Mokoša (Мокоша) or Mokoš (phonetically spelled as *Mokosh* for English speakers). The etymology of her name stems from the Common Slavic *mokru/mokra,* "wet," making her cognate with the East Slavic Earth Mother Goddess, Mati Syra Zemlja (Мати Сира Земља), literally "Moist Mother Earth."[82] Mokoša (see figure 1) is mentioned in numerous East Slavic historical records from the eleventh through the seventeenth centuries, especially ecclesiastical chronicles that chided women for their ongoing devotions to the goddess, especially on her day of the week: Friday. For Russian women in the sixteenth century, the act of contrition before a priest began by answering this question: "Did you not go to Mokosh?"[83]

The body of folklore from all the Slavic groups—East, West, and South—attests to shared beliefs that translated into uniform cultic practices among Slavic women eager to placate Mokoša. The goddess's aid was sought in various aspects of daily living, from ensuring happy marriages and the births

80. Gajić, *Slovenska Mitologija*, 43–44.

81. Cvetković, *Slavic Traditions & Mythology*, 493.

82. Gimbutas, *The Slavs,* 169.

83. Gimbutas, *The Slavs,* 168.

Figure 1: Mokoša

of healthy babies to works of healing magic needed for people, livestock, and the land itself (e.g., prayers to end drought)—she's even petitioned by women for help with the laundry![84] Women in East Slavic lands have been documented offering the goddess carded wool, woven pieces of linen, and hemp rope, which were prayed over and deposited into sacred springs.[85] Centuries after Christianization, Mokoša's recognizable image—a goddess whose lower body is represented by a long skirt, her long arms upraised (and flanked by birds or horses) or else stationed at her hips—continues to dominate the Slavic imagination in the living tradition of embroidery and other folk arts.

The Powers of Fate/Destiny and Other Slavic Goddesses

As a protectress of women, a goddess of weaving and spinning invoked for help during and after childbirth, Mokoša has attributes that place her in the company of the Goddesses of Destiny—the Roženice (Роженице) or Suđenice (Суђенице). The Common Slavic verb *roditi* (родити), "to give birth," is at the root of *Roženice,* while *Suđenice* derives from the South Slavic verb *suditi* (судити), "to judge."

Viewed as three distinct female personages ranging in age from young to elderly, the Roženice are thought to appear within the first three nights after a child is born to pronounce the length of its life and its fate.[86] Standing dressed all in white before the hearth of the home, the traditional dwelling place of ancestral spirits, with their long hair unbound as a sign of their magical power, the Roženice, to this day, are welcomed guests. Robust folk beliefs current at the time of this writing attest that the Roženice are still widely believed in, particularly in South Slavic lands, where rituals by the new mother and her attending midwife, if she has one, are performed to help ensure a long and healthy life and a good destiny for the newborn baby.

One such ritual requires the mother and her infant to sleep on the floor; the room must be candlelit. On a table a "meal" is set for the Roženice

84. Gimbutas, *The Slavs,* 168.

85. Cvetković, *Slavic Traditions & Mythology,* 453.

86. Conrad, "Female Spirits Among the South Slavs," 28.

consisting of three special honey cakes, three glasses of red wine paired with three glasses of water, and three cubes of sugar. A golden gift for the baby, such as a gold necklace with a small Orthodox cross pendant, is also set out. When the Roženice appear, likely through the home's chimney but also via any keyhole, they are thought to speak simultaneously while pronouncing the baby's destiny. The mother must be awake to carefully discern their speech; should she fall asleep, she must take pains to remember her dreams, for her child's future is encoded within them.

Once the child's fate has been set, the food can be consumed in the Fates' names by three women, if the baby is a girl, or by three men if it's a boy. The gold gift is presented to the baby as a magical token for it to have all its life. Sprigs of fresh basil are placed under the baby's head along with a small piece of the honey cake on the third night, and the icon of Saint Petka Paraskeva, the goddess Mokoša's Orthodox Christian avatar, is placed nearby.[87]

Ethnographic material such as these recorded folk beliefs but even folk songs can afford insights that aid Slavic Pagan reconstructionist efforts. The great Croatian linguist and philologist, Slavic ethnologist, and Indo-European comparative mythology scholar Radoslav Katičić (1930–2019) compiled folk songs related to Mokoša from lands across all three Slavic groups (West, South, and East Slavs) and made a strong case that the goddess is the wife of the sky god Perun.[88] The symbolism makes sense, as the thunder god's dispensation of life-giving rains brings fertility to the earth. However, Katičić went one step farther, and postulated that Perun and Mokoša are the parents of the vegetation god Jarilo (Јарило) and the goddess of winter and death, who is variously known as Mara, Morana, or Marszanna. Many Native Faith believers regard Jarilo and Mara as a sacred couple and do not accept this family genealogy theory for its problematic incestuous implication.

South Slavic folk songs do celebrate, during the traditional reckoning of summer starting in early May, the marriage between Jarilo/Juraj and

87. Conrad, "Female Spirits Among the South Slavs," 28.

88. Cvetković, *Slavic Traditions & Mythology,* 450.

Mara.[89] She's clearly the sovereign goddess of the land, but in the minds of most Slavic Native Faith believers, Mara is first and foremost a goddess of winter's darkness, ferocity, and death, the sovereign goddess of the land when it's seemingly lifeless. The famous contemporary East Slavic rituals held during *Maslenitsa,* or the Shrovetide carnival that precedes Lent, are renowned for their time-honored activity of the burning or drowning of an effigy that represents Mara, a grand gesture that symbolically "kills" winter.[90]

Spring's arrival, according to many South and East Slavic folk songs, is heralded by the warm southern breezes of Stribog, who ushers in the goddess Vesna (Весна) or Živa (Жива) on his breath; the name of the latter literally translates to "Life." Benevolently disposed toward the human race, Vesna is described as a beautiful, young, ample-bosomed and pregnant woman. With long hair that runs past her knees and bedecked with flowers, Vesna is described as rose-cheeked, always smiling, barefoot, and nude, save for the adornments around her body made of woven fern leaves. The fern is a very sacred plant among all Slavs; in Serbian belief, it has connotations of fertility. It figures prominently in Pan-Slavic folk beliefs surrounding the great Summer Solstice revels of Kupalo.

Wherever Vesna strolls across the landscape, causing vegetation to emerge in her wake, she wafts her enticing fragrance behind her, all the scents of spring. Her right hand always bears an apple, and on her right index finger, a lark is perched; this bird is a well-known harbinger of spring in Serbia. Vesna's left hand holds a bunch of ripe grapes on the vine as well as a bouquet of flowers—symbols of abundance and marriage, respectively.[91] For the Czechs, the goddess Živa taught human beings how to plow as well as how to guide animals to pasture in the spring, clearly attesting to her influence in agriculture and animal husbandry and her cultic importance among farmers and everyday people.

During periods of draught in the spring and summer months, there is a curious women-only ritual that's been documented by anthropologists

89. Cvetković, *Slavic Traditions & Mythology,* 298.

90. Ivanits, *Russian Folk Belief,* 6.

91. Gajić, *Slovenska Mitologija,* 64.

in rural Serbia as far back as the turn of the twentieth century—a magical practice performed in a group context with the intention of influencing the weather to summon needed rain clouds…a group rain dance of sorts. The ritual derives its name from the Serbian noun used to describe a group of young women: *dodole* (додоле).[92]

The dodole gather, dressed in old clothes and adorned with wreaths variously made of grasses, grains, and grape leaves. Walking barefoot, they visit each house in the village, ritually sprinkling water upon each threshold while singing songs such as the following trance-inducing chant:

Naša Doda,
Boga moli,
Da udari rosna kiša.

Our Doda,
Appeal to God
To properly strike and send dew and rain.[93]

The "Doda" addressed is none other than Vesna, and the dodole choose one among them to serve as their leader, the *Dodolka,* an avatar of Doda/Vesna, goddess of fertility. The women then abscond to the parched fields, where they discard their clothes (but keep the wreaths of flowers on themselves) and work themselves into a deeper state of trance with ecstatic dancing, chanting, and veneration of the Dodolka, who is asperged with water: This is the central ritual action. Men are forbidden to observe these proceedings, lest they be cursed.

The consensus is the "god" evoked in the prayer has nothing to do with Christianity and is obviously a reference to thundering Perun, who "properly" strikes the heavens with his sacred axe to deliver needed rains to earth. Furthermore, this god plays second fiddle to the goddess Doda, who is the one with the ability to grant the girls' request; she is the one with agency in this situation to undo the drought conditions.[94]

---

92. Gajić, *Slovenska Mitologija,* 64.
93. Gajić, *Slovenska Mitologija,* 64. The translation into English is the author's own.
94. Gajić, *Slovenska Mitologija,* 64.

With the notable exception of Mara in her wintry aspect as a death goddess, the goddesses noted thus far—Mokoša, the Fates, Vesna, Živa, Dodola—all are believed to be directly involved in the affairs of humans. Are there any Slavic goddesses who are patrons of wild, uncultivated spaces? Yes. The Slavs recognized a solitary, untamed goddess of forests, mountains, and indigenous wild animals whose name varied regionally. She may be called Devana (Девана; Serbo-Croatian), Dziewanna (Polish), or by the Old Common Slavic *Devica,* which is a noun rather than a name. It literally translates to "maiden" or "virgin," in the old sense of being unpartnered/"belonging" to no man, such as the Vestal Virgins of ancient Rome.[95] However, some modern Slavic Rodnovjerje believers eschew the virginity concept and choose to partner Devana with Veles, given their common associations with wild animals.[96]

Of course no roster of wild Slavic goddesses would be complete without mentioning Baba Yaga (Баба Јага), the iron-toothed crone dwelling in her magical forest hut that pivots on its chicken legs to face a fenced yard whose pikes are topped with human skulls. More than any other figure from Slavic mythology and folklore, she acts as an ambassador of sorts for quintessential Slavic-ness that is gendered as female—the ultimate *baba* (old woman) whose rough, calloused, and wrinkled exterior reflects a lifetime of earning the hard-fought wisdom that she is ready to pass down to younger generations, whether they're ready to undergo her initiations to receive that wisdom or not. She is the classic image of the child-endangering witch, a figure whose aura of menace has enabled Slavic parents for many generations across the global Slavic Diaspora to scare their children into obeying orders. "If you don't eat your peas, Baba Yaga will get you!"[97]

She's captured the imaginations of diverse groups of non-Slavic folks in the Western world, from feminists to Jungian psychologists to practicing

95. In contemporary Serbian, *Devica* is a term assigned to the constellation and the zodiac sign of Virgo.

96. Gajić, *Slovenska Mitologija,* 52.

97. I'm quoting the threat made to me by my very own parents when I was little and I hated eating peas!

witches and Neopagans.[98] The latter group have had quite an impact in how Baba Yaga is perceived today. By revering Baba Yaga as a "dark goddess" even though there is zero historical evidence for her ever having had a cult among the pre-Christian Slavs, today's witches and Pagans remind us that religions are not static entities; they evolve in the societies that practice them to meet the needs of the people. A thousand-plus years ago among the Kievan Rus', there certainly was no goddess named Baba Yaga. However, there definitely is a goddess named Baba Yaga alive and well in the aether today because of all the energies collectively poured into the mythic construct that *is* Baba Yaga by her countless devotees worldwide.[99]

Rod and the Concept of Rodu

As we've seen, Rod (Род) is the eponymous creator god whose name is at the very heart of Rodnovery/Rodnovjerje, contemporary Slavic Native Faith. As we saw with the Roženice, with whom he was always paired in medieval Orthodox denunciations of the Pagan celebratory feasts in their honor, the verb *roditi,* "to give birth," is cognate with his name, but *rod* in South Slavic languages and in Russian is the word for "clan," "kinfolk," "ancestry," "lineage" (in Ukrainian, it is *ríd).*[100] As a familial deity, his cult was essentially private and domestic, which is likely the reason for his exclusion from Vladimir's princely pantheon in Kiev. Some Slavic scholars maintain that the male, grandfatherly house spirit of later centuries commonly known as the *domovoi* is a transformation of the cult of Rod.[101]

Rod can be regarded as the locus and sum of one's ancestral line, or as scholar Kenneth Johnson puts it, "The collective psychic imprint of the

98. Dr. Clarissa Pinkola Estés's bestselling nonfiction book *Women Who Run with the Wolves* (Ballantine Books, 1992) presents a thought-provoking analysis of the well-known East Slavic folktale "Vasalisa the Wise," which features a classic hero's journey archetype. As insightful as Dr. Pinkola Estés's commentary is, there is no evidence whatsoever that Baba Yaga is a Slavic "horse-mother Goddess, associated with the power of the mare" (98).

99. Occultists familiar with the principle of how an egregore is formed as the result of unified intent and repeated ritual action on the part of a close-knit magical group understand this perfectly.

100. Gimbutas, *The Slavs,* 168; Ivakhiv, "The Revival of Ukrainian Native Faith," 231.

101. Ivanits, *Russian Folk Belief,* 14.

fathers of the family or clan."[102] But his importance lies far beyond one's own immediate family line. He is both a deity and a cosmic principle, a concentration of the Prav (Divine Law) energy that permeates the cosmos, linking the tripartite structure of the World Tree and the cycles of existence.[103] I see that unbroken connection of All That Is as a circle/kolovrat that unites not just the Slavic peoples in a shared cultural heritage I call the Circle of Rodu, but the sum total of humanity with *all* sentient beings—divine, animal, plant, mineral, etc.—in holistic kinship. That is the fullest expression for me of the ritual greeting, *Slava Rodu!*/Glory to the Kin!

Jarilo

As might be clear by now, with the notable exception of the cult of the goddess Mokoša, the "official Paganism" of Prince Vladimir's fledgling Kievan state in the tenth century seemed to have little in common with the Paganism of the countryside. There, the common folks may well have followed much older ways, revering their ancestors and the life-giving powers of the sacred sun and fecund earth.

The god Jarilo (also anglicized with the spelling of *Yarilo* or otherwise known as Jerovit/Juraj/Jure/Đurđev) embodies the vitalizing energies of both earth and sun. A god of vegetation typically depicted as young and fair-haired and associated with a white horse, he clearly has solar attributes, and in some sense he may be thought of as a life force–emanating warrior god engaged in battle against winter's barren darkness and cold.[104] Little wonder, then, that during the Christianization process of Slavic lands his imagery would easily translate into the well-known Christian iconography of the militant Saint George astride a white steed, skewering a dragon with a lance. Tellingly, Saint George's feast day (known as *Đurđevdan*) in Serbia is celebrated on May 6, the traditional date for the start of the summer half of the year.

Could the young god's mythic opponent in combat be none other than the chthonic Veles/Volos, the black dragon? According to some scholars,

102. Johnson, *Slavic Sorcery*, 143.

103. Perun Mountain, *Discovering Rodnovery*, 48.

104. Gilchrist, *Russian Magic*, 73.

Veles is reputed to be the young god's uncle or foster father; he imprisons Jarilo in the gloom of the Underworld until the agreed-upon date of his release in May, thereby ushering in the light and heat of summer and the growth of all plant life, most importantly crops.[105]

South Slavic celebrations of Saint George's Day rival those of the Celtic Beltane, the fire and fertility festival at the beginning of May that also marks the traditional Celtic start to summer. For pastoral Celts and Slavs, it's the time of year to put grazing cattle and sheep out to pasture. In Croatia, for example, on April 22, the eve of Jarilo's Day, or *Jariljdan*, bonfires are lit and processions of men and boys, blowing horns and whistles, escort their animals through village streets to their grazing lands, ensuring the animals cross over the threshold with their right leg first for good luck. Alternatively, they may be led to walk over an axe lying on the ground as a means of spiritual protection.[106]

In Slovenia, Jarilo or Zeleni Juraj/Green Juraj is represented by a man adorned in literal greenery/local foliage. He is the one who leads the procession in his village, not unlike Green Man or Jack-in-the-Green figures popular during Beltane revels in the United Kingdom and Ireland. The folks in his retinue, adults and children alike, sing cheerful songs announcing Jarilo's return and receive gifts from villagers.

South Slavic folk songs attest to a sacred marriage between Jarilo/Juraj/Đurđev and Mara, who takes on the form of a sovereign maiden goddess of spring, not the death-dealing goddess of winter she is typically known as being within the Slavic pantheon to modern Slavic Pagans.[107] These songs have striking parallels with documented Celtic and British Beltane customs centered around the choosing of a King and Queen of May, symbolic representations of deities of the land, whose union promotes fertility, abundance, and unbridled joy.[108]

According to contemporary Serbian Native Faith author Stefan Cvetković, the marriage of Jarilo and Mara "marks the peak of the vegetative

105. Cvetković, *Slavic Traditions & Mythology,* 295.

106. Cvetković, *Slavic Traditions & Mythology,* 288.

107. Cvetković, *Slavic Traditions & Mythology,* 298.

108. Matthews, *The Quest for the Green Man,* 81.

cycle, after which Jarilo is killed (harvested), while Mara becomes a terrible goddess of winter, because they find out that they are siblings."[109] This theory of the deities being siblings, as you'll recall, was promoted by the late Croatian scholar Radoslav Katičić. Other variants of the myth that I have heard orally transmitted from my own parents state that Mara kills Jarilo in the autumn in a fit of jealousy due to the young god's philandering ways (i.e., he cheats on her with Vesna). Regardless of Mara's motive, Jarilo's death is tied to the harvest cycle and Mara's transformation from a young, beautiful maiden to a horrible, death-dealing goddess of winter is ensured.

The Polycephalic Triglav Is Chernobog, the Black God

As with other Indo-European cultures, the Slavs venerated deities who were depicted as being polycephalic, having three or four faces on one head.[110] The two most well-known gods from the archaeological and historical records as well as extant ethnographic data, especially from West and South Slavic lands, are Triglav (Триглав) and Svetovid (Световид).

The literal translation of *Triglav* is "Three-Headed"; an alternate theonym among the East Slavs is Trojan (Тројан), "Thrice." In all likelihood, these terms are used as epithets in lieu of actual names out of taboo. Most Slavic scholars identify his three heads as representing his tripartite domain of the heavens, the earth, and the Underworld, or the three levels of the Cosmic Tree.[111]

While he may traverse or even possibly have dominion over the three realms of Prav, Yav, and Nav, Triglav is most associated with Nav, or the Underworld. We know this from a variety of sources. An eleventh-century chronicler named Ebo wrote about the religious practices of the West Slavic Vendii tribe and one of their major cultic centers in then-Pomerania (present-day Poland), the town of Szcsecin (or Štetin), where the Oder River flows into the Baltic Sea. According to Ebo, the Vendii's religious complex had four temples: the most important of them belonged to Triglav. Situated high on a hill, the temple had

109. Cvetković, *Slavic Traditions & Mythology,* 491.

110. Barford, *The Early Slavs,* 198.

111. Gajić, *Slovenska Mitologija,* 48.

walls that were painted and adorned with human and animal shapes; gold was kept inside the temple, as were musical instruments and elaborately carved drinking horns. The statue of the god Triglav was described as three-headed, made of gold, and veiled.

The temple was encircled by sacred grassland, in which a black horse was pastured. This horse was used in a curious divination ceremony: It was led between nine lances that had been driven into the earth. If the horse didn't touch any of the lances in its route, the omen was favorable. Sadly, in 1127, Bishop Otto of Bamberg, dedicated to converting the Pagans of Pomerania, ordered the Szcsecin "idol" to be smashed and for one of the heads depicting Triglav to be sent to Pope Honorius II in Rome.[112]

The color symbolism of the black horse and the gold-plated heads of Triglav's statue are also indicators of strong chthonic connotations, in addition to his three-headedness, a trait shared by the Greek Underworld guardian Kerberos and triple-faced Hekate. In South Slavic folklore to the present day, Triglav is associated with mining and precious metals. He is known as the Black Rider on a black horse, wearing a black cloak and a hat, carrying a magical rod and a hatchet. Wolves, the ancestors in animal form, follow him, and roosters (solar animals) crow to warn of his approach.[113]

The fact that his temple was situated on a hilltop in no way contradicts his chthonic energies. From the shamanistic paradigm, hills and especially mountains the world over are also symbolic of the Axis Mundi. They function as the World Tree does, demarcating the interconnected levels of Ultimate Reality. Intriguingly, the highest mountain (standing at 1,864 meters/6,115+ feet) in the Julian Alps of today's South Slavic country of Slovenia is known as Mount Triglav; it aptly has three peaks or heads.

Some scholars and even contemporary Slavic Native Faith believers propose that Triglav and Veles are different names for the same chthonic deity.[114] I personally don't share that view; to me, the two gods' energies feel very different. What I'm going to relate comes from my own UPG, which I as a contemporary Polytheist do use to inform my personal theo-

112. Šavli, "Triglav and Svetovit."

113. Ristić, *Balkan Traditional Witchcraft*, 185.

114. Ristić, *Balkan Traditional Witchcraft*, 431; Ristić, *Balkan Traditional Witchcraft,* 187.

logical beliefs. It's what I believe to be a direct download from Triglav that came to me in a dream or perhaps even a visit from him during my sleep the night of Friday, June 21, 2024—two nights after my Summer Solstice ritual.

My Dream of Triglav

I'm seated at a long wooden table in a dark subterranean space. It strikes me as an old tavern or restaurant, but I'm not entirely sure. I'm with a group of people who are presumably my friends, but I can't see anyone's faces. Suddenly a man comes bounding toward us, parting his way through saloon-style swinging wooden doors. He's illuminating the atmosphere somehow. A handsome man in the prime of his life, he has dark blond hair that reaches his shoulders. His shirt is so white it's almost blinding. His eyes, which are so dark that they appear to be black, twinkle. He sports a neatly trimmed, rather long handlebar mustache.

As he gets closer to my table, I can clearly discern a tattoo on his chest, as his shirt is unbuttoned. It's the image of the god Triglav—the three heads are unmistakable. I shout the god's name with delight and surprise, and the blond man comes and stands next to me. He's smiling broadly. I also notice that he's wearing a necklace with a kolovrat pendant. I return my gaze to his tattoo, admiring the beautiful line and shade work. But it's more than that—the tattoo seems alive, sentient.

Addressing only me, the man announces he's Croatian. I enthusiastically reply in Serbo-Croatian that I'm Serbian and add, "*Mi smo komšije!*/We're neighbors!" I lovingly place my hand on my heart, and I can feel the man beam with joy. His energy is electrifying, and I'm quite giddy.

Shot glasses filled with *rakija* instantly appear in everyone's right hands. We toast, *"Slava Rodu!"* Glasses clink joyfully.

Next, I jolt upright, catching my breath as I eye the familiar surroundings of my bedroom. I sit for a few moments in a state of happy surprise, processing it all. The din of the clinking glasses still resounds in my ears. It all felt and sounded so incredibly real.

I'm convinced that dream was more of a spontaneous shamanic journey of mine to Nav, Triglav's Underworld realm. I do believe it was his way of saying, "You're alright, kid. Your other ancestral gods and I know and appreciate you." Since then, extra time spent in meditation and prayer to Triglav has helped me deepen my relationship with him.

While I don't see Triglav and Veles as the same god, I can understand what some historians and mythology scholars claim is a Slavic god named Chernobog (Чернобог; Black God) as a theonym for Triglav. It all begins with the eleventh-century German monk and chronicler, Helmold, who worked with the missionaries converting West Slavic tribes settled along the Elbe River. He documented a custom of those Slavs at their feasts, passing about a bowl over which they thanked good fortune coming from their "white god" (Bielobog, Биелобог), and excoriating the bad luck doled out to them by their "bad" god, the "black god," or Chernobog/Černobog.[115] The dualism of the Slavic cosmology is reasserting itself here, as the existence of Chernobog implies the existence of an opposing deity or foil, per the polarities of light and darkness that interweave their omnipresent patterns on the cosmic loom of life.

The Polycephalic Svetovid Is Bielobog, the White God

That yang to Chernobog's yin is the "white god" or Bielobog/Byelobog, which is actually the theonym of the other major polycephalic god of the Slavs, especially the West Slavs: Svetovid. Also variously spelled (depending on the region) as *Svetovit, Świętowita, Svantevit, Sviatovyd, Su'Vid,* or

115. Cvetković, *Slavic Traditions & Mythology,* 368.

just *Vid*—Svetovid has many scholars' vote as the supreme god of the West Slavs. He is a god of light, divination, abundance, and war.[116] Whereas Triglav has three faces or heads, Svetovid has four.

The variants of spelling in the god's name can denote two different but complementary etymological meanings: in Common Slavic, the prefix *sve-* and its variants translate to "all," "the totality" of something. However, the distinct prefix of *sviato-* or *swieto-* means "holy, sacred." The variants of the suffix *-vid, -vit, -wita,* all derive from the verb *videti,* "to see." Hence Svetovid is the "All-Seeing" or "World-Seeing God" and Sviatovyd is the "Holiness-Seer."[117] Either way, the god's function of divination is inherently emphasized.

Slavic Temple Complexes and the Temple of Svetovid at Arkona

Historically, we know that the Pagan Slavs of the pre-migration period lived in small tribal societies that were clan based. They worshiped their gods and spirits in open, circular sites, typically enclosed by ditches or stones. At that level, there would have been no need to develop highly organized, elaborate, and hierarchical cults of deities with war or other "high" gods at the apex of the pyramid. However, during the centuries of the Slavic migration period and after—sixth to tenth centuries CE—as Slavic societies underwent massive transformation from small to large tribal units with more defined sociopolitical organization, religious cults evolved to meet those needs, resulting in more elaborate, organized, and hierarchical forms. Formal temple complexes within fortifications were not constructed prior to the tenth and eleventh centuries.[118] They were built in response to internal sociopolitical changes and external threats to the tribes' emerging Slavic states, chiefly well-established Christian nation-states seeking to violently expand their territories under the bloodstained banners of the "Prince of Peace."[119]

116. Ivanits, *Russian Folk Belief,* 14.

117. Ivakhiv, "The Revival of Ukrainian Native Faith," 231.

118. Zaroff, "Organised Pagan Cult in Kievan Rus'," 16–17.

119. Gimbutas, *The Slavs,* 151.

The most detailed description of a Slavic temple available to us in the historical record is of a temple that was dedicated to Svetovid. It was housed in a massive, fortified complex called Arkona, which was situated on the island of Rujana (or Rügen, in today's Germany) in the Baltic Sea, home of the Rugii Slavic tribe. Arkona was "the last bastion of West Slavic paganism against the forces of Christianity," Marija Gimbutas famously wrote.[120] The thirteenth-century chronicler Saxo Grammaticus in volume XIV of his *Gesta Danorum* (circa 1208 CE) provides us with detailed information about the temple and the cult of Sventovit, prior to its destruction by the Danish King Valdemar in 1168 CE.

The temple had two components: the external walls were ornamented in relief with all kinds of motifs that were roughly painted. The door to the temple was red, as was the roof. The colossal wooden idol or god-pole of Svetovit's elaborately carved four-fold faces (which depicted the god as clean-shaven and not bearded, per the grooming styles common to the Rugii) and bodies (depicted holding various cultic implements) stood in a sunken base in an inner sanctum. The roof of this interior space, which measured some 20 square meters or 215 square feet, was supported by four columns and had purple rugs in lieu of walls.[121]

The statue's side that faced the entrance to the temple was carved in such a way as to show the god's right hand holding a drinking horn, which was made of various metals. The horn was filled once a year, Saxo Grammaticus goes on to explain, during the harvest festival. The priest who assessed the level of evaporation of wine poured into the horn would prophesy concerning next year's crop—the higher the level of wine remaining in the horn, the better the prospect for a successful harvest the following year.

Elaborately made, large (almost as tall as a person!) honey cakes were also offered to Svetovid as thanks for military victories on land and sea, and warriors offered a third of their spoils of war to the temple's treasury. Svetovid received tribute from "all of the Slavic lands" and even neighbor-

120. Gimbutas, *The Slavs,* 151.

121. Gimbutas, *The Slavs,* 152–53.

ing Christian kings paid tribute, ignoring the injunctions from their clergy to not commit such "sacrilege." Indeed, Denmark's King Svein III, Valdemar's predecessor, donated "a wonderfully crafted cup" as an offering to the god. "This god also had other temples in different places, but none was so venerated as the one at Arkona," Saxo Grammaticus informs us.[122]

Adjacent to the statue were a bridle, saddle, and temple sword. A white temple horse was pastured within the first ring of fencing (there were two concentric circles of fences) that surrounded the temple. Only the temple priests could mount or lead the horses for a certain war divination ritual: to know the outcome of the Rugii tribe's next battle, lances "in three rows and in equal interwalls" were set up before the temple. Once prayers were made, the horse was led through the rows, with careful observations made of right-hoof- versus left-hoof-forward movements, with right-hoof-forward movements considered auspicious. The temple complex had stables housing up to three hundred sacred horses.[123]

Svetovid—god of war, god of divination, with his white cultic horse—is clearly a sky god, a foil to the black cultic horse and the Underworld energies of Triglav. He is the celestial Bielobog, or White God, four faces looking out into the universe from the cardinal directions. "It should be understood that the ability to oversee everything is inseparable from the characteristic of being ever-present, and therefore eternal, unbound by time," adds Serbian Rodnover Stefan Cvetković.[124] Triple-headed Triglav, not unlike the Greek/Thracian Hekate, is a chthonic deity par excellence, black colored and hence Chernobog, the Black God. According to some scholars, the blackness of Triglav/Chernobog symbolizes the unknown universe, while the whiteness of Svetovid/Bielobog represents "concrete life on earth."[125]

Perhaps the most famous statue ever to be discovered in the archaeological record as pertaining to the Pagan Slavs is the so-called Zbrucz idol, which was discovered in 1848 in the River Zbrucz in Galicia, southeastern Poland.

---

122. Šavli, "Triglav and Svetovit," 4.

123. Šavli, "Triglav and Svetovit," 4.

124. Cvetković, *Slavic Traditions & Mythology*, 372.

125. Šavli, "Triglav and Svetovit," 5.

Now the highlight of the Archaeological Museum in Kraków, the eight-foot-tall (244 centimeters), four-faced/four-bodied statue carved out of limestone is commonly believed by scholars to be a representation of Światowid.[126] As figure 2 shows, the statue is divided into three tiers with engraving on each side.

As with the depictions of deities and spirit beings on the famous Celtic artifact known as the Gundestrup Cauldron, the scenes engraved on the sides of this probable Svetovid statue have fielded a wide array of interpretations from scholars as well as present-day Slavic Native Faith believers. The middle and bottom tiers of each of the sides have fielded speculation that images of other Slavic deities, chiefly Perun—even the goddess Mokoša—are being portrayed in a narrative that has long since been lost to us. The male figure at the bottom with his arms extended is thought to represent Triglav emerging out of the cosmic waters, performing an Atlas-like gesture of upholding the sky.[127]

Places of power associated with Svetovid besides the isle of Rügen and Mount Triglav in Slovenia include Mount Borhyt in Ukraine's southwest Oblost Region and a variety of hilltop locations in Croatia and Serbia, including Vidova Gora (Vid's Hill), Vidov Vrh (Vid's Peak), Vidovica, and Sutvid. In Serbian lore, the dark historical memory of the Serbian Empire's loss to the advancing Ottomans at the Field of Kosovo on June 28, 1389, is known as *Vidovdan,* the Day of Vid.[128] Vid is supposed to represent the Christian Saint Vitus, *Sveti Vid* in Serbian, but the folk beliefs and current folk magical practices discussed in Chapter 7 show traces of the link to the god Vid/Svetovid and his function of divination. On Vidovdan, it's advised to perform healing works to treat the eyes, as well as seek prophetic visions. I like to perform a devotional ritual to the god Svetovid in which I light a ceremonial fire for him using "living fire" and I ask for his counsel through divination (chiefly a tarot reading).

126. Warner, *Russian Myths,* 10.

127. Cvetković, *Slavic Traditions & Mythology,* 143.

128. Ivakhiv, "The Revival of Ukrainian Native Faith," 231.

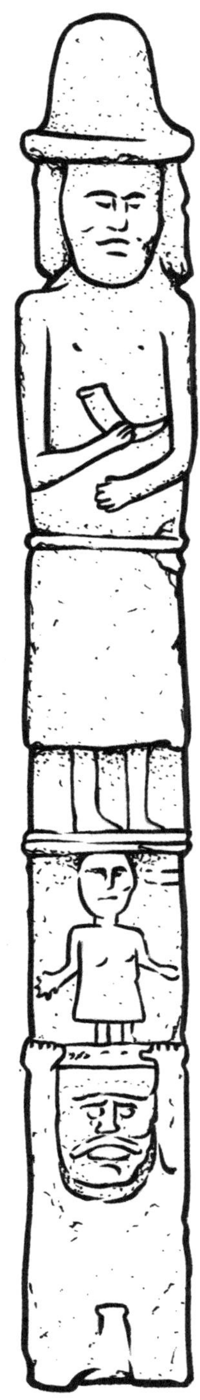

Figure 2

The Gods in Rodnovjerje/Ridnovira Today

As a form of contemporary Polytheism, Slavic Native Faith espouses a belief in the gods as literal, living, powerful, and awe-inspiring beings. They guide, protect, and inspire their devotees. They bridge the remote Slavic past and highlight ancestral roots while serving as devotional focal points for peoples across the global Slavic Diaspora today.[129]

Some groups and individuals honor a multitude of holy powers, while others may choose to solely focus on devotionals to a patron deity and their ancestral cult. Regarding patrons, from my own anecdotal observations, Perun and Veles appear to be the two most popular gods. Just as Heathen followers of the Teutonic gods may choose to wear a Thor hammer (*Mjöllnír*) pendant to display their devotion to Thor or a *Valknut* pendant to show their allegiance to Oðinn, Slavic Native Faith believers may adorn themselves with images of Perun's axe/hatchet or his *gromovnik* symbol (see figure 3). If they're devotees of Veles, who today "is certainly the major male deity of Slavic witchcraft," according to Serbian witch Radomir Ristić, they may wear the telltale contemporary stylized bull head that is associated with him (see figure 4).[130]

As with any devotional practice, aside from having an open and sincerely believing heart, the foundational pillars to operating in any Polytheistic practice are achieving consistency with prayer and devotional offerings. Chapters 11 through 13 in Part III will help guide you with getting your devotional practice started.

129. Perun Mountain, *Discovering Rodnovery,* 23.

130. Ristić, *Balkan Traditional Witchcraft*, 188.

Figures 3 and 4

Exercise
Make Homemade Clay Votive Offerings

Votive offerings to the gods are attested in the historical record by all Indo-European cultures. Symbols such as a kolovrat, Perun's axe, and cultic animal forms—such as a bull or serpent for Veles, or a horse for Triglav or Svetovid—made of biodegradable homemade clay can be fashioned and presented as offerings or forms of altar décor to the Slavic gods or made into personal jewelry for yourself. I first learned this recipe for homemade clay from my third-grade homeroom teacher at my Chicago Catholic elementary school, and I have been making little figurines, statues, and clay talismans ever since.

Here's what you'll need:

- A large mixing bowl and a wooden spoon
- 1 cup flour
- ¼ cup salt
- ⅓ cup water
- Plastic sandwich bags
- A rolling pin

- Wax paper
- A knife or cookie cutters
- *Optional:* paper clips, string, a pencil, poster paints and a paintbrush, sequins/beads/amber chips, clear nail polish

Procedure: Mix the flour and salt together in the bowl first, then add the water. Press out any lumps. Add a few more drops of water if the clay mixture feels too dry or crumbly; conversely, add a pinch of flour if it's too liquid. Shape the clay into a good-sized patty and store it in a plastic bag, which can then be refrigerated. Prior to sculpting with the clay, let it warm to room temperature.

Roll out the clay on a sheet of wax paper to a quarter inch in thickness. Using a knife or perhaps cookie cutters, cut out the shape of your talisman. You can press a paper clip into its back to create a bail or loop and then thread string through it to hang; otherwise, poke a hole with a pencil. For larger pieces, just use larger amounts of the clay and sculpt your figure accordingly. I've made a freestanding bull effigy for Veles that I keep on my shrine to him.

The clay image should be left to dry for about two to three days. Feel free to use children's poster paints, which are nontoxic. Pieces destined to be kept indoors may be decorated with sequins, beads, or especially nuggets of Baltic amber. If the piece isn't being deposited outdoors, a topcoat of clear nail polish creates an effective varnish.

You may choose to wait for the timing you feel is appropriate to consecrate and present the votive offering to the deity/deities of your choice. The new moon is always a good idea, as is the day of the week associated with various gods (Thursday for Perun, Friday for Mokoša, Saturday for Veles/Triglav and the dead, Sunday for solar deities such as Svarog or Khors, etc.). Or just follow your intuition and present your votive offering whenever. *Slava!*

CHAPTER 3
The Host of Spirit Beings in Nature

While the impact of Christianization in Slavic lands from the late ninth century CE onward supplanted belief in the pantheon of Slavic deities in established major cities and the administrative hubs of empires, in rural areas, the Church's process of trying to displace indigenous gods and spirits was a more complex, centuries-churning affair.

It could easily be argued that those beings were never fully displaced. The thriving, widespread folk beliefs attest that, even today, a panoply of divinities that compose various classes of nature spirits continue to animate the spiritual geographies of Slavic landscapes as well as the soulscapes of Slavic peoples.

Let us now turn our attention to these powers of Earth, Water, and Air.

Powers of Earth: Spirits of the Forest

The lore surrounding forest entities comes to us chiefly from South and East Slavic lands. Let's begin our journey in the Balkans.

Velika Šumska Majka: The Great Forest Mother

In South Slavic lore, perhaps the oldest spiritual being regarded as indigenous to the Balkans is the Great Forest Mother, or Velika Šumska Majka. She is well known even among non-Slavs, as the Romanian ethnic Vlach community in southeastern Serbia refer to her as *Muma Puduri* (Forest Mother). Whether she is a deposed goddess or an exalted spirit of the forest is open to academic debate and of zero importance to the rural folk who believe in her and respect her sylvan home and its denizens, natural and supernatural alike. Some speak of her as being in charge of the *vile*[131] or fairies, making her their queen.[132]

Not fond of the smoke from fires nor electric lights, the Forest Mother steers clear of villages and their human inhabitants. She can be sought out in her forests and has been known to appear to humans, but only after midnight. She is a beautiful woman with long, unbraided black hair and horns on her head. Her torso is characterized by "well-developed, even huge breasts."[133] She sports outrageously long fingernails. Normally naked, Velika Šumska Majka has also been reported clothed in long black or white dresses. If she doesn't want to be seen in her true form, however, she is thought to shape-shift into a female dog, a mare, a she-goat, sow, or cow—or even a haystack.

Like the spring goddesses Vesna and Živa, the presence of the Great Forest Mother is marked by a sweetly scented breeze.[134] Also like those goddesses, Velika Šumska Majka loves to sing, and the forests can echo with her alluring, Otherworldly voice. Oftentimes, mortal men fall prey to

131. Pronounced *VEE'-leh*.

132. Ristić, *Balkan Traditional Witchcraft,* 170.

133. Conrad, "Female Spirits Among the South Slavs," 30.

134. Ristić, *Balkan Traditional Witchcraft,* 170.

her seductive singing; as with the *vile* who serve her, she reputedly takes a fancy to handsome men. Tales abound of these lascivious encounters.

As a being in command of the regenerative forces in nature, a keeper of ecological balance, and a protector of wildlife and the land, she is not a force to be trifled with, however. She is also not blind to the concerns of women and is thought to be especially protective of those about to undergo childbirth; Serbian midwives and Cunning Women (*bajalice*) call upon the Great Forest Mother directly when delivering babies.[135]

The *Leshii,* Male Forest Spirits of the Slavs

During the nineteenth century in western Russia's Kaluga Province, a woman fleeing a forest fire filed a remarkable report with her local magistrates to describe her encounter with the most well-known forest spirits among the Slavs. As panicked animals from bears to squirrels darted out of the inferno that day, the woman was shocked to see that trudging behind them, the size of a literal belltower, was "he himself," the woodland's guardian and master of animals.[136] The "he himself" is none other than the *leshy,* plural *leshii*—also known as a *leshnik, leshovik, lisun,* or *lesnoi.*[137] In Serbia's densely forested Šumadija (*šuma*, "forest") district, an alternate name for this spirit is *šumnik.*[138]

As with the Great Forest Mother of the South Slavs or the spirits of the home and field, the leshnik presents anthropomorphically. Garbed in peasant attire—tellingly, without a belt—his stature can vary from tree-sized to small and pixie-like. There is some reversal magic on display with his clothing and footwear that tips off the unwary to his supernatural stature: shoes worn on the wrong feet, the left flap of his kaftan covering the right instead of the proper opposite way, and so on. In a nod to folk beliefs about the Devil, he may also sport black fur, wings, goat hooves, horns, and glowing red eyes. Also as with the Devil or other beings of a demonic nature, the leshy's sudden appearances were said to be accompanied by high winds.[139]

135. Conrad, "Female Spirits Among the South Slavs," 31.

136. Ivanits, *Russian Folk Belief,* 64.

137. Ivanits, *Russian Folk Belief,* 221.

138. Ristić, *Balkan Traditional Witchcraft,* 178.

139. Warner, *Russian Myths,* 40.

Accounts also usually mention him carrying a large cudgel or club, indicating his sovereignty over the forest animals. As with the Great Forest Mother, he can shape-shift at will. The animal forms he assumes can be wild or domestic. He can even appear as fungi; or, alarmingly, he can mimic the likeness of a person familiar to you. In Russia's remote Arkhangel'sk Province, ethnologists have recorded the preferred method by which country folk can summon the leshy—but only during July 6, the eve prior to Saint John's Day: Head into the forest and chop down an aspen tree so that its tip falls to the east. Climb on top of the stump, facing east, and bend down to look through your legs. Petition the leshy to appear, "not as a gray wolf, not as a black raven, not as a flaming fir tree," but as a person.

If he were to appear, it'd be hard to gauge his temperament, which can be capricious toward humans. A bit of a prankster, the leshy has a habit of leading people astray in the woods—a disturbing way that he does this is by mimicking the voice of a loved one in distress. In his angrier moods, especially if he's feeling vindictive toward hunters or woodcutters who chop down his beloved trees, he may hide knives and axes or dull their blades; he also has the power of *fascinatio* to halt teams of cart-pulling oxen and horses, rooting them to the spot. People who offend the leshy run the risk of serious physical illness or even death. On the opposite end of the spectrum, when he's feeling jovial, he might be inclined to tickle a person![140]

It only makes sense to try to get on his good side by propitiating him with offerings of bread and salt, the traditional gesture of hospitality in East Slavic countries.[141] Other offerings include eggs (especially those dyed red as during Orthodox Easter) and pancakes. These should be wrapped in a clean cloth that is tied in red string and then left at a forest crossroads.[142]

At the very least, it's recommended to consider yourself a guest in the leshy's forest and behave with respect: Boisterous behavior, swearing, even whistling, were frowned upon, as were the more obvious taboos of willfully trampling upon flowers, damaging trees, or going hunting during holy days in the Eastern Orthodox Church's calendar. It's only polite to ask the leshy's

140. Ivanits, *Russian Folk Belief*, 66.

141. Ryan, *The Bathhouse at Midnight*, 44.

142. Ivanits, *Russian Folk Belief*, 69.

permission before setting up camp for the night. However, should diplomacy fail and you find yourself in need of magical protection against a leshy, you can draw a magic circle around yourself in the ground with a hazel or aspen staff or stick and set up a fire within it. You can also make the Sign of the Cross,[143] shoot a bronze button at him, make him laugh by uttering a string of obscenities, or engage in reversal magic by turning your clothing inside out and placing your shoes on the wrong feet. Should those measures fail, calmly and carefully retrace your steps backward out of the forest.[144]

The ambivalent nature of the East Slavic leshy is split into "good" and "bad" male forest spirits known as *vedi* in Croatian folk belief. Like their East Slavic counterparts, the vedi physically present in humanoid form and can be stupendously tall; their bodies are entirely covered with hair. More social than solitary, they dwell in groups of their own kind in forests such as what dot the landscape of the Bilogora region some 43 miles/70 kilometers east of Zagreb.

"Bad" or forest-dwelling *(šumski)* vedi actually try to avoid humans, but if the latter were to trespass into the protected woods, beating or starvation from the vedi might ensue before release was possible! Conversely, each family is thought to have its own protective, good vedi that can be called upon for help. Ethnologists in the Bilogora region of what was then Yugoslavia during the 1960s and 1970s recorded a common exclamation of *"Daj, Bože, da nam vaši vedi pomognejo!"*/"God, allow it so that our vedi helps us!" It was believed that after uttering this short and simple prayer, the spirit would come quickly to the petitioner's aid.[145]

The *Vile*: Fairies of the South Slavs

The *vile* (singular *vila*) are nonhuman nature spirits who are envisaged anthropomorphically and gendered female: They appear as tall, thin women with long and loose, unbound hair that is either pale blonde or richly black.

143. The Orthodox way to do so is to group the index, thumb, and middle finger of the right hand and touch your forehead, your abdomen, your right breast, and your left breast. Catholics cross from left breast to right breast instead.

144. Warner, *Russian Myths,* 38.

145. Conrad, "Male Mythological Beings Among the South Slavs," 5.

Dressed in either gossamer white or inky black, the telltale colors of the Underworld, the alluring *vile* radiate a pale, Otherworldly beauty. In some parts of eastern Serbia, they may be considered a class of spirits subservient to the Great Forest Mother.[146] Like their queen, they are forest-dwelling beings for the most part, though they—in threes or in multiples of three, the Slavic magic number—certainly enjoy dancing the kolo in meadows, woodsy clearings, and even on the borders demarcating wild spaces from cultivated fields.[147]

As with other spirit beings in the Slavic soulscape, they could be helpful or harmful to humans. Serbian epic poems and tales feature *vile* as prominent characters, supernatural women of agency, who aid heroes like Kraljevič (Prince) Marko, not unlike the helpful goddess Athena to Odysseus in Homer's *Odyssey*. Many heroes, equipped with supernatural strength in battle and other powers, are thought to be the offspring of *vile* and mortal man "marriages."[148] Like the Valkyries of Teutonic lore, the *vile* are also babes of battle, equipped with arrows that can kill with instant ferocity or cause someone to waste away from an inexplicable disease; it's the Serbian equivalent of what the medieval Anglo-Saxons referred to as being "elf-shot."[149]

Other harmful activities of the *vile* relate to their aptitude for weather magic that results in crop-destroying hailstorms. They are likely to display their ire against those mortals foolish enough to approach or disrupt them when dancing, riding horses, working, or bathing nude in the moonlight. A common punishment is for the interloper to be struck dumb, returning to his village mute; far worse outcomes entail turning male victims into stones or trees or having their flesh torn apart in the cavernous lairs of the *vile*.[150]

However, a man's good looks might stay the fairy women's wrath. The *vile* are fond of seducing handsome men, but the latter have to keep quiet about their sexual adventures, lest punishment befall them. Men and

---

146. Ristić, *Balkan Traditional Witchcraft,* 190.
147. Conrad, "Female Spirits Among the South Slavs," 27.
148. Ristić, *Balkan Traditional Witchcraft,* 191.
149. Hall, "Calling the Shots," 195.
150. Conrad, "Female Spirits Among the South Slavs," 27.

orphaned babies plus lost children in the woods favored by the *vile* might be offered a special (breast?) milk to drink, which would endow them with superhuman strength and blessings of tremendous healing.[151]

While they're thought to be most active at the liminal times of dawn, dusk, and midnight—especially during new or full moon periods—*vile* can appear during the day but only in animal form: Butterflies, swans, falcons, deer, hares, or snakes are their preferred guises. They can also take the form of mist, a cloud, or an old woman, or become invisible. In terms of the seasons, their powers are the strongest in late spring to late summer—from *Biljini Petak* in early May through Saint John's Day on July 7.[152]

To this day, Serbian Cunning Women (*bajalice*) are thought to derive their knowledge of medicinal herbs and healing abilities from the *vile. Vile* are also renowned for their divination skills. Modern Pagans and witches who want to cultivate a relationship with the *vile* or form some kind of covenant with them may want to call upon the following names, which have been recorded in Serbian epic poems: Ravijolja, Angelina, Andresila, Andželija, Djudža, Janja, Janojka, Jovanka, Jelka, Jerina, Jerisavlja, and Nadanojla.[153]

Unless a person has the clout of a Prince Marko to harangue the *vile* into undoing their baleful magic aimed at them, it's best to always have a little bit of garlic in one's pocket when venturing into wild places. That, in addition to any iron implements (a horseshoe nail works well), is the way to keep the *vile* from targeting you with their arrows or luring you onto the wrong trails so that you get lost. But since everyone loves to dance and make merry, especially at the high summer holidays/feast days of *Đurđevdan* or *Ivandan*, when the *vile* are thought to be most active, I think the best course of action should you come upon a troupe of these dancing Fae women is to join right in and show them your fancy kolo footwork!

151. Conrad, "Female Spirits Among the South Slavs," 28.

152. Ristić, *Balkan Traditional Witchcraft,* 191.

153. Ristić, *Balkan Traditional Witchcraft,* 191.

Powers of Water: Spirits of Rivers, Lakes, Springs, and Wells

In Ukraine, Russia, and Belarus, the *vily* (plural) were supplanted by water nymphs known as *rusalki* sometime during the early Middle Ages.[154] It is to this next class of Elemental beings that we now turn, starting with their male equivalents.

The *Vodenjak/Vodeni Duhovi*

Given its central importance in providing physical sustenance and spiritual purification, water looms large in the Slavic mythic consciousness. As an Element, Water serves as the permeable boundary demarcating "this" world from "that" one of the Otherworld: Every well, holy spring dedicated to a saint, river, lake, and seashore can play host to a tutelary *vodeni duh* or grouping of *vodeni duhovi.* The two most widely known types of water spirits are the male *vodenjak* (the root of *voda* means "water" in most Slavic languages) and the female *rusalka.*

Also variously known as a *vodeni čovjek* ("water man" in Croatian), *nečastivi* ("evil one" in Serbian), or *vodianoi chert* ("water devil" in Russian), the vodenjak is almost universally regarded in the Slavic world as a dangerous being whose chief aim is to drown people.[155] Lacking the beauty of his female counterpart as well as her ability to switch habitats from water to trees, the humanoid-appearing vodenjak is thought to be ugly, green, bloated, bearded, scaly yet shaggy, and slimy. He largely stays confined to his own or neighboring waters, emerging no farther on land than the riverbank or the water mill, if there is one nearby.[156]

However, he can conjure a glamour about himself to appear as a handsome mortal man if his objective is to whisk away a beautiful human woman who captures his fancy. He is thought to be fiercely strong, so much so that escape from his grip is impossible. A century ago, peasants in Russia's Orel, Tula, and Kaluga provinces claimed to glimpse sightings of fantastic underwater crystal palaces where the *vodianoi* held court among their own kin and the ranks of the humans who died by drowning.[157]

154. Conrad, "Female Spirits Among the South Slavs," 27.

155. Ivanits, *Russian Folk Belief,* 70.

156. Charney and Slapšak, *The Slavic Myths,* 199.

157. Ivanits, *Russian Folk Belief,* 72.

Numerous villages throughout the Slavic world have their own repertoires of legends about the vodeni duhovi and how to avoid being drowned by them. In eastern Serbia's Bor District, near the town of Donji Milanovac, two of the main cautions include never mentioning the phrase "water spirit" for fear of invoking him—the epithet of *onaj stari,* "that old man," is used instead—and never answering if one hears one's name being called outdoors three times aloud at night, as this means the nečastivi is attempting to cast his net to drown a person. Other dangerous behaviors to avoid include gazing at your reflection in the water, as this enables the nečastivi to target you. Never make the mistake of taking a riverside nap, whether on the bank or even on a moored boat, as this can tempt the vodeni duhovi to dance their kolo around you and entrap you in their world.[158] Ethnologists in the field have recorded these kinds of accounts in the month of July in particular—the month in which the nečastivi is thought to be most active.[159]

Places where drownings had occurred were considered "unclean" and shunned, especially at night. In general, the learned habit of getting out of the water and avoiding swimming, fishing, and bathing in rivers and lakes at the taboo times of noon or after sunset were considered the most effective strategies of dodging the vodenjak's attention.[160]

But, just as with those for whom forming a pact with the Devil sounds appealing, there are always those who deliberately courted the vodeni duhovi for favors in exchange for their human souls. Successful fishing was one motivation. Another motive, sought by women only, was for the outcome of obtaining tremendous powers in witchcraft. That could only be obtained through sexual congress with the vodenjak. The water spirit's sexual appetite is said to be insatiable.[161] The price to be paid for this strange coupling is high: It might be the death of the would-be witch's husband, if she is married, or her fertility. The ultimate payment of death by drowning is reflected in the Serbian proverb of "*Došao Džavo po svoje*"—"the Devil came for his own." In the not-too-distant past, attempts

158. Conrad, "Male Mythological Beings Among the South Slavs," 6.

159. Bandić, *Narodna Religija Srba u 100 Pojmova*, 159.

160. Ivanits, *Russian Folk Belief,* 72.

161. Ristić, *Balkan Traditional Witchcraft,* 182.

to recover the bodies of drowning victims were thought to anger the vodenjak, as he wanted to hold on to his rightful "prizes." Bruises on the victims' bodies were interpreted as signs of struggles with the fearsome strength of the water spirit.[162]

Aside from successful fishermen and witches, another demographic suspected of having entered into pacts with the vodeni duhovi was the village miller. In fact, the miller was often regarded as a sorcerer for having a friendship with the local vodenjak. It was known that, as with the construction of the *bania* or bathhouse in East Slavic lands, a rooster (ideally black) would have to be sacrificed at the threshold upon the construction of a water mill. Millers were known to continue to make offerings at least annually in the spring if not more frequently throughout the year to keep the local vodeni čovjek pacified. Vodka, bread and salt, tobacco, ram and horse heads/skulls, or entire slain black pigs were thrown into mill streams and offered to the water spirit.[163] Smooth operations at the mill and ease in catching multitudes of fish were surefire signs of a happy, well-placated vodeni duh.

The *Rusalki*

As for the female, nymphlike rusalki, signs of their pleasure are much more obvious. In South and East Slavic lands, they even have an entire week named after them—*Rusal'nalia* Week (also known as Holy Trinity week, culminating in Pentecost Sunday)—wherein they are thought to be at the height of their powers of the year. They leave their underwater homes on the Tuesday leading up to Pentecost Sunday and can be seen, especially by those born on a Saturday, dancing a kolo by the river's edge or in forest clearings. Otherwise, they're seen and heard frolicking in trees, singing and laughing.

Hostile to humans, especially women, the rusalki punish those who trespass into their revels by driving them mad or making them physically ill to the point of death. Those unfortunate folks, in Serbian folk belief, are

162. Ivanits, *Russian Folk Belief,* 73.
163. Ivanits, *Russian Folk Belief,* 73.

said to be "taken" by the rusalki.[164] Considered throughout all Slavic lands to be the souls of unbaptized babies or women or girls who drowned (in either case, they are the "unclean" dead), rusalki, despite their physically beautiful appearances that closely resemble their land-dwelling nonhuman cousins of the *vile*, are nevertheless regarded as another manifestation of the *Nečistaja Sila*—the "Unclean Force."[165]

To this day in rural Serbia, protocols have to be followed, especially by women, for the entirety of Rusal'nalia Week to ensure that the rusalki stay away. Not only do women avoid bathing in rivers and their favorite local swimming spots, but they don't even come near the water, period. Nor do they court danger by napping outdoors. It's also considered wise to avoid engaging in spinning, weaving, knitting, doing laundry, working around the house, and gardening for that entire week.

If those chores, especially ones done outdoors like gardening that would put you in the line of sight of the rusalki, can't be avoided, the best insurance is to carry sprigs and roots of wormwood *(Artemisia absinthium)* on your person and have bunches of the herb on display throughout the house. This is the most apotropaic herb to keep the rusalki at bay.[166] Methods of rendering them harmless include making the Sign of the Cross, proffering garlic, or enclosing yourself within a magic circle drawn on the ground. However, some women in East Slavic countries go the route of trying to appease the rusalki with offerings of linen hung in trees.[167]

The rusalka is certainly a more complex figure than her male counterpart of the vodenjak. Combining traits that apparently fuse the Classical Greek mythological beings of the siren and the naiad with an indigenously Slavic forest spirit *and* with Christian folk religious superstitions about the dead who died unbaptized or unnaturally via drowning, the rusalka bridges the dualism that divides the Slavic goddesses we've profiled in the previous chapter as being *either* forces of life (e.g., Vesna) *or* forces of death (e.g., Mara).

---

164. Bandić, *Narodna Religija Srba u 100 Pojmova,* 156.
165. Ivanits, *Russian Folk Belief,* 187.
166. Bandić, *Narodna Religija Srba u 100 Pojmova,* 156.
167. Ivanits, *Russian Folk Belief,* 75.

The rusalka is a dangerous being, associated with the "unclean" dead, yes, but her ability to leave her underwater domain for the land (at least during the spring and summer months) attests to her powerful, Goddess-given, life force–promoting critical function of bringing new life to vegetation. She transfers the magic of life's inception, which occurs in water, from river or lake to forests and, more importantly, to fields of grain.[168]

Singing to the hauntingly beautiful aria ("Song to the Moon") in Act I of Czech composer Antonin Dvorák's 1900 opera that bears her name, the rusalka captivates us as she carefully balances the waters of life and waters of death within her. In this regard, I think of her as a wholly Slavic version of the female divine being often depicted in the Tarot's Major Arcana card of Temperance. She provides us with much to meditate upon about the cyclical nature of reality and our own ways of marking our celebratory stations with each unfurling of the spiral. *Slava!*

Powers of Air: Spirits of the Winds

Of all the Elements, the one with the most negative connotation in Slavic folk belief is Air.[169]

Elemental Air and the Unclean Force (*Nečistaja Sila*)

In its destructive form of wind (*vetar* in Serbian; *wiatr* in Polish; *viter* in Ukranian), air is the most palpable, this-worldly manifestation of the Unclean Force. Slavic Christians can point to the Bible passage of Ephesians 2:1–2, which alludes to Satan as the "Prince of the Power of the Air."[170]

That negative predisposition toward air finds expression today in the very widespread belief across all Slavic lands that exposure to cold drafts can lead to all manner of devastating sicknesses, paralysis, even death. Throughout much of the former Yugoslavia, the name for that disease-bearing cold draft is *promaja,* and many a baba, including both my grandmothers when they were alive and now my elderly mother, caution against opening windows and carelessly exposing your sensitive skin to this dreadful current of air.

168. Ivanits, *Russian Folk Belief,* 75.

169. Warner, *Russian Myths,* 32.

170. King James Version.

When I was a small child, I was also taught the very old belief that little whirlwinds that pick up and scatter dust or dried leaves in the warmer months and snow drifts in the colder ones are actually animated by devils.[171] The method of magically protecting myself and dispersing the whirling wind, per my mother's instructions, was to place my right hand into the "fig sign" hand gesture (known as *šipak* in Serbian) with the thumb protruding from between the curled index and middle fingers (figure 5). The verbal charm to accompany the gesture is the Serbian taunt of *"Evoti—na! Evoti šipak!"* Translation: "Here—have at it! Here's a šipak for you!" Another method to disperse these little whirlwinds is to stab them with a pocket knife.[172]

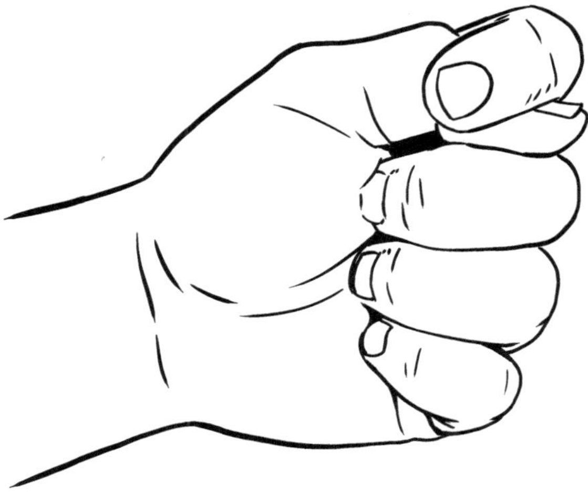

Figure 5

Given that sudden, violent wind gusts are thought to herald the arrival of sinister spiritual beings of all stripes, human and other-than-human, it's not surprising to learn that workings of malefic magic are often sent on the winds. The annals of occult history in Russia are rife with such examples. A sixteenth-century reference to wind-borne magic entails the Tatars of Kasan' as trying to bewitch from a distance the besieging Russian army, as

171. Warner, *Russian Myths,* 32.

172. Ryan, *The Bathhouse at Midnight,* 36.

noted by Prince Kurbskii. As late as the mid-nineteenth century in Siberia's Tiumen' Province, a tailor was accused of starting a cholera epidemic as *nasylat' po vetru*—"sending on the wind."[173]

Closer to our own time, in Orašac, Serbia, a twentieth-century bajalica or enchanter named Desanka Matijašević gained renown as a Cunning Woman skilled in healing a variety of diseases (including jaundice, eczema, and anthrax), which are collectively known as "the nine winds." She and her neighbors perceived these illnesses as originating in the Otherworld and disseminating through our world via the unclean powers of the wind (vetar). It is to the unclean "other place" where the diseases originated from that they are returned.[174]

Slavic Cunning Folk fortunately had at their disposal the spiritual and physical properties of animals both wild and domestic to aid them in their work. It is to these powerfully loaded symbolic repositories of shared meaning across Slavic lands and cultures that we now turn.

173. Ryan, *The Bathhouse at Midnight,* 36.

174. Foley, "Spellbound," 121.

CHAPTER 4
The Powers of the Animal World

To exhaustively list every animal that has accrued significant symbolic currency in Slavic mythology and contemporary Native Faith as well as in Slavic folk beliefs is beyond the scope of this book. I would like to emphasize the ancestral cultic importance of a trio of wild animals—the serpent, the wolf, and the bear—whose lore is best suited for adapting to spiritual practices informed by Paganism.

Serpent Lore in Serbia: The Guardian Snake of the House

According to Serbian anthropologist Dušan Bandić, of all animals the serpent *(zmija)* has the greatest hold on the Serbian imagination. Folk belief holds that snakes were either created by the Devil or by a terrifying supernatural creature called the *ala,* feared for its limitless gorging abilities, or by the world's first dragon (i.e., Veles). The snake's supernatural powers can be felt from the creature's intense gaze. Those powers could be evoked even by simple sympathetic magical methods, such as engraving wavy, zigzag patterns that mimic a snake's shape and movement onto talismans, etching those lines and imbuing everyday objects—from farming implements to weapons and even Easter eggs!—with the serpent's powers of healing and fecundity. While it was taboo to kill a snake, Serbian witches still use snakes' heads, fangs, vertebrae, blood, and shed skins in healing medicines and protective spells, as well as in curses.[175]

The most important snake in Serbian belief, the one accorded the highest respect and propitiation, was the snake living in a family's dwelling. These naturally wild but people-friendly snakes were thought of as home guardians and were variously called *kućnim zmiijama, kućaricama,* or *čuvar kućama.* These are all euphemistic epithets (forms of the phrase "watcher of the house") because it's a huge taboo to utter the word *zmija*/"snake."

When it comes to tracing the ancestral connection, the greatest epithet for this type of snake is *cjen novite*, which means "full of soul" in the Old Slavonic language. In other words, the house-dwelling snake actually has a *human* soul. The animal serves as the embodiment of an ancestor, probably the first head of that family. This ancestor-guardian snake lived either under the foundation of the house (near the threshold) or near the hearth, the focal point of a villager's modest house. The presence of the house-guardian snake would guarantee the protection of the household from all danger.

All manner of taboos, grounded in the culturally important rules of hospitality and the host-guest relationship of reciprocity, surrounded the human-snake interaction in the household. Great care was taken to never offend the snake. Words were chosen carefully in addressing the snake with a preference given to speaking in rhyme! Foul language was prohibited; the snake ought to never witness one's loss of temper. Offerings of food were always deposited in places where the snake would be seen coiled up and

175. Bandić, *Narodna Religija Srba u 100 Pojmova,* 30.

resting. The greatest fear was offending the snake to the degree that it would decide to leave.[176]

If it did depart the household, the family's ruin was ensured. Losses *(šteta)* and ill luck *(zlo)* were sure to follow: crop failure, disease (affecting people and livestock), poverty, and even the deaths of the head of the household and children. No Pagan or Christian magic could counteract the egregiously ill effects or even the sense of hopelessness wrought by the guardian's departure.

Exercise
Shifting Your Consciousness with the Serpent's Breath

This exercise can be done on its own—perhaps throughout the course of the day to get you into the habit of mindfully breathing—or as a prelude to beginning a devotional ritual to your ancestors. This simple practice can help you shift your consciousness into more of an altered state.

Seated comfortably either on the floor, cross-legged, or upright in a chair that supports your back and with your feet firmly on the floor (ideally barefoot), bring your hands together in a classic prayer pose with fingers raised upward and palms touching. Feel the mounds of your thumbs gently resting upon your chest cavity.

Breathe in through your nose, slowly and deeply to a count of six. Pause and hold your breath for a count of two. Then slowly exhale out your mouth with your lips gently parted and *hiss out* your exhalation for a count of six to eight.

Repeat this process as many times as you like. When you feel you have reached an energetically charged, mentally clear state, continue the hissing breath but raise your hands, still in prayer pose, from your chest to above your head, with your elbows bent to whichever degree is most comfortable for you. Visualize yourself as a conduit for ancestral serpent energy, a gift of the god Veles, rising from the Underworld, through the floor or chair where you sit, up your spinal column, and out through the tips of your fingers. Now you have become the Axis Mundi, the World Pillar that connects all the realms of Nav, Yav, and Prav.

176. Bandić, *Narodna Religija Srba u 100 Pojmova,* 33.

When you are ready, say the following out loud:

> *"Slava Rodu: Those who have gone before me!*
> *Slava Rodu: Those who will come after me!*
> *Slava Veles, Grandfather!*
> *The Sacred Serpent who holds us all in an unbroken circle of connection!*
> *Mir svima—peace to all!"*

Lower your arms, and when you are ready, slowly rise. If you wish, you may journal about your experiences.

Wolves in Serbian Folk Belief: The Ancestral Magic of Winter

Feared but equally revered, wolves were and still are widely believed to have supernatural powers—so much so that to even say the word *wolf* (*vuk*) is still quite a taboo in many places for fear of unintentionally invoking one. Instead, one would resort to using nicknames or euphemisms, which, incidentally, are the same ones for the Devil(!), such as *Nepomenik* (Unmentionable), *Kamenik* (the One Made of Stone), *Pogan* (the Unclean One), *Onaj iz Gore* (the One from the Woods), and other terms.[177]

Magic, *vračanje,* was performed apotropaically to prevent wolves from attacking. Simple sympathetic acts of magic could include taking one's shears for shearing sheep and closing them on the eve before the feast day of Saint Demetrios, a.k.a. *Mitrovdan* (November 8 in the older Julian calendar, October 26 in the modern Gregorian one), the traditional Serbian reckoning of the start of winter. This act magically prohibits wolves from having access to one's livestock.

Placating Vengeful Wolf Spirits

The winter season from Mitrovdan onward brought misery to country folk. Aside from the rigors of maintaining heat (through humble wood-burning stoves, for the most part) and other resources for months on end,

177. Bandić, *Narodna Religija Srba u 100 Pojmova,* 25.

family farmers had to watch out for wolves. In the hilly terrain of the village of Gornji Milanovac, my father's ancestral land, wolves were known to descend from the mountains in packs and kill livestock. My father's winter of 1944 boyhood was filled with episodes of being given a shotgun at the ripe age of eight years old so that he and his twelve-year-old brother Mirko could patrol their village, guarding various families' pens of livestock against wolves, while gunfire rang out in the snowcapped hills above between invading Nazi ground forces and Marshal Tito's Communist *Partizani* Yugoslav defense forces.

As my father sat by the roaring fireplace in the subterranean family room of his and my mom's Chicagoland home on Mitrovdan of 2014 and shared these traumatic anecdotes with me, time and place melted away in the flickering firelight. The shadows cast by my father's hands, his wide-eyed look that haunted me at the time, and his trembling voice brought his boyhood terror vividly to life. I can't even begin to imagine what he and my mother's families and millions of other Europeans endured. My father confessed he didn't know what scared him more in that dire winter of 1944—the prospect of encountering a wolf or a Nazi infantryman in the hills above Gornji Milanovac.

The Yugoslav government recognized that wolves posed a problem to rural families like my father's whose livelihoods depended upon the survival of their herds. Poisons were doled out to villages and people were instructed to use them to bait wolves. But my father said his father and their neighbors refused to do it. It was wrong on so many levels. Wolves were scary and posed definite threats to livestock, yes, but the idea of being subject to the *wolves' vengeful spirits* was even more frightening. This was something the Communist Yugoslav government, of course, neither understood nor could eradicate: centuries of peasant superstition.

For country dwellers like my Deda Miloš and my father, it was taboo to kill a wolf. Wolves were greatly respected and feared, especially after their deaths. The belief was that if you killed a wolf, the spirit of the wolf would become enraged and would want to exact revenge, not just on you as a defender of your livestock or as a hunter but on your entire village. It makes sense that a pack animal would want to target a group.

My mother's work as a civil engineer in Yugoslavia often took her to the Republic of Bosnia-Herzegovina. While working on a highway project in the autumn of 1966 in Borija, northwest Bosnia, she told me she'd encountered hunters in a horse-drawn wagon who had a quarry of slain wolves. The beautiful creatures had been shot as nuisance animals. My mother burst into tears and tried to shame the men for their actions. She told me that the men then emptied their shotguns of live rounds and tossed the guns over the carcasses of the wolves across the bed of the wagon, saying, "Here is your enemy! Not me, but *this!*" A striking act of sympathetic magic done in broad daylight, before dozens of witnesses.[178] The hunters' words implied, "Hey, wolves, I didn't shoot you, the rifle did! So don't come back after me! Go after the rifle."

However a wolf met its end, its pelt and other parts were put to apotropaic magical use. If shot, the wolf would be skinned and then paraded into homes, and people had to offer the wolfskin gifts. Women offered carded wool and finely spun linen. And men in the village offered money, placing it atop the wolf's head.[179] The reason for these gestures is clear: Pay the spirit of the slain wolf for taking its life. Appease the spirit almost as if you're befriending it.

To enhance magical protection, talismans were made from the slain wolf's eyes, heart, fur/hair, claws, and teeth.[180] But to really harness the animal's power, thankfully in a way that doesn't take the lives of wolves, women still name their sons Vuk. It's a popular nonbiblical Serbian name. In the old days, my father said, the reason for doing so was due to higher infant mortality rates in rural areas like his village. If a mother had stillborn children or ones that didn't survive their infancy, she was strongly advised to name her next newborn son Vuk, especially if it showed signs of being a sickly child. Again, sympathetic magic is at work here. The child will, it is hoped, acquire the same powers as the animal: strength, immunity from sickness, and the ability to ward off malevolent spiritual forces.

178. Milanka Urošević, interview with the author, June 7, 2024.

179. Bandić, *Narodna Religija Srba u 100 Pojmova,* 27.

180. Ristić, *Balkan Traditional Witchcraft,* 203.

Figures of wolves were engraved on swords in Serbia and Montenegro to make the swords deadlier for their intended foes in battle as well as to protect the wielder of the sword from evil people and demons. Swords could also help women conceive babies if they were infertile; they merely needed to touch one if they wanted to get pregnant.[181]

At country weddings as recently as the mid-twentieth century, men pretending to be wolves would attack the groom's house. They formed a single chain, howling and singing, warning the groom to take care of his bride to protect her from them as both young men and wolves. The wolf-men wouldn't leave until someone from the house threw them a package of food. Around Christmas time and during the *Koleda* winter festival season in many Serbian villages, wolf skins were stuffed with straw and men would create fantastical masks and adorn themselves in wolf pelts and go from house to house, caroling and collecting gifts. In Kosovo, families were known to bake a ritual bread on Christmas Eve (January 6) as an offering to wolves. In Serbia, Bosnia, and Croatia's Dalmatian coast, people would bring wolves a ritual supper after sunset to one of three places: on the threshold of pastures, at a crossroads, or where garbage was burned outside the village.[182]

During the whole length of winter and the spring season to Saint George's Day, the traditional reckoning of the start of summer, wolf magic was strong. Visits from actual wolves and spirit wolves took place, especially during major feast days in the Eastern Orthodox Church. It was assumed that spirit wolves were everywhere and your behavior toward them would affect how you'd be treated by real wolves as well as how the spirits would treat you. Good behavior meant exuding the widely acclaimed Serbian trait of hospitality, especially to strangers.

When a lone wolf descended into a village from the mountains on a winter night, it was often regarded as an embodiment of the ancestors—not just the dead members of a given family or community, but all the dead.[183] Chthonic Slavic gods such as Veles and Triglav, as we've seen, are associated

181. Bandić, *Narodna Religija Srba u 100 Pojmova,* 30.

182. Ristić, *Balkan Traditional Witchcraft,* 203.

183. Bandić, *Narodna Religija Srba u 100 Pojmova,* 27.

with wolves. Not unlike Wotan or Odin of the Teutonic peoples, these dark lords are masters of magic and the mysteries of death. I have felt their spectral presences course across the winter night skies with iron resolve.

Bears: Kin of Humanity

As we've seen so far, to say the name of the spirit being or the sacred animal in question is a taboo out of the fear of inadvertently conjuring it. That taboo is so prevalent in Slavic countries concerning the word *bear* that the Serbian and Russian nouns for the animal are *themselves* euphemisms: In both languages, *medved*, "bear," literally means "the knower of honey."[184] To downplay the animal's supernatural connotations, diminutive nicknames are used instead, especially when speaking aloud. In East Slavic lands such as Russia and Belarus, the masculine diminutive of *Mishka* is used, while in Serbia and neighboring Bosnia—even in regions where, tragically, the animal has been hunted to extinction—the feminine diminutive title of *Tetka,* "Auntie," is used. It is, according to Russian folklore expert Cherry Gilchrist, "from this mixture of playfulness and fear, respect and defensiveness" that the Slavic consciousness of the bear as a sacred animal is developed.[185]

As with serpents and wolves, bears—in this case, the European brown bear *(Ursus arctos)*—are also tied to the cult of the ancestors. In far northeast Europe, the bear cult dates back far into the mists of prehistory, quite likely as the result of human-bear coexistence (however wary for both parties) in shared cave systems.[186] The closeness of humans and bears finds expression in the folk beliefs of peoples in Serbia, Bosnia, and Montenegro relating to bears' origins: Humanlike in their cleverness and curiosity, in the ferocity of their protective mothers, and in their stature (when standing on hind legs), bears are thought to have once been human. Intriguing folklore from the Bosnian city of Mostar and surrounding areas states that humans caught kneading dough with their feet instead of their hands as well as bakers who

184. Gilchrist, *Russian Magic,* 116.
185. Gilchrist, *Russian Magic,* 117.
186. Gilchrist, *Russian Magic,* 117.

appeared before the throne of God with unwashed, flour-coated hands were turned into bears as punishment.

Folktales also are rife with disturbing episodes of the mating of humans and bears that resulted in the births of supernatural male heroes who were human in appearance but bearlike in indomitable strength. In the Bosnian capital of Mostar, these strong, strapping lads were called "bear-built" (*Međed gradio*). Solitary human women out foraging for mushrooms in desolate forests ran the risk of being abducted by male bears and taken back to their caves to produce these supernatural offspring: The Serbian clan of *Međedović* has this as their striking mythic origin story.[187]

The spirit of the bear continued to be venerated well into the late twentieth century, with many customs related to bear-lore performed on Saint Andrew's Day (December 13 in the Julian calendar/November 30 in the Gregorian). The saint's feast day is actually known as *Mečkin Dan* or *Mečko Dava,* the "Day of the Bear." Taboos pertained to refraining from working with leather goods/tanning, especially repairing or making new shoes, as it was thought the vengeful spirit of the Mother Bear, again, diminutively referred to as Auntie or Tetka, will kill (by strangulation!) any cobblers who violate this taboo.

To ensure a harmonious relationship with Tetka, even in regions where the brown bear has died out, the eldest or most authoritative woman of the household would scatter several cobs of corn as well as pieces of wood meant to be burned in the stove on her house's rooftop. She would also scatter corn kernels around the perimeter of the house on Saint Andrew's Eve. The following morning, the children of the family would be brought outside to be shown how the corn has disappeared, proof of Tetka's visit overnight. Taking up a barren cob, the mother would then dunk the cob in wine and everyone from the household had to drink from the glass to ensure their protection against physical harm and spiritual malevolence.[188]

East Slavic hunting customs of bears show a strong overlap with the superstitions and taboos we've previously seen concerning slain wolves in Serbia: fearful of the bear's vengeful spirit, Russian hunters would decry

187. Bandić, *Narodna Religija Srba u 100 Pojmova,* 35.

188. Bandić, *Narodna Religija Srba u 100 Pojmova,* 36.

their involvement and claim the fatal shooting came from another source. "Another rather more eerie custom was to take the bear's skin into the house by passing it through a window," Cherry Gilchrist informs us. "This prevented its spirit from following the skin indoors, as it could only enter through a doorway."[189] Respect had to be shown to the dead animal by holding a feast in its honor and having each guest pay their respects to the bear by touching their foreheads to its muzzle.

Properly placated, Bear as a spiritual animal brings the blessings of healing, renewal, and fertility from the Underworld/Otherworld. In wedding ceremonies of some parts of Russia, both the bride and the groom are still referred to as bears. In Belarus, an act of apotropaic magic to protect one's house against fire involves leading a (presumably tame) bear around the house clockwise three times. Bear droppings found in the barn are viewed as a sign of good fortune, and bears' heads used to be buried in fields and pastures to assist with the growth of crops and the protection of the herds, respectively.[190] Not surprisingly, bear claws, whole paws, hide, and teeth are highly desired amulets by Slavic magical practitioners.

While the spirits of magical animals certainly play their role in helping ensure things go smoothly in the home, devotional attention chiefly belongs to the house spirits themselves to keep peril and spiritual malevolence at bay. Let us learn of these sacred powers next. *Slava!*

---

189. Gilchrist, *Russian Magic,* 118.

190. Ryan, *The Bathhouse at Midnight,* 112.

CHAPTER 5

The Spirits of the Home and Farmstead

Spirits that can be either helpful or harmful to humans don't just exist in nature: to the Slavic peoples, as with many other cultures around the world, there is an array of spirits associated with one's home and property. It's a wise idea to develop a relationship with these spirits and curry their favor for domestic harmony. The most well-known of these is the *domovoi* (Russian; домовой) or *domovyk* (Ukrainian; домовик); the root of *dom* means "house" in many Slavic languages and is cognate with the English word *domicile*.

In Serbian, the spirit is known as a *kućnih duhova* (кућних духова), literally "house spirit," and it is thought to be an invisible dwarf that is attached to a given family rather than to the house/structure wherein it dwells, per se.[191] This would be another indication

191. Podunavski, *Tradicionalno Balkansko Veštičarstvo*, 162.

that the domovoi's origins ultimately link to the pre-Christian cult of the ancestors.[192]

Domovoi, the House Dwarf

As it is a taboo to call a potentially dangerous creature by its name, an endearing epithet that expresses kinship such as *Deda* (Serbian) or *Dedushka* (Russian), both meaning "Grandfather," is the most common way to address a domovoi and acknowledge it as a representative of the former head of the family.[193] Given the implied blood ties, forged however remotely in the past, with the current living family, a domovoi is thought to be favorably disposed toward the living and serves as a diligent household guardian and invisible helper. Like the screeching banshee of Irish lore, he can even be thought to sound an alarm when the family is about to face a dire calamity.[194] Unlike the wilder spirits of nature, a domovoi isn't perturbed by the sight of Christian religious objects such as crucifixes, icons, and blessed beeswax candles; nor does the rooster's crow at break of day unnerve him and send him running, as it would to any spiritual manifestation of the Unclean Force.

Thought to reside either near the stove, under the threshold, in the cellar, in the attic, or in the stables if the family resides on a farm, the domovoi goes about his daily tasks unseen, but the sounds he makes—footsteps on the stairs, doors or cabinets opening and closing, knocks, and even singing—can be heard by the people in the house. Though he prefers to be invisible, he can make himself seen by the family in his true form if he wishes, especially during the first night when the family moves into a new home. He is also likely to disguise himself as the family dog or cat.[195]

To ensure a happy relationship with your home's domovoi, a little hospitality goes a long way. Set aside a special place for him in your kitchen and speak to him out loud, addressing him as "Grandfather." Historically,

---

192. Ivanits, *Russian Folk Belief,* 52.
193. Gilchrist, *Russian Magic,* 54–55.
194. Podunavski, *Tradicionalno Balkansko Veštičarstvo,* 162.
195. Ivanits, *Russian Folk Belief,* 52.

offerings to him include a bowl of porridge, a thick slice of bread, tobacco, or juniper sprigs.[196]

You'll be able to feel when your domovoi is content and there's a sense of your household functioning smoothly, with peace in the home experienced by all who live there. By contrast, if your domovoi feels neglected or is upset by the behaviors he sees in the home (e.g., bickering, adults swearing, adults or children being untidy), the signs of his displeasure can range variously. There may be an increase of quarreling in the home accompanied by strange phenomena of lights flickering on and off, objects suddenly and mysteriously disappearing from their usual resting places, and doors slamming shut for no apparent reason. Even more disturbing indications of what appear to be poltergeist activity include the smashing of china and glassware, even windows. Farmers with an upset domovoi would discover signs that their livestock had been abused overnight, from tangled horses' manes to knots tied in cows' tails! If the domovoi becomes too enraged or disgusted, he'll simply leave the family, the worst outcome imaginable.[197]

As guardian of the family, the domovoi could be counted on to predict the family's fortune. If the domovoi were to take the form of a cat at night and rub against the head of the household, the textures of warm skin and smooth fur were a good omen; a cold, prickly touch could serve as a death omen, however, as could the domovoi making himself visible and extinguishing lights. Happy portents were associated with the sounds of the domovoi laughing or singing and especially his fondness for plucking the teeth of a comb as a musical instrument; this could foretell a wedding in the family.

Great care has to be taken to ensure that the domovoi is successfully transferred from one home to another. An actual declaration—"Grandfather, Grandfather! Don't stay here, but come with us to our new house!"—accompanied by an offering is a common practice. Ritual gestures to transfer the domovoi are the head of the family's responsibility and can include offering him a plate of fresh-baked bread and salt—the quintessential East Slavic gesture of welcoming a guest—or transferring embers from

196. Gilchrist, *Russian Magic,* 54.

197. Ivanits, *Russian Folk Belief,* 54.

the old house's fireplace or woodburning stove to the new. This connection between the spirit and the domestic fire also clues us in to the spirit's likely origin in the pre-Christian Slavic cult of the ancestors.[198]

Kikimora, a Female House Spirit

Also referred to as *šišimora,* the kikimora (кикимора) is a female-gendered house spirit that may be considered the wife of the domovoi, or else a spirit in her own right. She was thought of as anthropomorphic in appearance and may be arrayed in traditional women's attire—but her hair would be unbound and uncovered, a signifier of wild magical power.[199] In Serbian folk belief, she is a bit of a grotesque, chimerical figure with attributes of a fox and a duck in her facial features: squinty eyes and even a duck's bill instead of human lips.[200]

The traditional province of Slavic peasant women—spinning, needlework, tending to chickens—falls under the kikimora's purview of the household as well. She could punish women who failed to observe the taboo of spinning on Fridays as well as damage or destroy the needlework carelessly left around the house. She might also take out her frustrations on the livestock; to halt the kikimora's nocturnal tormenting of chickens, a hagstone would have to be found in the fields and hung above the chicken coop.[201]

Kikimora were especially thought to haunt abandoned or otherwise empty houses. To transfer one as a form of punishment to living people into a new home undergoing construction, disgruntled carpenters and other contractors angry with their clients might entice a kikimora to occupy a small doll, which would then be buried in the new house's foundations. This spiteful ritual act is thought to impart a rough start for the new homeowner.[202]

---

198. Ivanits, *Russian Folk Belief,* 56.
199. Ryan, *The Bathhouse at Midnight,* 80.
200. Gajić, *Slovenska Mitologija,* 188.
201. Ivanits, *Russian Folk Belief,* 57.
202. Ryan, *The Bathhouse at Midnight,* 43.

The Malevolent *Bannik,* Spirit of the Bathhouse

Of all the spirits of place most overtly hostile to living humans, the bannik (банник) historically was the most feared among the East Slavs. Numerous taboos and stipulations were imposed on the use of the bathhouse or *bania.* Far from being a mere outdoor structure on one's property that served as a sauna meant for weekly steam baths—Saturday being the preferred day—the bathhouse was a spooky, even sinister, place, the equivalent of a crossroads wherein evil spirits, witches, and Unclean Forces might come to gather or even be deliberately conjured up.[203]

A location that might serve as the last bastion of Slavic Paganism in countries where Eastern Orthodox Christianity is the dominant religion, the bathhouse was the one place on their private properties or communal village zones of liminality where Orthodox Christians would not hang an icon. Such a sight would likely offend the bannik. Additionally, prior to steaming themselves, people had to remove their necklaces of blessed crosses as well as their belts, items thought to be imbued with powers of spiritual protection.[204] People were thus at their most spiritually vulnerable, so it is no wonder that the bathhouse and its resident spirit of the bannik came to be feared.

However, given the Slavic rules of hospitality that prescribe not just how to be a good host but a good guest as well, the bannik could be placated upon visiting the bathhouse by presenting him with offerings of soap, fir branches, and a little water. It's also the sign of a good guest to say out loud, "Thank you!" to the bannik upon exiting the bathhouse. Concern for the bannik also extends into certain behaviors while taking a steam bath: Boisterousness, loud talk, and singing are not encouraged. The third round of the steam, which has to conclude before sunset, is the final round for living humans. The bannik himself took his turn at the fourth round, and he was likely to invite other nonhuman spirits to join him. People, especially women, were forbidden from going to the bathhouse at night and could never enter alone at any time of day.[205]

203. Gilchrist, *Russian Magic,* 58.

204. Ryan, *The Bathhouse at Midnight,* 51.

205. Ivanits, *Russian Folk Belief,* 59.

But that last rule certainly didn't stop magical practitioners from performing their workings, as the bania acquired a reputation as one of the most powerful places to perform either positive workings of ritual purification or curses and other types of *malefica*. An example of the latter in Russian lore has the sorcerer (variously known as a *znakhar*, *koldun*, or *volkhv*) take the measure of his target's footprint with yarn or thread and bring that artifact to a bathhouse at midnight to perform a working with the goal of killing his target.[206]

Divination with the bannik was an occurrence saved for New Year's Day or when a bride-to-be wished to know the destiny of her marriage. The bold querent had to stand, either fully naked or with her posterior otherwise exposed, at the threshold with her back to the bathhouse and ask for the bannik to tell her fortune with his touch: A soft touch was a good omen; a cold or prickly touch, the opposite.[207]

Fearful attitudes surrounding the bania may stem from the fact that historically, animal sacrifices were conducted at the threshold when building one: A black hen, suffocated and feathers left unplucked, was laid in the foundation as an offering to the bannik.[208] If a bania were to ever burn down, its replacement would have to have the sacrifice repeated, though at a new site, as the former would be considered unlucky at best and evil at worst. In Belarus, this belief of tainted places extends to other places considered as sites of misfortune—especially anywhere blood has been spilled during a tragic event's unfolding, or anywhere in a forest where a tree has been uprooted or blasted apart by lightning. Regardless, a koldun or znakhar would have to be employed to select a new location to erect a bania for village folk.[209]

For urban dwellers today who are wealthy enough to have a bania inside their modern homes or who have access to modern banias in their cities, magic can be made through intentionality and self-care: Aromatherapy, ritual purification with an herbal bundle known in Ukraine as a *vinyk* (віник),

---

206. Ryan, *The Bathhouse at Midnight,* 36.
207. Gilchrist, *Russian Magic,* 63.
208. Ivanits, *Russian Folk Belief,* 59.
209. Ryan, *The Bathhouse at Midnight,* 51.

and even divination performed under the watchful gaze of the bannik are ways to keep the age-old East Slavic traditions of the bathhouse alive.[210]

The *Ovinnik*: Spirit of the Grain-Threshing Barn

With its likely origins in a pre-Christian Slavic fire cult, most certainly tied to Svarog, the East Slavic spirit known as the ovinnik (овинник) is unquestionably the most dangerous of the domestic spirits. This is the spirit that presides over the threshing barn, the critical structure of the farmstead that had to be positioned as far as possible from the family dwelling because of the severe fire risk it posed. In places like the far north of Russia, this barn was a two-level structure with a crude furnace, partially dug into the earth, on the ground level. The second level's floor would be covered with sheaves of grain for drying.[211]

The ovinnik is a spirit with a tremendous amount of agency, and rural families consider it a mission-critical objective to get on his good side. It's widely thought that he forbids the stoking of the furnace on days when the winds are strong as well as on certain feast days in the Orthodox liturgical calendar, such as *Krstovdan* (the Day of the Holy Cross, September 27 in the Julian calendar) or the Dormition of the Virgin Mary (August 28). Failure to abide by such taboos could lead to the disastrous consequence of the burning down of the barn, perhaps with the head of the household inside of it.

Beliefs surrounding interactions with the ovinnik overlap with the bannik, especially concerning the ritualized offering of sacrificed animals, chiefly roosters; their heads would be chopped off over the threshold and the blood sprinkled in the four corners of the barn. The November feast day of the magic-working twins or *Vračari*, Saints Cosmas and Damian, on November 14 (old Julian calendar) or November 1 (modern Gregorian), is considered the most auspicious day for this butchery.

Also as with the bannik, one could engage in divination with the ovinnik on New Year's Day simply by requesting his touch: A soft-textured

210. Pamita, *Baba Yaga's Book of Witchcraft*, 237.

211. Ivanits, *Russian Folk Belief*, 60.

touch foretold good luck and happiness, but a cold, prickly touch foretold disaster—even the death of the querent.[212]

To this day in some rural corners of the East Slavic world, the Pagan practices of prayers and ritual offerings performed to the ovinnik in the threshing barn have been impossible for the Orthodox Church to eradicate.

The Spirits of the Fields: *Polevoi* and *Poludnitsa*

There's a pattern that you may have detected by now regarding the names of these spirits: They're largely determined by their habitat, with the domovoi related to the house, the bannik to the bania or bathhouse, and so on. It's no different with this outdoor-but-still-residing-on-human-territory class of spirits known as the male polevoi (полевой) or the singular female poludnitsa (полудница). These are the spirits of the fields.

The anthropomorphic appearance of the polevoi reflects regional variations. In Russia's main agricultural regions such as the Orel Province, the spirit's body may be black like the soil, with long green grass for hair, and he isn't clothed. In the far northern woodland landscape regions, he is a luminous being attired in white, not unlike the slender birch trees surrounding his fields.

Some theories advocate that the polevoi, attached to a family more so than a geographical location, can make himself visible to warn of impending doom. This is a trait shared with the domovoi. By other accounts, the polevoi has more in common with the tricksterish leshii, especially when it comes to the practice of leading people astray outdoors.

Other viewpoints in the Slavic mindset go one level past tricksterishness and assign pernicious natures to the polevoi, asserting that these spirits are manifestations of the Unclean Force, and it's best to avoid them and the sites they defile. Care should be taken to avoid the liminal zones of the boundaries of the fields, and for field workers to especially not take their afternoon siestas at those in-between places, for those are the areas where the horse-mounted polevoi gallop about or where their spectral children

212. Ivanits, *Russian Folk Belief*, 61.

like to play; in either case, contact with these spirits poses physical danger for the humans.[213]

The magical time of day associated with polevoi and poludnitsa activity is noon, the opposite of midnight. It was from my mother that I first learned about noon as a hazardous, no-less-eerily-magical-than-midnight time when supernatural creatures can make their presences known and terrify you.

This is her story: One early autumn day in 1960, somewhere on the outskirts of the hilly southwestern Serbian village of Kotraža, where she was working as the team lead civil engineer in a highway expansion project, she violated the taboo of sojourning alone in the fields at noon and something invisible pursued her on foot, terrifying her. She says she actually heard heavy stomping boots directly behind her, crunching the stubble of wheat stalks in the harvested fields; of course, when she turned around, there was no one there.

She ran and ran with her invisible pursuer still on her heels until she saw her colleagues dining outside at a local *kafana* (pub). Everyone asked her what was wrong; she was as pale as a sheet. She said nothing. The savvy kafana owner sat her down indoors, and over a warm plate of homemade *sarma,* he quietly confided that he understood the nature of her terror—many have experienced the disturbing phenomenon prior to her, including himself—and it would be wise going forward to avoid making shortcuts through the fields, especially when she's alone.

I have to admit, as a ten-year-old girl listening to her strange and harrowing anecdote, I was initially incredulous. *How can something ghostlike and scary take place in broad daylight? Especially when her coworkers were enjoying their lunch just a couple of hundred feet away?* I just couldn't wrap my mind around it, so I had a hard time believing her. Now, as an adult spirit worker, I don't doubt the existences of the polevoi and poludnica one bit. Such spirits to me are potent *genii locii,* beings of awareness and agency.

Regarding any spirit of place, my policy is to cultivate a humble and respectful attitude as a necessary prerequisite prior to venturing into their territory. The language of reciprocity, of giving offerings as thanks for the

---

213. Ivanits, *Russian Folk Belief,* 74.

gift of safe passage in unfamiliar territory, is something I think spirits of place speak and understand very well, no matter where you are in the world and what your spiritual tradition may be.

Exercise
Cultivate a Relationship with Your Home's *Domovoi*

If you've ever watched the popular 2019 Netflix series *Tidying Up with Marie Kondo,* you may have felt as deeply moved as I have during the moments when Ms. Kondo would ask the homeowners' permission to commune with the in-dwelling spirit of the house before she could commence her decluttering work. The American homeowners, perhaps due to not being familiar with Japan's indigenous Shinto religion, always seemed so stunned by Ms. Kondo's request; quizzical eyebrows arched in response to the mere mention of a house spirit. Thankfully, however, the homeowners would acquiesce.

As they watched Ms. Kondo perform her simple ritual of kneeling on the floor, closing her eyes, and communing with the house's spirit guardian with her hands folded in prayer, they seemed to be deeply affected for the better. Some folks were even moved to tears, perhaps recognizing even at an unconscious level the healing power inherent in creating and maintaining a relationship with one's house spirit. Whether they're new to their dwelling place or have been living in it for decades, homeowners and renters alike would benefit from cultivating a devotional relationship with their home's domovoi.

The history of the hearth/fireplace as the locus of ancestor veneration in Slavic countries translates into setting aside a little zone in the kitchen—on a cupboard shelf, windowsill, section of countertop, or small corner table—as the shrine where the domovoi can be honored. The domovoi doesn't just guard the physical space of the home, but the luck and well-being of the residents too. Hence you may want to also consider adding elements of a household prosperity shrine, even if it's just a piggy bank or glass jar that everyone dumps their loose change into. Be sure to do so mindfully, though, with a "Thank you, Grandfather, for growing our wealth!" kind of greeting to the domovoi when coins are added.

On the night of a new moon or a young moon, when the slender waxing crescent is first visible after a new moon (usually three nights after), gather the following items:

- A white plate, however large is up to you, with either a small round loaf of *pogača* (see appendix D) or three slices of fresh-baked bread
- Butter or *kajmak* for the bread
- A clear glass with clear, still water in it—spring water is ideal
- A small bell or rattle
- Matches or a lighter
- A beeswax candle (taper or votive) in its burner atop a fireproof surface, such as a ceramic saucer
- A bottle of either vodka, *šlivovica*, *krupnik*, whiskey, or mead
- A shot glass
- *Optional:* images of the domovoi[214]

Stand at your newly created shrine space for the domovoi and ring the bell or shake the rattle in groups of threes to announce to the house spirit as well as to your deep mind that you're leaving behind mundane consciousness to open a portal into the Otherworld, where spirit contact is possible. Take a deep, cleansing breath and light the candle.

In a calm but clear voice, say aloud:

"*Slava Rodu*—Hail the Elder Kin! Grandfather, come! Watcher of the house, I bid you welcome! I, *[state your name]*, who live under this roof with you as your neighbor, have set aside this space for you; please come and make your abode at this hearth! With joy and friendship, I offer you a meal of *[name offerings as you hold them aloft, pour the alcohol into the shot glass]*. Please come and eat and drink your fill! I thank you for lending your spirit of tranquility and order to the goings-on in this home. Stand watch in peace,

214. I have a wonderfully detailed, hand-carved linden wood statue of a domovoi that was made in Czechia by the artisans of Wulflund.com.

Grandfather! Put to flight the *urok*[215] and all disguises of the Unclean Force. Allow only energies of health, abundance, joy, and friendship to enter this home! May it be so! I look forward to building many years of friendship with you as I care for this home as well. To your good health, Grandfather! *[Raise offerings.]* May peace and harmony always be between us! *Slava!*"

Ring the bell or shake the rattle to seal your prayer. Let the candle continue to burn down as long as you can but certainly extinguish it (with your fingers—don't blow it out) before leaving the house or retiring to bed for the night. Ensure that no pets or small children have access to the space.

No later than the third day after doing this ritual of welcome, take the offerings outside: Crumble the bread for birds, pour the water onto plants, and pour the alcoholic beverage onto the ground. Make the act of refilling the glass of water a daily habit, along with addressing the domovoi first thing in the morning and right before retiring to bed. Ask him to watch over the home when you leave the house, especially if you'll be gone for a while. Repeat the ritual activity of giving him the food and alcohol offerings on new and full moons as well as during sacred days—he certainly deserves to be spoiled with extra goodies for all the good work he does!

The more you integrate interactions with the domovoi into your daily routine, the faster your household will be on the road to domestic harmony and to receiving serendipitous forms of abundance as well as plain old good luck! Remember, an attitude of gratitude goes a long way toward keeping your domovoi content; consider adding this or a similar statement to your prayers: "Thank you for the blessings you've sent and thank you for the ones that are on their way! *Slava!*"

With its amalgamation of ancestor reverence and animism and its adaptation to the Christian concept of a Slavic family's protecting saint, the cult of the domovoi is perhaps the most well-known example of Dual-Faith Tradition in practice. It is to the history of Dual-Faith that we now turn. *Slava!*

---

215. Pronounced *OOH'-rawk*, it's the Serbian term for the evil eye.

PART II
THE DUAL-FAITH TRADITION

(Народна Веровања)

CHAPTER 6

Christianization and the Dual-Faith Compromise

In the early sixth century CE, as Western European tribes and warring kingdoms sought to fill the vacuum left by Rome's collapse, the Slavs in their ancient homeland (modern-day southwest Ukraine) began the first of three major phases of expansion over the next two centuries. They would spread out in four directions: along the east flank of the Carpathians (through Moldavia and east Romania) toward the Danube plain and the Balkans, including a large swath of Peloponnesian Greece; along the north flank of the western Carpathians (through southern Poland); along the south flank of the western Carpathians (west Slovakia and Moravia to Bohemia and through to Polabia), toward the Danube and Elbe Rivers; and pushing eastward into Ukraine.[216]

216. Barford, *The Early Slavs*, 47.

The Early Slavs: The View from Byzantium

Wherever they migrated and settled, family and clan life continued for the Early Slavs much as they had from centuries prior. Insights into the home-life and kinship systems of the Early Slavs can be gleaned from sociological and linguistic evidence from present-day South Slavs, which distinguish between a nuclear family's home (Serbo-Croatian *kuća inokosna)* and a *kuća zadružna,* or joint/multigenerational household.[217] *(Družina* means "community" in Serbo-Croatian.) This more communal sense of a household (a *zadruga)* describes the homes of the Early Slavs, which were patrilineal with related families living in collective settlements. Everyone worked and shared the fruits of the land, which was regarded as common property. Tellingly, it wasn't until the end of the Pagan period that the concept of private land ownership began. The zadruga's affairs were presided over by a council of family chieftains who assembled with other chieftains to form clans and, subsequently, tribes.[218]

Skilled metallurgists, the Slavic peoples had the implements necessary for land cultivation as well as weapons for hunting and fighting. Their primary occupations were raising livestock, hunting, fishing, agriculture, and beekeeping. In search of fresh lands to till, they may have frequently changed their dwellings. However, they were not nomadic, unlike the Huns and Khazars, Turkic-speaking peoples who neighbored them in the southern steppes of what is now Russia.[219] Slavic merchants sold their honey, beeswax, amber, and animal skins to the merchants of Byzantium as well as to the Vikings of Scandinavia and to their neighboring Balts in the far northeast, their closest cultural and linguistic cousins among the Indo-Europeans.[220]

The earliest written observations on Slavic civilization were by sixth century Byzantine writers, especially Procopius of Caesarea (d. 562). He wrote about the Sclaveni and Antes tribes as they poured into the Balkans,

217. Gimbutas, *The Slavs,* 133.

218. Dvornik, *The Slavs*, 57.

219. Dvornik, *The Slavs*, 53.

220. Johnson, *Slavic Sorcery,* 13.

peacefully for the most part, commenting on how they favored democracy in lieu of the rule of one strong man and that their warriors traveled light, on foot, and fought without armor (poison-tipped arrows being a favored weapon). More than a millennium and a half later, his work offers us intriguing descriptions of the Early Slavs' religious practices, even dabbling a bit in comparative religious studies in the process and comparing the Sclaveni's beliefs and practices to the only other "barbarians" (non-Romans) he bothered to provide considerable detail about: the inhabitants of "Thule," i.e., Scandinavia. This passage from *The Wars of Justinian* could very well be the oldest written testimony of the Slavic cults of the storm god Perun, as well as the rusalki: "They believe that one god, the maker of lightning, is the chief ruler of everything, and they sacrifice to him cattle and all other victims... But they also revere rivers and nymphs and some other spirits, and they sacrifice to all these too, and they make their divinations in connection with these sacrifices."[221]

In describing the religion of the Slavs, Procopius resorts to an *interpretatio graeca,* using a vocabulary and context he knew from Classical texts to find parallels to ancient Greek religion—a henotheistic Polytheism with Zeus as the prominent deity among many. Hence the Slavs must be henotheists as well, he reasoned, with their unnamed thunder or sky god as their main deity. And the water spirits the Slavs offer sacrifices to and use divination to learn of the sacrifices' acceptability must surely be similar to the nymphs of Classical lore, such as Daphne.

As a member of the urbane, educated elite, Procopius and others of his class in Constantinople at the time would have known as a matter of course that their version of Christianity was *itself* heavily influenced by Pagan philosophical thought, which centered on ideals of human virtue and public duty, transcendental and earthly beauty (with a focus on sacred images: icons), and mystical contemplation that leads not just to a union with Ultimate Divinity but *becoming* it (the doctrine of *theosis* in Eastern Orthodox belief).[222]

221. Quoted in Drapelova, "Procopius on the Religion of the Early Slavs," 177–200, 179.

222. Jones and Pennick, *A History of Pagan Europe*, 191.

Meanwhile, across the class divide among the uneducated working people of Constantinople—and by extension, all of Byzantium—animistic beliefs (a "lesser" Polytheism), plus the belief that some humans were inherently born with magical healing powers, were still prevalent. It therefore becomes easy to see how the eventual cult of the saints would become so widespread and fervently clung to, especially among Slavs baptized into the Eastern Orthodox Church, the religious emissary of Byzantium.

Christianization and Its Malcontents

The decisions rulers made to convert themselves and their populaces from Paganism to Christianity were largely dictated by political machinations of the highest Machiavellian degree. "The Christian religion as practiced in early medieval Europe was a strong and effective supporter of a centralized political system, and thus was an advantageous ally for a leader wishing to concentrate power in his hands," explains historian P. M. Barford.[223] Time and again, European history bears this out, and the conversion of the Slavs was no exception.

Rome and Constantinople served as the twin anchors of Christendom and centers of European trade and commerce. Pagan leaders, looking for more than localized political alliances, saw the central governing aspects of Christianity as beneficial to the long-term survival of their nascent states. Of course, forging political and economic links to Christendom came at the cost of sovereignty, but leaders such as Rotislav (846–869), Prince of Greater Moravia (today's Czechia and parts of Hungary), found that the hard bargain was worth it.

Pressured by the Frankish and Carolingian Empires to the west and a rising Bulgar Empire to the east, Rotislav in the year 862 turned to the Byzantine emperor Michael III for aid, asking for Orthodox missionaries who could speak the Slavic language to be sent into his lands. Little did Rotislav know that this decision would have far-reaching consequences, not just for his state and its people but for European history as a whole.[224]

---

223. Barford, *The Early Slavs,* 213.

224. Dvornik, *The Slavs*, 81.

The following year, a contingent of monks led by brothers Constantinus (born ~826/827 CE, he assumed the name Kiril/Cyril on his deathbed in 869) and Methodius (born ~815 CE), bilingual natives of culturally Slavic-dominant Thessaloniki (Slavic Solun), Macedonia, arrived and began to preach the Gospels to the Slavs. To the ire of Pope Nicholas I (858–867), who resented the incursion of Byzantine influence so close to Catholic Frankish territory, Constantinus and Methodius organized a national church with services in Slavic. More importantly, they translated the Bible and key ecclesiastical texts into the Slavic dialect spoken in the region of Thessaly and adapted them to the dialect of Rotislav's Moravian Empire.[225]

This first literary language, called Old Church Slavonic, penetrated almost all Slavic lands during the ninth through eleventh centuries. Constantinus-Cyril developed an initial Slavic alphabet called Glagolitic, which adapted and modified mainly Greek characters (or some combination of them); however, this alphabet was refined by the late Methodius's students in Bulgaria in the year 885, aligning it more closely with Greek and naming it the Cyrillic alphabet, which is still used by all Eastern Orthodox Christian Slavs today (see appendix A).[226] "As a consequence of [Cyril and Methodius's] mission, the Old Church Slavonic language developed into the common Slavonic literary language. Thus, Slavic culture was enriched and a new era in Slavic history was inaugurated," the archaeologist Marija Gimbutas noted.[227]

But Slavic Paganism had no opportunity to develop a literature of its own to control its own narratives. Croatia and Serbia underwent Christianization in the late eighth century, Moravia in 863, Bulgaria late in the ninth, Poland in 966, and the Kievan Rus' in 988.[228]

As mentioned in Chapter 2, Prince Vladimir of Kiev implemented a state-based Polytheism that lasted a short eight years. In the year 988, Vladimir, aware of the long-term political and economic gains to be made

225. Dvornik, *The Slavs*, 84–85.

226. Dvornik, *The Slavs*, 121.

227. Gimbutas, *The Slavs,* 170.

228. Gimbutas, *The Slavs,* 151.

by jettisoning tribal Paganism in favor of a centrally organized, trade route–linked variant of one of the Abrahamic religions, came up with the idea of a religious scouting mission for teams of emissaries. Some he dispatched to Jerusalem to investigate Judaism, the source of Christianity. Other emissaries were sent to Western Europe to investigate Catholic Christianity as practiced in the Frankish/Carolingian Empires. Closer to his own territory, he sent still more emissaries to investigate Islam among the Khazars in the region of the Volga River. Lastly, he wanted to learn more about *the* Orthodox Church in Constantinople, the Hagia Sophia, and he sent envoys there.

According to the report of the monk Nestor in his *Primary Chronicle,* the emissaries found life among the Muslim Khazars "dull" and "joyless" because they repudiated drinking and dining on pork meat; the Islamic tenet of praying five times a day, facing Mecca, was also deemed excessive. Vladimir ruled out Judaism also because of its prohibition against eating pork. Roman Catholic Christianity as an institution was viewed with suspicion due to its growing temporal power. But even the emissaries' experiences of attending Mass were negative, mainly due to the aesthetics. The Frankish churches to them seemed uninviting, austere; they lacked beauty and emotional warmth.

But in the capital of Byzantium, Vladimir's retinue was awestruck by the beauty (not to mention the gold) and the elegant solemnity of the liturgy performed inside Hagia Sophia, the Church of Holy Wisdom. Built by Emperor Justinian in the sixth century, the holiest place of worship in Eastern Christendom was already more than four hundred years old when Vladimir's messengers set foot in it. Conversion to Eastern Orthodox Christianity and an alliance with Byzantium it would be, Vladimir decided (it didn't hurt that he was offered the hand of the emperor's own sister, Anna, in marriage as part of the deal).[229]

Baptized himself that year by a Greek metropolitan (archbishop) who was stationed in Kiev on order of the Byzantine emperor Basil II, Vladimir issued an edict requiring large-scale baptisms of the Rus' and the destruction of all Pagan "idols," first and foremost the enormous wooden statues of the Slavic pantheon that he'd commissioned to be carved and established

229. Jones and Pennick, *A History of Pagan Europe,* 185.

outside of his palace and outside of his brother's palace in Novgorod eight years prior. In fact, he even ordered the statue of Perun, with its gold-plated mustache and beard, to be *flogged* by a dozen men once it was toppled. The Russian *Primary Chronicle* goes on to say how the faithful devotees of Perun wept to see the representation of their god so dishonored before it was cast into the Dnipro River. (The site downstream where the statue wound up subsequently became known for centuries as Perun's Shore.) Then the entire population of Kiev was itself marched into the river to be forcibly baptized en masse.[230]

"Byzantine influence gave the Russians a developed system of law, art and literature, which made up for its comparative dormancy during the centuries when its western allies had been part of the Roman Empire," explain historians Prudence Jones and Nigel Pennick.[231] When Constantinople ultimately fell to the Ottoman Turks in 1453, Kiev lost importance and the power passed to Moscow, which now saw itself as the inheritor of Byzantium, a holy imperial city. Ivan the Great (1462–1505) would adopt the title of Tsar (Caesar), and he added the two-headed eagle of the Roman Empire to the Russian national arms.[232]

But even among the ruling elite, the conversion to Christianity was a hard sell. Prince Sviatoslav of Kiev, Vladimir's predecessor, refused to accept Christianity when Byzantium first sent missionaries to the Rus' in the 950s. He remained a steadfastly Pagan warrior prince. His brief lone rule was mainly spent in successful military campaigns in the Caucasus. He waged several attacks against Byzantium itself, but the peace treaties he swore with the empire in 971 were ratified, as we learned in Chapter 2, under oaths sworn to Perun and Veles.[233]

Among the common people of Slavic Europe, revolts against Christianity and the cultural imperialism that it represented were not uncommon. The Pagan priests, the *volkhvy,* often led these rebellions, especially during times of famine or pestilence, which were interpreted as punishments or

---

230. Ivakhiv, "The Revival of Ukrainian Native Faith," 214.

231. Jones and Pennick, *A History of Pagan Europe,* 185.

232. Jones and Pennick, *A History of Pagan Europe,* 186.

233. Barford, *The Early Slavs,* 245.

revenge from the native old gods for their expulsion by the foreign missionaries of the wholly alien Christian god.[234]

The most famous Slavic Pagan rebellion against Christian conquerors occurred among the Polabian Slavs (led by the volkhvy of the Lutici tribe) of what is now far northeast Germany, in the hinterland of the Baltic coast. Commenced on June 29, 893 CE, during the reign of the Frankish emperor Otto II, the rebellious bands of Slavic tribes destroyed the Frankish strongholds and churches and completely drove out the Christian ruling elite. They developed an independent Pagan Slavic state that remained so until the early twelfth century.[235]

During smaller-scale, volkhv-led uprisings, sometimes Christian clergy and the nobles who supported them were targeted by the Pagan majority and murdered, as happened in the Russian city of Rostov in 1070 CE, to give one example.[236] Of course, the response by the Church would be disproportionately brutal, as it was against the Slovenes in 1331 (on the borders of modern Slovenia and Italy), when the Catholic Church under Pope John XXII mounted a full-scale crusade against the Slavs who retained their Paganism.[237]

The Gradual Development of *Dvoverovanje,* or Folk Orthodoxy

In the early decades of the conversion, Christianity was mainly restricted to the noble classes in urban areas. In rural districts, especially in the large swaths of territory of the East Slavs, Christianity simply lacked the ministry infrastructure, and so the New Religion was extremely slow to take root. Archaeological and ethnographic evidence point to ancient Pagan practices such as the cremation instead of the inhumation of the dead continuing for centuries.[238]

234. Ivanits, *Russian Folk Belief,* 86.

235. Barford, *The Early Slavs,* 259.

236. Ivanits, *Russian Folk Belief,* 86.

237. Jones and Pennick, *A History of Pagan Europe,* 190.

238. Barford, *The Early Slavs,* 225.

But when Christian influence in Eastern Europe increased, it, in turn, absorbed Pagan customs, such as ancestor veneration (as seen in the present All Souls' Day Polish *Zaduszki* and Serbian *Zadušnice* customs of feasting with the family dead at their graves); celebrations tied to seasonal changes and shifts in the agricultural/pastoral cycles; and practices such as the sanctification of fire, water, and food. Hence, according to the Ukrainian Native Faith scholar and adherent Adrian Ivakhiv, "Christianization was less a process of replacement or 'conversion' than one of syncretic mutual accommodation, with Pagan traditions continuing under a new veneer and a new or hybridized form of Christianity emerging as its outcome."[239]

Polytheistic Paganism is by its very nature inclusive, and for its part in fostering syncretism with non-indigenous beliefs throughout its long history, it has a proven record of absorbing many gods and spirits into its evolving pantheons in a manner that is just incomprehensible to exclusivist Christian ideology. The initial activities of the Christian missionaries were aimed at destroying the cults of the major Slavic gods, building churches atop their former sacred sites, and providing Christian substitutes for religious worship via the cultic devotionals to a panoply of saints, the goddess-like Virgin Mary, and, to a much lesser extent, Jesus Christ himself. And thus, worship of Perun evolves into the cult of Saint Elijah, Veles morphs into Saint Blaise and/or Saint Nicholas, Jarilo becomes Saint George, Svetovid becomes Saint Vitus, Mokoša becomes Saint Friday or Saint Petka Paraskeva, and so on.

Yet Slavic peasants, whose lives were dictated by their intimate ties to the cycles of the land and the powerful forces of nature, never gave up their animistic worldview. The commingling of a Pagan worldview and nominally Christian devotional practices has been called Dual-Faith (Russian: *Dvoeverie* [Двеверы]; Serbian: *Dvoverovanje* [Двоверовање]). As a phenomenon, it's mostly identified with the East and South Slavs, nations Christianized by the Eastern Orthodox Church as opposed to the Church of Rome. Why? For one thing, the country folk in these lands were isolated culturally and in many instances geographically from the mainstream of their nation's

239. Ivakhiv, "The Revival of Ukrainian Native Faith," 215.

development. Second, these South and East Slavic nations where Orthodoxy dominated "experienced neither the intellectual upheaval of the Renaissance nor the purging of ancient superstitions of the Reformation," according to Slavic scholar Linda Ivanits, like their Catholic-influenced counterparts did.[240]

In the case of Orthodox South Slavs in the Balkans—such as the Serbs, Bosnians, Macedonians, and Bulgarians (as well as their Albanian and Greek neighbors)—five centuries of occupation by the Islamic Ottoman Empire from the fourteenth to the nineteenth centuries ensured that they were effectively frozen in time, locked out of the cultural developments occurring in Western Europe such as the Renaissance. Paradoxically, the cultural presence of Islam preserved Dual-Faith and older Pagan practices simply because the Orthodox churches in those Balkan nations were themselves suppressed. Without the political power or resources required to stamp out Pagan practices, those practices continued unabated; this is largely why there was no "witch craze" in those lands either. The situation was the exact opposite in wealthy Catholic countries, which had the robust infrastructure and the resources, financial and political, to successfully combat Pagan practices and tragically hunt down suspected "witches" and other heretics (e.g., Jews, Gnostic sects like the Cathars) with brutal Inquisitions.[241]

Eastern Orthodox Saints as the New Guises of the Gods

Perhaps the most underdiscussed aspect of Slavic Paganism's survival in folk Orthodoxy is the veneration of icons. With their likely origins in the funerary portraits inside the sarcophagi of the dead in Hellenized Egypt, icons are essentially three-dimensional, easily portable nexus points of art and Spirit.[242] "The icon is not only a holy picture... According to Orthodox belief, an icon is a place of the Gracious Presence. It is the place of an appearance of Christ, of the Virgin, of the Saints, of all those represented by the icon, and

240. Ivanits, *Russian Folk Belief,* 4.

241. Jones and Pennick, *A Pagan History of Europe,* 193.

242. Bulgakov, *The Orthodox Church*, 144.

hence it serves as a place for prayer to them," the twentieth-century Russian Orthodox priest and theologian Father Sergius Bulgakov wrote.[243]

In Orthodox services (known as Divine Liturgies) today around the world, icons are censed with incense, sprinkled with Holy Water, and presented with offerings of flowers and apotropaic herbs—especially on the feast day of the saint depicted in the icon. Pious believers routinely kiss icons before and after prayers petitioning aid of the saint or biblical personage depicted. Father Bulgakov conceded that in devotional practice among Orthodox believers who may fall prey to superstition, without the proper religious education to serve as context, icon veneration can indeed "bring us near to Polytheism and near a 'syncretism' where Pagan vestiges exist tranquilly, side by side with Christianity."[244]

Unique among all the Slavic peoples today, Orthodox or Catholic, is the tradition observed only among the Serbs—wherever they are in the Diaspora—of honoring one's family protector saint. This tradition is known as *Slava* (Glory) or *Krsna* (Baptismal) *Slava.* Widely acknowledged by religious scholars as well as by Serbian Orthodox clergy to be derived from Paganism, especially the cult of the ancestors, Krsna Slava is said to commemorate the date of a given saint's feast day whereupon a Serbian clan or network of clans collectively accepted and became baptized into Orthodox Christianity.[245] To that family protector, passed down generation after generation in patrilineal fashion, the saint receives homage every year with special rituals and specifically prepared and consecrated ritual foods on its Slava date.

Given that the central ritual food is a boiled wheat dish known as *žito,* which is served to the dead during Zadušnice (All Souls' Days) Saturdays, and given that the majority of family Slava dates fall during the winter months, a period of time connected to chthonic and ancestral forces, it is easy to see why scholars speculate that the origins of the day lie in ancient celebrations of the divine progenitor of one's family, which after Christianization was replaced by a saint (such as Saint Nicholas, Saint Demetrios,

243. Bulgakov, *The Orthodox Church,* 140.

244. Bulgakov, *The Orthodox Church,* 122.

245. Cvetković, *Slavic Traditions & Mythology,* 335.

Saint Stephen, the Archangel Michael, etc.).[246] The cultic devotional focal point of what was once a wooden idol of the ancestral god evolved into the veneration of the family saint's wooden icon.

In an uncertain, chaotic world, the anchor point of a Serbian family holding Slava once a year provides that family comfort and the assurance of spiritual protection. Showing gratitude to the family saint is the right thing to do. The Slavic spirit of reciprocity is evoked. As the Serbian proverb states, *"Ko Slavu Slavi, tome i pomaže."*/"Whoever celebrates the Slava, them the Slava assists in life."

The Slavic virtue of hospitality is also a hallmark of a Slava celebration. Once the family's private audience with a visiting priest—who blesses the icon, the žito, and the ritual bread known as a *slavski kolać* (figure 6) and who also performs a brief memorial service for the dead members of the family during his stay—has ended, everyone is welcome to the celebrating family's home and table, where a huge feast will be laid out in honor of the saint. Godparents, distant relatives, neighbors, even total strangers off the street are cordially welcomed to partake of the bounty and goodwill.

My family's/clan's Slava honors John the Baptist and celebrates him on January 20, one day after Orthodox Epiphany, when folk magic customs and winter purification rituals that feature the Waters of Life are prevalent. Ever since I was a little girl, I welcomed this festive and magical break from winter's tedious gloom. I believed the spirit of John the Baptist, the "Forerunner," manifested itself in the icon my father would reverently display on the dining room table. I instinctively knew I mustn't swear or otherwise misbehave in front of the saint. Both my parents encouraged me to pray to the saint so I could continue to do well in school, ace my exams, and so forth. My devotional piety was strong and long lasting, seeing me all the way through graduating *summa cum laude* with my bachelor's degree in English and beyond!

---

246. Cvetković, *Slavic Traditions & Mythology,* 335.

Figure 6

John the Baptist was the family saint of my father, and his father before him, and so on. As I didn't marry into a Serbian family, I never forfeited my father's saint in lieu of the saint honored by a would-be husband carrying on his paternal Slava tradition. Some of my father's icons of John the Baptist are themselves antique, handmade heirlooms that I treasure. I take great pride in continuing the Slava tradition as head of the household, my father dead a few years now and my frail elderly mother not able-bodied to do the work herself. As I imagine myself lying in my eco-friendly coffin someday, nestled deep in the bosom of my Mother Earth, I dare say it's a safe bet that I'll have among my grave goods one of those heirloom wooden icons.

As we wend our way into the intricacies of the Dual-Faith Tradition in the subsequent chapters of this part of the book, we discover that "in the beliefs and customs of ordinary people, the Orthodox saints often contain an extraordinary mixture of Christian and pre-Christian characteristics," according to historian Elizabeth Warner.[247] The strands of Eastern Orthodox Christianity's canonical emphasis on the cultic veneration of the Blessed Mother and the saints are tautly woven together with folk religious devotions and magical practices that reflect a vibrant, lived understanding of the Wheel of the Year. The cycles of time find their markers in seasonal celebrations, in key points of the agricultural and animal husbandry cycles, and in the feast days of the Julian calendar–observing Orthodox Liturgical Year.

Not unlike the ancient Celts, my Christian Serbian ancestors, pastoral farmers all, initially only reckoned two seasons—summer and winter—as dividing the year.[248] Let us now turn to the saints and celebrations of the light half of the year. *Slava!*

247. Warner, *Russian Myths,* 19.

248. Zaroff, "Measurement of time by the ancient Slavs," 13.

CHAPTER 7

Gods, Saints, and Celebrations of the Light Half of the Year

Even a cursory glance at a monthly calendar page in the Serbian Orthodox liturgical year reveals that there's usually more than one saint or holy martyr assigned to each day. To detail the feast days associated with each personage is beyond the scope of this book. Rather, the focus is on the saints whose natures and functions clearly hearken to displaced Slavic gods, saints whose feast days were grafted onto the rhythms of day-to-day life established by the agricultural and pastoral cycles. These time-honored feast days attest to the Pan-Slavic commonality of hardworking people living close to the soil and being highly attuned to the natural world and to the spiritual forces acknowledged as undergirding the observable phenomena in the natural world—the forces acknowledged as being the providers of both blessings and bane.

Let's begin this journey by focusing on Dual-Faith celebrations of spring and summer.

Lazareva Subota and Easter

In Serbian Orthodoxy, the Saturday before Palm Sunday carries a robust folk tradition, which can be hinted at from the holiday's names of *Vrbica* (Pussy Willow Day) and *Lazareva Subota* (Lazarus Saturday). With this latter name, the Serbian Church's intention was to allude to the biblical miracle of Christ's raising of Lazarus from the dead. But the common people with their mythic interpretation of historical events associated the day with the late medieval Serbian ruler Tsar (Czar) Lazar Hrebejanović (1329–1389), beloved for his courageous if doomed defense of the Christian Balkans against the invading Ottoman Empire. Tsar Lazar's refusal to accept vassaldom to Sultan Murad I led to the bloody Battle of Kosovo on June 28, 1389 (June 15 in the Gregorian calendar), wherein both he and the Sultan died as a result, but the Ottoman conquest of the Balkans was ensured.

Tsar Lazar looms large in the Serbian mythic imagination, a King Arthur–like figure who inspired epic folk ballads that are still sung to this day. Apparently, he's inspired a considerable amount of folk magical practices as well, ones that have since been tenuously assigned to the lead-up to Easter.

The Curious Folk Magic of Lazarus Saturday

Lazarus Saturday is first and foremost a day associated with divination, especially ornithomancy, or divination by observing birds. The bird in question is the cuckoo, colloquially referred to as the *kukavica* (кукавица) in Serbian, the bird that mourns (the verb *kuka* means "to wail, to keen"). In the immediate aftermath of the Battle of Kosovo, so the folk beliefs go, the daughters of Czar Lazar shape-shifted into cuckoo birds to avoid capture and rape by the invading Ottomans. The lamentations of these princesses are thought to be heard in the cries of the cuckoo bird.

At dawn on Lazarus Saturday, the cries of the cuckoo carry an ominous tone: How and where you see and hear the bird can affect the nature of the news you receive. It's considered bad luck to hear the cuckoo while one's stomach is empty, so preparing a quick, vegan breakfast (given the Lenten food taboos) is recommended. Should the cuckoo fly into one's house, that is a dire phenomenon indeed and serves as an unequivocal death omen.

To purify oneself against any bad news received and as an overall health tonic, it's recommended that people light fires on their property to banish evil while they go searching for apotropaic herbs and flowers.[249] The herbs and flowers are then soaked in spring water and this water should be drunk as the morning advances, but definitely before the sun reaches high noon. Incidentally, this plant medicine tonic is a practice adopted even in cities, not just in rural areas. If you can wear green and adorn yourself with early blooming wild vegetation, such as the flexible bands of willow and pussy willow branches, even better. An alternate name for Lazareva Subota as a holiday, in fact, is *Vrbica* (Врбица), Day of the Pussy Willow.[250]

At remote parishes, it's common to see Serbian parents tie little bells around their children's necks (as if they were lambs?) while the kiddos stand outside the church door, pussy willow branches in hand, singing songs about Tsar Lazar's courageous stand against the Turks—again, nothing to do with the biblical story of the raising of Lazarus at all. People naturally associate Easter with children and the games and egg hunts devised for them. But in rural Serbia, Lazarus Saturday is organized by and for women, culminating in a special Rite of Spring ritual procession that has a very carnival-like feel to it.

The Lazarice, a Women's-Only Magical Theatre Troupe

Preteen girls to young unmarried women to married women of various ages compose the procession of the *Lazarice* (Лазарице). They all dress up in curious costumes and perform specific songs and dances at each house in their village, pronouncing blessings tailored to the families who dwell therein. The preparations, from sewing the costumes to rehearsing the songs and dances, span several weeks beforehand.

Every home is eager to have the Lazarice stay and sing for a while and it's hoped that the Lazarice part with some aspect of their wardrobe, especially the white veil worn by the flower-bedecked lead *Lazarica*, to the benefit of the family members in the house. The garments and herbs

---

249. Depending on the region in Serbia, these can range from chamomile, Saint John's wort, hemp, or lilies of the valley.

250. Bandić, *Narodna Religija Srba u 100 Pojmova,* 318.

worn by the Lazarice are thought to be imbued with supernatural powers. It's considered great luck to the household to obtain anything the singing, cross-dressing women wear.[251]

Cross-dressing? *Da!* Well, for several of the performers, at any rate: The roles of the sword-wielding Tsar Lazar, his foe the Sultan Murad I, and Serbian and Turkish cavalry officers with their respective hats and pants mean that several performers pretend to be men and swagger around while singing and swinging their prop swords. The woman playing Tsar Lazar is accompanied by Lazarica: Think of the two of them, if you will, as Lord and Lady of a mummer's troupe. As befitting a divine couple bearing the renewing energies of spring, they're naturally at the head of the procession. As much as Tsar Lazar gets top billing in this curious theatrical procession, the Lazarica, who looks like an Otherworldly goddess or the queen of the *vile* in her all-white ensemble, complete with opaque veil and floral crown, is the real star of the show. Her veil is the most coveted magical article of the day.

The women begin their village procession at dawn and the entire experience is thought to serve as an initiation rite for young unmarried women. If single women of marrying age, for whatever reason, choose *not* to participate in the procession of the Lazarice, it's thought to bring severe misfortune to them, not the least of which is the curse of never finding a spouse and getting married.[252]

The songs the troupe of Lazarice performers sing have to do with banishing evil and dangers to the villagers' well-being, including the common seasonal hazard of snakebites from venomous pit vipers, newly awakened from their winter brumation periods. Below is one such song. I'll note it in the original Serbian first because it rhymes; then I'll provide the English translation, which, sadly, loses the rhyme scheme.

Beži zmija, plazara,
Eto Svetog Lazara!

251. Bandić, *Narodna Religija Srba u 100 Pojmova,* 321.
252. Bandić, *Narodna Religija Srba u 100 Pojmova,* 318.

I on noci tavinu,
Običeti glavinu!

Get away, snake with protruding tongue,
Here comes Saint Lazar!
And he's carrying his staff,
He's going to konk you on the head with it![253]

With every house they approach, the Lazarice, once they have finished their song and blessing specific to that family, is welcomed inside and treated to refreshments, where the Easter staple of a red-dyed, hardboiled egg is the first food to be consumed for its symbolic magical potency of renewal. As an interesting inverse, seasonally and in terms of gender, during the Winter Solstice–related folk observances of *Koliada* or *Koleda,* an all-male theatrical procession performs a similar function of expelling evil and bringing blessings to families' homes, and one of the actors cross-dresses as a bride. Those men collectively represent the return of the ancestors, while the women of the Lazarice procession appear to be avatars of Vesna or Živa, the goddess of spring, announcing the arrival of the forces of rebirth now that the spell of winter has been broken.

Easter Sunday Customs

The Orthodox Divine Liturgy for Easter (*Uskrs*; Ускрс) Sunday is almost unendurably long, especially because you have to stand on your feet the entire time. However, if you can cultivate a steely resolve, there is a reward to be had: Along with obtaining your piece of the Eucharistic bread, the bishop or deacon leading the service dispenses into your outstretched and welcoming hands your talismanic red-dyed Easter egg.

My parents taught me a long time ago that the blessed egg you obtain at the end of Divine Liturgy on Easter morning shouldn't be eaten; it needs to be kept as the *čuvar kuća,* the "watcher of the house," preferably on or very close to the family ancestor altar. This talismanic egg is thought to ward off the evil eye/urok and other disasters that might befall the house.

253. Bandić, *Narodna Religija Srba u 100 Pojmova,* 320.

Using the eggs that are dyed by the family, it's customary to play a popular game called *kuc-kuc,* or "knock-knock," which is common throughout the Balkans and Greece as well. Each participant grabs a red egg that they think has a strong shell. They take turns striking each other's eggs with a single tap or knock; the person with the least amount of dents in their egg "wins" the game. Win or lose, everyone enjoys gobbling their eggs afterward.

Biljini Petak i Đurđevdan: Saint George's Day and the Start of Summer

The Slavs initially only recognized two seasons: summer and winter. The crucially important markers for those seasons, in Serbian culture, found expression post-Christianization in the feast days of Saint George (May 6) and Saint Demetrios/Mitrov (November 8), respectively. These dates can be thought of as opposites on the axis of the year. Of tremendous importance to rural populations dependent on animal husbandry more so than agriculture, Saint George's Day (April 23 for Slavs who observe the Gregorian calendar) marked when herds could be let out to pasture.[254] Conversely, in the spiritually precarious days leading up to Saint Demetrios's feast day, the herds had to be escorted back to their farmsteads for the winter.[255]

At the same time when much of the Pagan world in the Northern Hemisphere celebrates the well-known Celtic Fire Festival and Great Sabbat of Beltane, the first week of May also holds tremendous significance for Serbian people who identify as Slavic Native Faith or Dual-Faith adherents.

Biljini Petak

Every year, the Friday before May 6 bears witness to a rich and diverse array of folk customs that attest to very old and widespread Native Faith beliefs preserved in rural as well as urban Serbian communities. This Friday that comes but once a year has a special name: *Biljini Petak.* The word *Petak* means "Friday" and *biljini* is the adjective "wild" but in relation to botany; hence, *Biljini Petak* can be best translated as "The Friday of

---

254. Bandić, *Narodna Religija Srba u 100 Pojmova,* 327.
255. Bandić, *Narodna Religija Srba u 100 Pojmova,* 292.

Wild Herb-Gathering Before Saint George's Day." Given that Slavic peoples, descending into the Balkans as early as the seventh century CE, settled into lands where Celtic civilizations once thrived, perhaps it shouldn't come as a surprise that cultural overlap exists between Slavic and Celtic observances at the start of May.[256] Clearly, there's a shared Pagan past.

As with Serbian Cunning Craft, or *bajanje*, in general, the activities surrounding *Biljini Petak* fall under the provenance of "women's work."[257] There's a deeply moving element to the mentoring involved, as my mother relayed to me. Early in the morning, older women lead younger women and girls out of their villages and towns and into wild, uncultivated meadows and fields. Everyone sings together. First on their agenda is the act of literally rolling about in the morning dew. Aside from being thought of as a way to enhance one's beauty, this action is considered to be an extremely important apotropaic gesture, one that helps prevent sickness. For those looking to get pregnant, the dew is thought to help facilitate conception and an eventual safe, uncomplicated birth.

The bulk of the women's time together was spent identifying and harvesting specific medicinal plants to be put to use throughout the year. It would have been taboo to harvest these plants earlier in the spring. My mother reports that in the fields surrounding the city of Novi Sad, where she spent her formative years, she was encouraged to gather chamomile, mint, wild thyme, Saint John's wort, cowslip, rosehip, elderflower, yarrow, nettle, linden flowers and leaves, young willow branches, and hellebore, which she only knew by its folk name of *kukureka*—related, magically, to helping hens lay plentiful eggs.[258] She also collected wild strawberries and was taught to stain her cheeks with their juice to create a natural blush.

---

256. Barford, *The Early Slavs,* 47.

257. Bandić, *Narodna Religija Srba u 100 Pojmova,* 328.

258. Milanka Urosevic, interview with the author, June 7, 2024. The sound a clucking chicken makes is said, in Serbian, to sound like *ku-ku-re-ka*. Additionally, the penalty for violating the taboo of harvesting kukureka prior to Biljini Petak was the curse of infertility for the hens.

Thankfully, plant diversity thrives in tiny Serbia.[259] In the 2010 Fourth National Report to the United Nations Convention on Biological Diversity filed by Serbia's Ministry of the Environment, the data show that there are four thousand indigenous species of plants, with more than seven hundred considered medicinal.[260] Not bad for a country that's roughly the size of the state of Wisconsin. Best of all, due to the history of "low input agricultural production," especially in the mountainous (and thus less cultivated) southern part of the country, wild herbs are not affected by pesticides, heavy metals, fertilizers, or other harmful agents. It's good to know that the magic of *život*/life force in these wild-growing herbs continues much as it did for my parents in the mid-twentieth century.

The Magic of *Đurđevdan,* or Saint George's Day

During the feast day and major Slava date for the families with Saint George as their protector, the herbs that the women have gathered on *Biljini Petak* get "worked" on *Đurđevdan*. The first traditional day of summer is viewed as an extremely auspicious time to perform helpful magic. Starting first thing in the morning, a women's-only outing to the nearest flowing body of water culminates in the ritual "drowning" of wreaths woven from flowers. This action magically ensures that there will be adequate rainfall for the year's crops.[261] Incidentally, according to the weather lore taught to my father, as he used to tell me, if it rains on the morning of Saint George's Day, the entire summer is going to be parched and pestilential.

An overwhelming majority of the customs are apotropaic in nature, magically ensuring protection on the pastoral as well as the agricultural fronts. With apologies to Shakespeare, there's much ado about livestock. Sheep take center stage on *Đurđevdan*—especially the sacred slaughter of lambs. According to my father, lambs were said to stop suckling their mothers' milk at this time of year, and that was the cue that they could be killed by the head of

259. Vukov et al., "Habitat and Plant Species Diversity Along the River Danube in Serbia," 130–131.

260. Republic of Serbia, "Fourth National Report on the United Nations Convention on Biological Diversity, 2010," 8.

261. Bandić, *Narodna Religija Srba u 100 Pojmova,* 328.

the household for their meat as well as to ensure *sreča,* or good luck, for the home, the fields, and the herds for the remainder of the year.

For example, my father recalled how, in his native village of Gornji Milanovac, the strongest young men performed a great community service on Saint George's Day that was meant to ward off hailstorms: The men would run clockwise around the village and the fields, carrying ashes, which would be strategically dispersed. When they returned to their starting point, a farmer would donate his finest young lamb for slaughter. The lamb's blood would be sprinkled on the periphery of the fields as well as marked on the walls of houses.

My father also reported that sometimes the lamb's ears were cut and placed in a local large anthill. This was a gesture meant to placate the forces of pestilence and prevent illnesses from striking the herds.[262] He would also help his brother and father tie crosses out of hazelnut branches; these were hung in barns and animal pens to provide an additional layer of magical protection for all livestock. Hung above the front door inside the house, next to the sprig of Christmas Eve *badnjak,* such a cross would also protect against lightning and hail. This custom reminds me of the Celtic one of tying rowan wood branches together with red thread to fashion similar apotropaic crosses.

Another custom involved the firing of shotguns over pens of livestock, or the wild areas where the livestock were free to roam and graze in the summer months. Upon firing their shells, the men would say, "As far as this gunshot goes, so too may all sickness and predatory animals be kept as far as possible from my animals." To protect the animals against witchcraft, wooden barrels were dismantled and the metal hoops were held up for small livestock to pass through, thereby invoking the apotropaic power of iron. Ashes from the woodburning stoves and cauldron hearths were also scattered in circles around animals' pens to keep the baleful magic of one's enemies at bay.[263]

With the slaughter of the lambs not just for protection but to honor Saint George with communal feasting, *Đurđevdan* is known for being a

---

262. Bandić, *Narodna Religija Srba u 100 Pojmova,* 328.

263. Bandić, *Narodna Religija Srba u 100 Pojmova,* 330.

festival of food. The winter taboos in Eastern Orthodoxy surrounding what types of foods can be eaten are broken; everyone is free to indulge in fresh meat and the fresh milk of cows and sheep, as well as the fruits of the season. For Serbian families that honor Saint George as their patrilineal protector during their Slava, the feasting is even more elaborate, with the *slavski kolać* or saint's bread specially baked and then ritually consecrated in church before being shared in a large feast with one's family and neighbors.

Once ritual observances conducted by Orthodox priests concluded, the day's business of having a good time outdoors came into full focus. Again, as with Beltane customs, daring young couples could leap over bonfires. Folks court each other; established couples dash off into the woods and meadows for some frisky business. Everyone is bedecked in flowers and arrayed in bright colors. It's an unhindered, all-out celebration of the life force.

Outdoors or indoors, *Đurđevdan* celebrations call for *kolo* dancing (figure 7): Circle dances meant, when done clockwise, to mimic the sun and honor the living; a counterclockwise kolo is *mrtvaćki,* for the dead. The folk costumes' elaborate details vary regionally in Serbia as they do in other Slavic countries, especially when it comes to the symbolism in women's embroidery. However, the red and white hues worn by the men unequivocally inform us that we are in the presence of the life-giving, sun-kissed Slavic god *Đurđev* or Jarilo, he who brings vegetation to life with each of his steps. As the Serbian folk song states, *"Gde Đurđev hodit, tam vam polje rodit."*/"Where *Saint George* walks, there your field gives birth."

Whether it's because of the etymological connection of their names (*Đurđev* and George) or the symbolism of the white solar-associated horse and the defeat of the dragon, which, some scholars surmise, is tied to the serpentine form of Veles, it's not hard to see the connection between the Slavic god and the saint so widely venerated in Eastern Orthodox Slavic countries.[264] (Saint George is Russia's patron saint, for example.) May 6 is a powerful time to intentionally carry on these time-honored customs. *Slava!*

264. Marjanić, "Dragon and Hero or How to Kill a Dragon," 131.

Figure 7

The Ecclesiastical Folk Magic During *Duhovi* (Spirits)/Pentecost

Whereas the folk magical practices discussed thus far are performed outside of church, on Pentecost Sunday, the fiftieth day after Easter, a profoundly unique Dual-Faith talisman-making/-consecrating practice takes place *inside* church *during* the peak ritual moment of the Serbian Orthodox Divine Liturgy. In fact, the magical activity can't occur without the presence of the officiating bishop, whose lofty presence is required instead of the parish church's typical officiating priest or deacon because of the level of theurgy performed.

The event is something I look forward to every year, despite the pain my arthritic knees endure from the protracted sessions of kneeling on the church's bare floors. (I think of it as my sacrifice needed to obtain the magic.) It's a special ritual to participate in, and I always feel better—physically and emotionally—after attending it. My Pagan friends who are aware of this Serbian folk magical practice, especially my best friend, Richie, ask me to create talismans for them during the service that I can subsequently mail to them.

The magic entails weaving a grass wreath called a *venac* (венац) while, toward the end of the Divine Liturgy, the bishop ritually evokes the Holy Spirit to descend upon everyone gathered. During the series of powerful evocations (three, of course), able-bodied parishioners are expected to kneel and bow their heads to receive the blessings. It's during that time that the venac is woven using the tall blades of wild grasses that are locally harvested and strewn all over the floor.

As you weave your venac, you set your magical intention and pray. I create separate grass wreaths for each intention: First I make them for the dead to ensure my loved ones are at peace (I leave a venac for my father and one for my brother on their graves), then I make one for my mother's health, one for my prosperity, one for peace in the home, and however many more I need to make for friends who request them.

Clearly, this is a custom with very old, pre-Christian origins. Since the Serbian Orthodox Church at some point discovered that it couldn't eradicate this ritual, it wisely incorporated it into the liturgical calendar. I'm pretty sure the grass wreaths embody the solar magic of vitality, health, and spiritual protection, especially since the time of year when Pentecost occurs propels us toward late spring, depending on how late Easter occurs in a given year.

Each woven venac (figure 8) is kept for a year until the next Pentecost, during which time the old one can be burned, buried on one's property, or pitched into a river with gratitude for its service. As my special annually crafted magical talisman, my venac is well worth any discomfort or impatience I experience during the church service when it's being fashioned.

Figure 8

The Orthodox Christian holiday's name of *Duhovi* (духови), "Spirits," is meant to refer to the scriptural passage in the Acts of the Apostles (Acts 2:1–4) when Jesus's disciples have the Holy Spirit descend upon them during the first Pentecost. Little tongues of fire land on the devotees' heads, causing them to enter an ecstatic state of consciousness and begin speaking "with other tongues, as the Spirit gave them utterance," to quote the King James version (verse 4).

However, Pentecost, which lasts three days, also serves in Serbian folk religion as a high point for the year in spirit mediumship. The specific ritual performed to speak with the dead is called *rusalje* (русаље). A communal ritual conducted in rural villages, especially in the northeast of Serbia, it's performed outdoors near the closest river and it's witnessed by the entire community, especially by families who may have recently lost a loved one. The ritual is performed exclusively by young girls and women of any age or marital status; the ones who spontaneously fall into ecstatic states of trance and ultimately allow themselves to become possessed by the spirits of the dead are called the *padalice* (падалице), literally "those who fall, collapse."

The widespread belief is that certain Serbian families have always had an aptitude for mediumship; it's in their DNA as assuredly as other genetic traits that get passed down generation after generation. These families see it as their responsibility to their respective communities to have their psychically gifted women and girls serve as mouthpieces for the dead once a year during the Feast of Pentecost.[265]

Why this time of year? The day before Pentecost Sunday is one of the biggest Serbian *Zadušnice*, or All Souls' Days, of the year. There's a widespread belief that the ancestors return not just in autumn, but during the springtime, too. In Poland, there's a spring *Dziady* celebration that occurs after Easter as well. The Serbian Christian belief is that during the week leading up to Pentecost, graves open and the dead desire to communicate with their living family members. The living clean their loved ones' graves and bring a candle to light the way of the dead, as well as the kolać round loaf of bread, red wine, and frankincense as offerings to their deceased relatives. The graves are also decorated with leafy branches of the walnut tree, the tree most associated with witchcraft in Serbian lore.[266]

There are telltale signs as to which girls or women facilitating the rusalje ritual will be chosen by the spirits to become the padalica: Eyewitnesses report that prior to collapsing, the chosen padalica becomes deathly pale and starts trembling uncontrollably. As her agitation worsens, she emits incredibly loud and horrible sounds. Once on the ground, she kicks and shrieks, then briefly loses consciousness before transitioning into singing or speaking with a profoundly altered appearance, demeanor, and voice as she rises from the earth, signs the dead have gained control of her.

265. Bandić, *Narodna Religija Srba u 100 Pojmova,* 335.

266. Ristić, *Balkan Traditional Witchcraft,* 293.

Family members of the newly dead can directly address their departed loved ones and find out how they are faring in Nav, the Spirit World. They may even present the dead with gifts, placing them in the padalica's hands. The padalica can have multitudes of spirits speak through her, and she will often deliver messages to specific individuals, or even deliver a prophecy for the entire village.[267]

When she has no further communiqués from the dead, the padalica collapses once more, totally losing consciousness. She is left in that state for several minutes as a dancing troupe composed of young and single-but-looking villagers—three elaborately costumed women referred to as *Kraljice* (Queens), and three elaborately costumed, young, and sword-bearing men called *Kraljevi* (Kings)—come and dance a clockwise kolo around the padalica. Should the latter not emerge from her trance by the time the dance concludes, the Queens and Kings carry her to the river, stopping and placing her on the ground three times while they are en route.

Chewing the root of wormwood *(Artemisia absinthium)* in their mouths, the Kings and Queens will lightly spit, for a total of three times, on the padalica. If, by chance, the medium still hasn't returned to ordinary consciousness by this point, the attending Queens and Kings will put a spoonful of honey with minced garlic in her mouth and wait for her to come out of her trance.[268]

The rusalje ritual is said to bring profound healing to the community, especially to grieving families, as well as physical healing to any ill members of the community who witnessed it. As for the padalica, she would be congratulated by her immediate family for having so successfully undergone such a powerful, public initiation into bajanje, or healing witchcraft.

Clearly, there is more than just an etymological connection between the Serbian rusalje ritual and the wild female river spirits of East Slavic lands that are called *rusalki*. In fact, in Belarus, Ukraine, and Russia, the week leading up to Holy Trinity Sunday is called Rusal'nalia Week. The rusalki are believed to exit their watery abodes and reside on land for the coming summer months. Girls in rural communities decorate birch trees with ribbons

---

267. Ristić, *Balkan Traditional Witchcraft,* 293.

268. Ristić, *Balkan Traditional Witchcraft,* 336.

and beads and then dance the *khorovod* around them, welcoming the rusalki, who are sure to bring fertility to the land owing to their life-giving, watery associations. But the rusalki, like fairies the world over, are clearly connected to the human dead as well, as one of the highlights of Rusal'nalia Week is holding a special funeral service for the unclean dead.[269]

Vidovdan and the Summertime Rituals of Divination

The Slavic god Svetovid/Świętowita/Su'Vid is a deity of light, divination, abundance, and war. When and why his cult was grafted onto a supposed fourth-century Sicilian saint named Vitus, who is petitioned for protecting people against dog attacks, is quite a mystery. (Even the Catholic Church admits the man's hagiography is pure legend.[270]) Perhaps it's because the saint's feast day in the Catholic Church, June 15, replaced the earlier Pagan celebration of Svetovid.

Intriguingly, in South Slavic folk magic, it's the Slavic god and not the Catholic saint who is addressed in divinatory spells and healing magic focused on people's eyesight. These workings can be performed on June 15 per the Catholic Gregorian calendar or June 28 per the Serbian Orthodox Julian calendar. On either date, or both, the first magical act of the day is to rise very early in the morning and pluck the plant whose folk name is *Vidovčica trava,* "Vid's grass," which is composed of both varieties of pimpernel: scarlet (*Anagallis arvensis*) and blue (*Anagallis foemina*). Those flowering plants are placed in a vessel containing spring water, and folks ought to wash their faces with it to prevent optical diseases.

Near the Fruška Gora mountain in Serbia's far northern Vojvodina region, ethnologists in the field have recorded this variation of the Vidovdan face-washing ritual among carpenters and woodworkers by trade: As the men wash their faces, they say, *"Oj, Vidove! Vidovdan! Što ja očima video, to ja rukama stvorio!"*/"Oh, Vid! Vidovdan! All that my eyes see, my hands may create!"[271] By magical inference, then, their talents will have no limits.

269. Ivanits, *Russian Folk Belief,* 9.

270. Catholic.org, "Saint Vitus."

271. Bandić, *Narodna Religija Srba u 100 Pojmova,* 338. The translation is the author's own.

A slight variation on this spoken charm, now involving a mother and a daughter, has been recorded further northeast in the same Serbian region, in the village of Banatski Dvor. A mother takes her daughter out to the fence post that borders their field; they wash their faces and say together, *"Vido, Vidovane! Što god očima vidim, sve da znam raditi."*/"Vido, Vidovane! All that my eyes can survey, I will know how to work."[272] In other words, Vid will magically endow the women with whatever knowledge they need to be able to carry out their work. As they survey a limitless horizon, so too will their skill sets be limitless.

The colors red and blue, based on the pimpernel flower varieties, repeat themselves in other magical acts, carrying symbolic currency. This leads some scholars to speculate that red and blue could very well have been the cultic colors associated with the worship of the god Svetovid/Vid, at least among the South Slavs (the god's cult was strongest among the West Slavs). In a dream incubation ritual recorded in Bosnia by single women looking to dream of their future husbands, both varieties of the pimpernel flowers are placed under their pillow. The woman drinks a cup of rosehip tea (more red symbolism) while brushing her hair before her bedroom mirror. She says the following before immediately going to bed:

O moj Vide, Viđeni,
O moj dragi suđeni,
Ako misliš jesenac da me prosiš,
Dođi večeras, u prvi sanak na sastanak.

O my Vid, the All-Seeing,
O my dear fated one,
If you're thinking of proposing to me in the autumn,[273]
Come tonight instead, we'll rendezvous in my first dream.[274]

272. Bandić, *Narodna Religija Srba u 100 Pojmova,* 338. The translation is the author's own.

273. The most favored time of the year for marriage among the South Slavs. It's a time of abundance and celebration, as the harvest has ended.

274. Bandić, *Narodna Religija Srba u 100 Pojmova,* 339. The translation is the author's own.

Again, as the first line reveals, the Slavic god is addressed directly (the future husband then is addressed from the second line onward), and his functions related to divination and his ability to see in the four cardinal directions has remarkably survived intact in South Slavic folk memory more than a millennium after Christianization.

Ivandan: John the Baptist's Nativity and Summer Solstice Magic

If contemporary Slavic Paganism could be defined by just *one* image, it would likely be that of East Slavic folks in particular adorned with wreaths of wildflowers in their hair, having a grand old time dancing a khorovod around or leaping over a bonfire. Conversely, the focus could be on the Elemental opposite: splashing about in a river or lake during the great holiday of Ivandan, also variously known as *Ivan Kupalo, Kupalo, Noć Kupaly,* or Kupala Night. It's the ancient celebration of the Summer Solstice (July 7 in the Julian calendar; June 24 in the Gregorian) subsumed under the Christianized guise of cultic reverence for John the Baptist (known as *Ivan/Jovan Krstitelju*), whose "birthday" in Slavic folklore occurs this time of year. His symbolic connections to this important seasonal marker, specious as they are, largely stem from the folk magic practices involving sacred bathing (Kupalo is related to the proto-Slavic verb *kupati,* "to bathe"), not the tremendous body of lore related to solar/fire magic at this time.[275]

As with so many holidays, the magic actually starts on the eve before. In fact, the Polish name for this Summer Solstice celebration is *Noc Świętojańska*, the Night of Saint John. The Ancient Powers truly are alive, and magic is definitely afoot!

All Slavic lands' folktales speak of a magical plant that blooms only once a year as this sacred portal into the Otherworld opens the eve of Ivandan; many scholars have described the plant as a type of fern, but one that is imbued with a supernatural radiance that causes it to glow or appear fiery. For the brave soul, equipped with a hazel twig and a wreath of nettles for spiritual protection, who happens to behold the "fire flower," the magical action must be taken to draw a protective circle around themselves and

275. Bandić, *Narodna Religija Srba u 100 Pojmova,* 340.

the fern with the twig. This keeps out the demons who will cause a ruckus all night.[276] But the brave person will be rewarded as, at dawn, the fern will reveal where a buried treasure containing immense wealth lies nearby. The sunrise itself is also significantly magical as the heavens are said to open three consecutive times and pour forth blessings upon the righteous who stand ready in wait.[277]

As with Biljini Petak two months prior, Ivandan is the time to collect wild herbs and plants for magical and medicinal purposes. Two plants in particular are highly sought as they may not have matured enough to have been plucked when Biljini Petak occurred: the wild grasses known as yellow bedstraw (*Gallium verum*) and field broom (*Cytisus scoparius*). These grasses are used to weave apotropaic wreaths that can adorn homes and livestock pens. As this herb-gathering activity is almost exclusively the provenance of women, some scholars surmise that if Ivan Kupalo had a presiding deity at all in the remote Pagan past, it was likely a goddess of wild places.[278]

But the fire-centric activities, so symbolic of celebrating the summer sun at its zenith of power, were meant for entire villages to enjoy, young and old. Fires had to be living fires, meaning they were caused by friction from flint rocks or by rubbing oak or hazel (two "masculine" trees) and linden (a "feminine" tree) wood together. They were deliberately set at four types of liminal locations in particular: on hilltops, in valleys at the outskirts of villages, on the shoreline of a body of water, and at the crossroads.[279]

Young couples who were engaged to be married acquired good fortune by leaping over the flames. When the flames burned low to the point that glowing embers remained, animals would also be brought to either make the leap themselves or be carried in the arms of the farmers who leapt to ensure the health and spiritual protection of their livestock. Most critically, still-glowing embers had to be carried home to serve as a means of transferring the solstice magic of the living fire to each villager's individual house. This was a surefire way to keep evil spirits at bay.

---

276. Gilchrist, *Russian Magic,* 155.
277. Bandić, *Narodna Religija Srba u 100 Pojmova,* 340.
278. Ristić, *Balkan Traditional Witchcraft,* 288.
279. Bandić, *Narodna Religija Srba u 100 Pojmova,* 341.

There was an Elemental balance to the focus on masculine Fire by also prioritizing feminine Water in Ivandan magic. Offerings of floral wreaths would be floated atop a body of water to placate the vodeni duhovi or rusalki. If appeased, such spirits, normally very contemptuous of people, might bless babies subsequently bathed in the water with beauty and good health. Adults also bathe in lakes and rivers on Ivandan out of the belief that the magic of the sun, which is said to dance in the skies three times on Ivandan, penetrates the local waters and imbues them with healing. Ritual bathing has to be completed by sunset, however, as once the sun's light dissipates, humans run the risk of overstaying the water spirits' welcome![280]

Whether celebrated on June 24 or July 7, Ivandan/Ivan Kupalo is living proof today across all Slavic lands of the ancient and enduring belief in the connection between this world and the spiritual or invisible Otherworld, a connection heightened at these turning points in the seasons and the agricultural calendar. "Thus the rhythms of human life and of the Earth itself merged into an elegant mandala of time and space which symbolized the flow of Darkness and Light that sustained the Universe," reflects Slavic scholar Kenneth Johnson.[281]

Vračari: The Mid-July Serbian Feast Day of Saints Cosmas and Damian

In Serbian folk belief, there are two days of the week that are ideal for "throwing" magic: Tuesdays and Fridays. The Serbian Orthodox feast day of the *Vračari* takes place twice a year, which is fitting for honoring a pair of saints who function as divine twins: Cosmas and Damian (*Kozma i Damijan*). Should their summer feast day of July 14 or their autumn feast day of November 14 fall on either a Tuesday or a Friday, magical potency gets elevated to a whole other level.

The official Eastern Orthodox Church lore regarding this esteemed pair (my Brazilian-imported statue depicting them adorns my ancestor altar, as shown in figure 9) is pretty scant. My catechism taught me that they were

280. Bandić, *Narodna Religija Srba u 100 Pojmova,* 341.

281. Johnson, *Slavic Sorcery,* 43.

Figure 9

doctors renowned for supernatural healing skills. Magnanimous men of integrity, they didn't accept payment for their miracle cures. They lived and were martyred sometime in the third century CE. They supposedly even wound up healing the nasty man who sentenced them to death.

This is where folklore becomes much more of a reliable indicator of the importance of these saints in Serbian culture than official Orthodox Church doctrine. These saints referred to as *Vračari*—"the Sorcerers"—are petitioned by everyday people (but *especially* postmenopausal women) to expedite their personal magical workings. Those workings can be of a self-directed or externally oriented nature, of course. Given that Saints Cosmas and Damian served as healers, spells to effect personal healing or direct healing toward someone else are, not surprisingly, the chief reasons why folks invoke the Vračari.

But, as any devotee of the goddess Sekhmet can tell you, that which can heal can also be summoned to destroy. And so, as with the case of so many other folk saints in world cultures, the Vračari can also be invoked in magical workings that fall under the rubric of the morally dubious, if not the outright malevolent. As Neli, my first cousin who lives in Beograd, likes to say, "Scratch a Serb, and you'll find a witch lurking underneath the skin."

Ultimately, despite accepting the catechism that these individuals merited their sainthood because of the "good" lives they once led, Serbs know that there's an ambivalent quality to Cosmas and Damian; with a title like Vračari, it's a given that they would also be invoked to oversee hexes and similar workings that would make other saints in the Orthodox canon recoil in horror. As I've been taught many times by my mentors in magical communities over the years, there is no such thing as "black" or "white" magic; there is only effectual and ineffectual magic. In other words, is what you're doing endowed with *život* (life force) or not?

During my girlhood spent visiting relatives in Serbia, I clearly remember observing my maternal grandmother's engagement with folk magic. While Nana Milojka certainly saw herself as a devout Serbian Orthodox Christian and she would have spurned any associations with Pagan beliefs (she would have *never, ever* called herself a "witch"), I can clearly see now that she straddled that liminal line of religious belief that we now call Dual-Faith. On Tuesdays and Fridays, especially when neighbors came over, she would tell fortunes via Turkish coffee cups overturned, their mucky contents having already been consumed and the swirly patterns in the grounds read.[282] She also used regular playing cards as a tool for divination.

I'll never forget the *Sveti Kozma i Damijan* feast day in July 1983 when, while she was living with us in Chicago for the first year and a half into her widowhood, my Nana found evidence of *vračanje* (black magic) on my parents' front porch. *Really?* I was amazed. *People did that here, in Chicago? We're nowhere near my Nana's stucco-wall cottage in Užice, with its cute lizards that liked to sun themselves on the front gate of the plum tree orchard's enclosure in the summertime.*

What to me looked like an ordinary piece of black rope tied in seven knots—how it wound up on the concrete front stoop of our Chicago apartment building was a bit of a mystery, admittedly—was something my Nana literally hissed at, and then she immediately made the Sign of the Cross upon her person. I then heard her use some very unladylike language before she actually spat upon the rope. Then, pointing at it with her right index and middle fingers extended, she started yelling the name of the woman who she was convinced was responsible for this "sending." She said that with God and Saint Gabriel (the patron saint of her father's family) as her witnesses, this horrible woman who delivered the "sending" was going to pay!

Naturally intrigued, I went right up to the rope and offered to pick it up for my Nana with a stick that had fallen from the sycamore tree on the front lawn, but Nana was stern: I was under no circumstances to touch it, even indirectly. She would dispose of it, and that was that. My hopes dashed at serving as her witch's apprentice that day, I sullenly nodded.

I'll certainly never forget that display of her righteous indignation. And I'm sure she wound up invoking Saints Cosmas and Damian that day in whatever "uncrossing" spell she executed. I wish I knew the intricacies of her working.

---

282. She had a neighbor across her dirt road to the north who kept a very loud, brilliantly beautiful male peacock as a pet! I was convinced that woman was a witch, too.

Fiery Mary and Saint Elijah: The Saints of Summer's Destructive Heat

In *Dvoverovanje*, the period leading from the end of July to the beginning of August is a hazardous time. For rural folks in Serbia and elsewhere in Eastern Europe, it's an intense time of arduous physical labor to process the harvest. It's also a spiritually precarious time where the goal is to avoid the unwanted attentions of the folk saints known as Fiery Mary *(Ognjena Marija)* and her "brother," Sveti Ilija/Saint Elijah. Searing drought or a dangerous hailstorm sent by either of them can destroy the as-yet-unharvested crops.

Soaring temperatures at that time of the year, whether in the Balkans or the Midwest USA, can certainly augment a collective sense of anxiety. Serbian folk beliefs pertaining to this pair of Fire Saints take on a whole new level of alarming significance in this age of undeniable climate change and globally destabilized weather patterns, one of whose manifestations is the preponderance of out-of-control wildfires that last for months at a time.

A Slavic Sky Goddess in Disguise? The Folk Saint of Fiery Mary

A cursory look at the folklore surrounding Fiery Mary and Saint Elijah can translate into fascinating case studies of much older, fiercer, earth spirituality–centric Powers subsumed into the Dual-Faith visual representation of Byzantine iconography. The fixed date of July 30 (per the Julian calendar) marks the feast day of *Ognjena Marija*. As seen in figure 10, her telltale red robes, fire motifs (usually in the background), and her stern visage give her away in Orthodox icons, signifiers that are consistent in color symbolism and artistic form from Serbia all the way northeastward to Russia.

As is the case with many other Slavic folk saints, the details from her official hagiography are scant. Sveta (Saint) Marija, who also goes by the name Marina, is referred to in Serbian catechetical lore as a *Velika Mučenica*—a "Great Martyr." She hailed from the ancient Phrygian city of Antioch. She was put to death, supposedly for rejecting Pagan suitors, sometime during the reign of Emperor Diocletian (284–305 CE). The official story doesn't have much else to say.[283]

283. Bandić, *Narodna Religija Srba u 100 Pojmova,* 214.

Figure 10: Adaptation of fifteenth-century Russian Orthodox icon depicting Ognjena Marija, showing her surrounded by massive fires and pre-Christian solar symbols of hexafoils.

Fortunately, the folk beliefs surrounding her abound in details that speak of a unique, perhaps mythologically unprecedented, Slavic sky *goddess*. She's said to be the sister of the Old Testament prophet, Elijah. Sharing his quick temper and fondness for fiery cataclysms as a default response to human immorality, she'd gladly set the planet ablaze.[284] She is also said to use a heavy sledgehammer(!) to punish wicked people, smite devils, as well as hurl lightning, skills she shares with her "brother" and which certainly

284. Any devotees of the Egyptian goddess Sekhmet will surely recall the myth known as "The Destruction of Humanity," wherein Ra dispatches Sekhmet to incinerate the human race as punishment for wickedness.

put us in mind of the Slavic thunder god, Perun. She punishes dishonest women by cursing them with infertility.

In rural areas of Serbia, various taboos rule her feast day and people know better than to do any serious chores—especially labor out in the fields. It's best to stay indoors, period. And for women, that means no spinning of wool for use in the winter months to come, lest they draw the fiery ire of Ognjena Marija.

Saint Elijah the Thunderer: Avatar of Perun

The feast day of Fiery Mary's "brother," Sveti Ilija Gromovnik/Saint Elijah the Thunderer, arrives two days later, on August 2 (Julian calendar; the Gregorian date is July 20). As the star Sirius makes its heliacal rising, bringing with it the hottest weather of the season, Sveti Ilija Gromovnik arrives in his chariot of fire, reminding us that the old Slavic thunder god, Perun, is remembered, honored, and more than a little feared in the guise of this Old Testament biblical personage.

Where I live, it does seem to almost always thunderstorm on August 2. From the time when I was a little girl to well into my adolescence, I would listen with rapt attention during thunderstorms to my mother's tales of bad things that befell her neighbors in her hometown of Užice, Serbia—people who were punished at this sacred time of summer's intensity. I heard stories of people's orchards set ablaze in an instant during freakish storms and other sudden forms of loss incurred for violating the taboos of Sveta Ognjena Marija and Sveti Ilija.

It was even taboo, I learned to my astonishment, to make the Sign of the Cross during a thunderstorm! Sveti Ilija doggedly pursues the Devil around the world. Severe thunderstorms and lightning strikes occur when the fearsome saint, thundering past in his chariot, hurls his bolts like lances, hoping to zap the elusive Devil once and for all.[285] The cunning Devil knows that the normally effective apotropaic gesture of making the Sign of the Cross suddenly has no effect for the scared human hoping to keep evil away. Ever the opportunist, the Devil would like nothing better than to use a frightened child in a thunderstorm as a human shield. Making

285. Marjanić, "Dragon and Hero or How to Kill a Dragon," 129.

the Sign of the Cross can send the wrong signal—*the Devil is hiding behind me!* The Thunderer is pitiless and has no qualms with the concept of collateral damage ensuing from his righteous work. Thus, if Sveti Ilija were to hurl a lightning bolt, the child and not the Devil would be struck!

Eight-year-old me was horrified at the thought of being an unintended target of Saint Elijah's wrath; during storms, whether at home or at school, I made sure to stay away from windows so as to not be seen by the saint passing overhead in his chariot of fire. And no matter how loudly the peals of thunder boomed and how frightened I became as a result, I never, *ever* made the Sign of the Cross to allay my fears and ask for Jesus's or the Virgin Mary's help in the moment. It was just too risky a move.

"If Ognjena Marija and Sveti Ilija had their way, the planet would be burned to cinders," my mother would tell me, her eyes wide with alarm. "Totally destroyed! They love fire and will stop at nothing to punish evildoers!"

Wow, the whole world! Those two mean business! My young imagination visualized horribly burned pizza crust and then magnified that a *bazillionfold* to calculate, in my mind, the scale of what the fiery destruction of the world would entail. It occurred to me that Saints Fiery Mary and Elijah seemed to be more powerful than God himself, who apparently chilled out considerably after that Great Flood business, at least according to what the Dominican nuns in my Chicago Catholic elementary school taught me. *Jeepers!*

As an adult, I'd say it's quite clear that reverence for Saint Elijah took over the widespread cult in Slavic lands of the god of thunder and justice, Perun. A well-known Pan-Slavic epithet for the god, as we've seen with the saint who arrived on the mythological scene centuries later, is *Gromovnik:* "Thunderer."[286]

We learned that the World Tree in the Slavic cosmos is an oak, and it's in the topmost branches where Perun, in eagle form or accompanied by an eagle, likes to perch before setting out in his chariot to cause storms that ensue from engaging in combat with his serpentine enemy, the god Veles, Lord of the Underworld, who is often coiled at or beneath the World Tree's roots. This is where my mother's stories stem from: During the Christianization of the Slavs in the late ninth to the late eleventh centuries, Veles

286. Ivanits, *Russian Folk Belief*, 29.

easily became transformed into the Devil, and the early Christian Slavs saw in the iconography of Saint Elijah the form that Perun would take as all the Elements were there—thunder, the chariot of fire, and the hurling of divine wrath in the form of lightning bolts.[287]

Was Perun the most important god worshiped by all Slavs before the conversion period began?[288] In the resurging Slavic Native Faith communities springing up in Eastern Europe today, Perun receives universal praise as the chief deity—he's much more in the modern Rodnover consciousness than merely a god of storms. The centuries-old religious craft of carving god-poles as images of the gods meant to receive devotional offerings has been steadily making its way into public sites of worship again, from Poland to the Czech Republic to Croatia and Serbia to Ukraine and Russia.[289]

As the Serbian folk observances show, these folk saints and the gods who preceded them are dangerous and necessary, governing the tightly woven skeins of life and death, being and nonbeing, past and present. The destructiveness of Ognjena Marija and Sveti Ilija/Perun showcase the precariousness of life: A lightning-spawned wildfire can and does devastate late-summer crops in the fields. It does destroy homes. We approach these dread and majestic personages, if we know what's good for us, with a generous helping of humility.

Watery Pacification Courtesy of the Magdalene: *Blaga Marija*

Perhaps if Sveta Ognjena Marija and Sveti Ilija had their way, the planet would, indeed, be engulfed in flames. But in the Serbian calendar, relief from destruction arrives two days after Saint Elijah's feast day with the feast day of Elijah's other "sister," *Blaga Marija,* or "Mild, Benign, Gentle Mary." She is equated with Mary Magdalene in Serbian Dual-Faith Tradition and she switches the Elemental focus from destructive Fire to healing Water.

In terms of the agricultural cycle, there's a Serbian saying that goes, *"Od svetog Ilije, sunce sve milije."* Translated into English (losing the clever rhyme scheme in the process), it means "From Saint Elijah's Day onward, the sun becomes more gentle." If Ognjena Marija and Blaga Marija are two faces of

287. Marjanić, "Dragon and Hero or How to Kill a Dragon," 129.

288. Dvornik, *The Slavs*, 48.

289. Ivakhiv, "The Revival of Ukrainian Native Faith," 230.

the same primordial Slavic sky goddess, as some scholars suggest, the switch from Marija's *ognjena* (fiery) nature to her *blaga* (benign) one could herald the seasonal transition from summer to the first stirrings of autumn.[290]

Sveta Marija Magdalena is first and foremost a protector of women. Serbian Orthodox Christians pray to her for healing, especially concerning reproductive issues. On August 4, her feast day, people make pilgrimages to one of many sacred springs and wells, found flowing beneath or adjacent to churches, that are named after her throughout Serbia. The devout seek Holy Water to anoint themselves with as well as to consume, either unceremoniously or in the context of a bajalica's prescribed healing ritual. In rural communities, on the day of Blaga Marija, the taboos against laboring in the fields and chores involving the spinning of wool and other "women's work" apply.

The most obvious adaptations of celebrating these folk saints' feast days today entail rounds of spiritual cleansing, by fire and by water, respectively. On the dates of July 30 and August 2, I ask Saints Fiery Mary and Saint Elijah to purge and purify me, physically and spiritually, and to clear out of my life that which has served its purpose. I prefer to conduct my spell work at my indoor woodburning fireplace or outdoors at my backyard firepit.

When Blaga Marija's feast day comes around, I enjoy taking spiritual baths to bring sweetness into my life. I'm also fond of excursions to nearby Lake Michigan, seeking out my favorite lonely beaches wherein I can meditate on the profound powers of Elemental Water. I tend to drink the Holy Water that I obtain at my local Serbian Orthodox monastery as a health tonic also. It's also a traditionally appropriate activity to honor each saint on their feast day by cleansing their icons with Holy Water and adorning them with sprigs of fresh rosemary, hyssop, and basil—the trifecta of apotropaic herbs in Serbian folk magic.

As summer shifts into autumn, the Year-Wheel focuses on the outer activities of gathering the harvest and the domestic activities of preparing canned goods and other provisions that will be needed to make it through the long, dark winter. The saint who presides over these affairs is the one who stepped into the goddess Mokoša's proverbial shoes: Sveta Petka Paraskeva, the mysterious Saint Friday. Let us turn to her curious lore in the next chapter.

---

290. Bandić, *Narodna Religija Srba u 100 Pojmova,* 215.

CHAPTER 8
Gods, Saints, and Celebrations of the Dark Half of the Year

The traditional reckoning of winter in Serbian culture begins on November 8 with the Feast of Saint Demetrios. I'm expanding the winter half of the Year-Wheel time frame by a few weeks beforehand, however, to incorporate the late October feast day of Saint Petka Paraskeva, a folk saint revered as the preeminent protector of women throughout the Slavic lands Christianized by the Eastern Orthodox Church.[291]

The Feast Day of Svetka Petka: The Saint Friday of Orthodoxy

In my Serbian culture and in other Orthodox Slavic countries, we honor a curious eleventh-century female ascetic saint of the Balkans on her feast day held on the Friday closest to October 27. She's a protector of women

291. Ristić, *Balkan Traditional Witchcraft,* 285.

and patroness of spinning and weaving. Her name is derived from the Old Common Slavic term for the fifth day of the week, *Petak.* She is Saint Friday, Sveta Petka. Sir James Frazer's well-known quip about Saint Brigid of Ireland—she's "an old heathen goddess of fertility, disguised in a threadbare Christian cloak"—seems applicable to the ancient and mysterious Saint Petka.[292] She is also called Petka Paraskeva (figure 11). In Greek, *paraskevi* means "preparation," referring to the injunction to keep holy the Sabbath Eve. Her name, a Dual-Faith fusion of Pagan and Christian elements if ever there was one, is a clue to her origins, which are far older than Christianity.[293] It's clear that her cult places us in the goodly company of weaving goddesses known throughout Old Europe: goddesses of Fate.

Historian and feminist religious scholar Max Dashu informs us that "the old Goddess of the Pagans" was known by many avatars across Europe and that "Friday was observed as her holy day, beginning with its eve on Thursday night."[294] She's the oldest recorded leader of the Wild Hunt in folk belief, being especially active in "the dark of the year," and her symbol of the distaff signifies her role as the Fateful Spinner, known by various names and "beloved of the common people" well into the Middle Ages and beyond. She may simply be called Old Goddess, for she is "like the weathered Earth, ancestor of all, an immanent presence in forests, grottos and fountains."[295]

Not surprisingly, Saint Petka's healing energies are ascribed to holy wells and springs throughout Serbia—another telling clue that speaks to her earth goddess origins—including a very famous spring that flows under a well-known chapel dedicated to the saint in the middle of downtown Beograd, Serbia's capital.[296] Many legends exist about the origins of the spring, ranging from a fairy's show of gratitude for medieval chivalry to the deeds of a mysterious trio of "sisters" (the Roženice?) who erected a chapel to show their devotion to Christ, throwing in the healing spring as an added bonus to

292. Frazer, *The Golden Bough*, chap. 10, para. 29, line 22.
293. Rybakov, "Pagan Rites and Celebrations of the 11th–13th Centuries."
294. Dashu, "The Old Goddess," para. 2, lines 1–2.
295. Dashu, "The Old Goddess," para. 3.
296. Ivanits, *Russian Folk Belief*, 33.

pilgrims.[297] I've visited the chapel of Saint Petka Paraskeva every time I've visited family in and around Beograd, and I've tasted the spring's waters. There is definitely a loving sense of Presence in the entire environment.

Figure 11: Saint Petka Paraskeva, "Saint Friday," protector of women, holds a distaff, imagery that links her to the goddess Mokoša and to the Fate-weaving Roženice.

As a weaver, Saint Petka in Slavic lore has dominion over the women's-only fiber arts of wool carding, thread spinning, and weaving. On her feast day, however, one must not engage in those activities nor activities such as housecleaning or washing linens, lest she punish the household.[298] In

297. In this origin story, a traveling knight beheld an injured woman lying in a meadow, and as a show of thanks for his kindness, she told him to tap the ground with his lance, whereupon the healing waters ushered forth from the earth.

298. Ivanits, *Russian Folk Belief,* 33.

Serbian folk religious observances, it's customary to offer the ritual food of boiled shelled wheat grains with honey known as *žito* before her icon at the family altar—the same ritual food offered to the ancestral dead, which has me thinking Petka serves as a guardian of the female ancestral line, not unlike the *disír* revered in Heathenry.

Saint Petka's major roles, as might be expected, are those of protecting women in the autumnal marriage season—promoting abundance, averting the evil eye, and ensuring the women's fertility—but she's especially protective of expectant mothers. Her intercession is invoked to ensure a safe and complication-free delivery of healthy babies. To this day, in rural Serbian households, a whole slew of taboos are observed for home births. Many customs involve the strategic placement of hatchets and shears—the latter sometimes opened, sometimes closed—within the delivery room. It's also customary to offer newly carded wool before the household icon of Saint Petka.[299]

Tellingly, this feast day of Saint Friday falls near the start of the ancient Serbian reckoning of the season of winter, and the major All Souls' Day *(Zadušnice)* on the Saturday that precedes it. I'm more convinced than ever that Sveta Petka/Saint Friday is a Christian incarnation of Mokoša, a beloved, wise, and powerful mother.

Mitrovski Zadušnice and *Mitrovdan*: Ancestral Lore During Winter

Ancestor veneration and rituals to simultaneously propitiate and ward against the restless dead are among humanity's oldest and most globally recognized forms of religious expression.[300] We know that the ancient Romans had calendar days devoted to warding against the *Lemures/Larvae,* the restless, harmful dead.[301] In China today, the ancestors' graves are swept clean and laden with bountiful feasts every spring during the Qing Ming festival.[302] Every November, Mexican culture vibrantly celebrates Día de los Muertos, when the living

299. Bandić, *Narodna Religija Srba u 100 Pojmova,* 212.

300. Lecouteux, *The Return of the Dead*, 52–53.

301. Gill, "Spirits of the Dead."

302. Zhao, "Qing Ming 2025."

joyfully bedeck themselves as colorful *calaveras* and picnic with the dead.[303] Peoples of Afro-Caribbean descent and others who follow the traditional African religion of Ifá and its New World offshoot of Santería have an extensive roster of ceremonies for appeasing both the ancestral/known dead (*eggun*) and the communal, unknown dead (*eggungun*).[304] This small global sampling illustrates the deeply ingrained, worldwide belief that the dead have an interdependent relationship with the living.

Looking through the framework of my own Serbian culture, Days of the Dead known as *Zadušnice* (Задушнице) occur quarterly. They always fall on a Saturday, the day of the week associated with death. While each *Zadušnica* (singular) holds tremendous importance for Serbian families, the one that precedes Mitrovdan/Saint Demetrios's Day is unquestionably the most critical one of the year to observe.

The date of November 8 is the Feast of Saint Demetrios in the Julian calendar, October 26 in the modern Gregorian. It serves as the traditional start in the Serbian folk calendar to the winter half of the year, and the Saturday that precedes it is the largest All Souls' Day/Zadušnice of the year. The hagiography of the early fourth century CE Thessalonian-born commander of the Eastern Roman army-turned-Christian saint, while fascinating, offers us few clues as to how and why his feast day was grafted onto Pagan Slavic celebrations of the onset of winter, which have to do with providing great feasts for the dead.[305] However, there may be a link in that these elaborate feasts may have originally begun among the Slavic tribes as tributes to fallen warriors/the military dead, which Christian apologists in East Slavic lands certainly complained about in their medieval sermons and treatises.[306]

And so the iconography of Saint Demetrios, who is always depicted as an Eastern Roman Empire soldier bearing a spear and a shield, tracks with this theme of hailing fallen warriors. Tellingly, in Catholic-influenced Western Europe, the month of November features the feast day of another

303. Dobrin, "Dia de los Muertos Comes to Life Across the Mexican Diaspora."

304. De La Torre, *Santería*, 21.

305. Saint Demetrios Greek Orthodox Church, "Saint Demetrios Feast Day Celebration."

306. Helvin, *Slavic Witchcraft*, 176.

fourth-century Roman Empire soldier-turned-saint, Saint Martin of Tours (the patron saint of France). His feast day is known as Martinmas in the West (in Croatia, *Martinje*, and it's a day when regional wine gets ceremonially blessed!) and occurs on November 11, which, at the end of World War I on November 11, 1918, acquired the profound added layer of remembrance through Armistice Day, or, as we know it in the United States, Veterans' Day.

For regular country folk, whether in Eastern or Western Europe, the first half of November was the time of ensuring that winter provisions to sustain families through the lean and trying times of cold, darkness, and snow were readily available. That meant that livestock thought not to be able to survive the months ahead were slaughtered and their carcasses smoked and stored for future use. From the Middle Ages onward, roast goose appears to have been the traditional cultic food for devotees of Saint Martin in France and elsewhere in Central Europe and the United Kingdom; for West, South, and East Slavs, whether honoring Saint Martin or Saint Demetrios, the main meal stars that Slavic staple of smoked ham, reflecting the status of the pig as a cultic animal in Serbia.[307]

For the Slavs, as god of livestock as well as the shepherd of the dead, Veles figures prominently in these early winter celebrations. His gifts of music and storytelling around the hearth fire would also endow the Slavic peoples the ability to while away winter's dark, sometimes tediously long hours in the almost unendurable wait for the signs of returning light and life after the Winter Solstice. As Master of Wolves and Bears, Veles also instills in us the wisdom of treasuring our companionship with each other—cultivating a pack mentality—and balancing that with the need for stillness and solitude, healing and peace, which a mindful retreat into winter's embrace can grant us.

This time of year with its focus on the dead and on the gods and goddesses of the dead and the Underworld certainly falls within what many a modern witch would call "Spooky Season." With her corpse-white skin, harbinger of the snow and freezing cold to come, the goddess Mara/Morana/Marszanna steps into her own as a revered and feared death goddess: a fearsome, relentless presence who stalks our dreams as the original

307. Ristić, *Balkan Traditional Witchcraft*, 65–66.

night mare.[308] Hers are the mysteries of the waxing darkness that lead up to the Winter Solstice.

Notice how this sacred time of Mitrovdan overlaps with the period of the Celtic Samhain, that liminal and even spiritually dangerous period when at the ending of one year but before the beginning of the new, the fissures demarcating the Worlds widen considerably and spirits of the dead and denizens of the Otherworld mingle freely with us, the living, in this world.[309] It is a heightened time of spirit activity and for communing with the ancestors—while also trying to avoid the attention of less-than-friendly spirits, hence the time-honored custom of donning masks to disguise your identity, which has endured as a staple of modern-day Halloween celebrations worldwide.[310]

Sacred masks, known as *karaboszka,* were a staple in Polish celebrations of the *Dziady*, or "Forefather's/Grandfather's Eve" festival, which historically was celebrated on October 26–28 but nowadays runs from October 31 to November 2, to coincide with the holiday of Halloween and the Catholic observances of All Saints' Day (November 1) and All Souls' Day (November 2).[311] As with the Serbian ancestral observances on Žadušnice, Dziady centers around the ritual activity of picnicking on the graves of one's family dead and offering various kinds of symbolically charged food for the dead to eat, such as bread and honey.[312] "The Slavs believed that the souls of the dead would rejoice at these activities," states Soviet-born witch Natasha Helvin.[313] The widely held belief was that the dead could return to visit their living descendants during these liminal times when the Year-Wheel shifts and the seasons are about to change.

Our relationships with our ancestors tie us in threads of symbiosis and loving support. Indeed, as Kenneth Johnson notes, "To serve the dead was to serve the living."[314] This is for the spiritual elevation of all parties

---

308. Gajić, *Slovenska Mitologija,* 65.
309. Ravenwolf, *Halloween*, 7.
310. Ravenwolf, *Halloween*, 49.
311. Culture.pl, "The Polish Halloween."
312. Culture.pl, "The Polish Halloween."
313. Helvin, *Slavic Witchcraft*, 185.
314. Johnson, *North Star Road,* 186.

involved, and this serves as the basis for divine right order. I believe our task as human beings is to get our heads and hearts into as receptive a state as possible, so we never turn down moments of mystery and wonder when they present themselves before us at the behest of our beloved dead. I feel that awe and grace keenly when I continue my cultural tradition of solemnly observing each Zadušnice, as my diary entry from the Mitrovski Zadušnice of 2022 relays.

Dispatch from the Zadušnice Front Lines of Grief: November 6, 2022

Yesterday, November 5, was this year's Mitrovski Zadušnice, the biggest All Souls' Day of the year. It turned out to be a day of great pride but also great anxiety for me. With Mama so frail, the mantle of responsibility for ensuring a successful Mitrovski *Zadušnice* fell squarely on my shoulders alone. Given that it's the ten-month anniversary of Tata's death, I felt tremendous pressure from wanting "to do right" by him first and foremost—this sense that he can see what I am doing on behalf of the family line—and since I am the end of that line, when I die, this cultural observance dies out with me. It's a sobering, sad realization, but it is what it is. As the oft-quoted contemporary Heathen prayer from *The Sigrdrífumál* tells us, we petition the gods for "the gifts of speech and healing hands *while we live*."[315]

From my opening prayers to my named family dead to the prayers upon the poured spring water to the prayers of the adding of honey at the prescribed times with even more prayers to my family dead, the boiling of the wheat/the making of the *žito* took me five solid hours on Friday evening. It was an intense process, and I meditated on the concept of magick as *seething,* the idea behind the shamanic magical practice of Old Norse *seiðr.*

315. Emphasis is mine.

The Serbian church service was a whopping two-and-a-half hours long; my feet ached like crazy![316] But there was a real sense of holiness in community during the conclusion when the *parastos* was sung and everyone's žito received individual blessings. In the antiphonal call-and-response-style swelling with a chorus of voices, we sang "*Večnaja Pamjat,*" "Memory Eternal," as Brother Serafim and fellow clergy intoned the names of the dead associated with each bowl of *žito* brought to blessed. I looked with pride at my neatly written index card with the names of the dead written out; the card stuck out easily from underneath the žito bowl for Brother Serafim to retrieve it. Seeing the beeswax candles lit lifted my spirits.

I fed Tata and Mark *žito* at their graves afterward. Thankfully, foul weather held itself at bay until *after* I'd packed everything up and was safely back in my car, then a powerful thunderstorm unleashed itself against all of Chicagoland. As soon as I got home, I meandered about the expanse of the yard as the foul weather continued to rage (sixty-mile-per-hour wind gusts!). I felt tremendously pleased with how the day had turned out, and in my heart felt that my family dead, especially Tata, greatly approved of my efforts to make this *Mitrovski Zadušnice* a resounding success, even though I was the sole living ambassador of the family in the United States to commemorate it.

Exercise
Cook *Žito* for Your Own Ancestors

What Serbs know as žito (жито) is called *kutya* (кутя) by East Slavs. It's "an ancient pagan dish" whose primary ingredient of boiled wheat represents

316. Orthodox churches typically don't have pews. There may be chairs along one or two walls to accommodate persons with disabilities/the elderly, but able-bodied folks of all ages are expected to stand.

"the resurrection of the dead," explains Soviet-born witch Natasha Helvin.[317] "In ancient times it was believed that on certain days of the year the souls of the deceased could return to their native places and even affect the lives of the living in a certain way. The Slavs believed that the dead could influence the harvest and fertility of the earth from their place in the underworld."[318] As with the life in the fields, so, too, do the dead continue on, hopefully germinating in the Underworld to "rise" in a sense and evolve from the bewildered newly dead into communally embraced ancestors. A few minutes spent meditating on the symbolism of the wheat is a worthwhile activity.

If you'd like to incorporate the ritual food of žito to offer to your own ancestors, here's a good recipe. This is what you'll need:

- 1 pound granulated sugar or confectioners' sugar
- 1 pound walnuts, ground (not chopped)
- 1 pound white wheat grain (I use shelled wheat by the brand Ziyad here in the United States)
- Hand-cranked grain grinder that can be affixed to a flat surface
- 2 packages vanilla sugar
- 1 teaspoon vanilla extract
- 1 tablespoon honey
- 1 package almonds, raisins, or chocolate chips for decoration

Reserve two rounded tablespoons of sugar and ground walnut mixture and set aside for topping. Clean and wash the wheat (I use half the bag's contents) thoroughly in cold water. Pour out the cold water and bring the wheat to a boiling point. Keep it covered while cooking. Lower the heat to a simmer and cook for thirty minutes. Recite the names of your family dead and pray for them and to them with petitions. Drain the water and add fresh water and bring to a boil again.

Repeat the above process two more times (everything blessed comes in threes in Serbian lore), then let cook until the wheat is tender but not

317. Helvin, *Slavic Witchcraft,* 177.

318. Helvin, *Slavic Witchcraft,* 185.

mushy. Drain and rinse with cold water. Spread the wheat on a clean, dry cloth to dry for one hour, then grind the wheat in a hand-cranked grain grinder. Combine the wheat, sugar, ground nuts, vanilla extract, and honey (the glucose-laden ingredients are symbolic of the sweetness the living hope to impart to the dead). Shape into a mound on a serving dish—use your finest crystal; your beloved dead are worth it!

Sprinkle the sugar and walnut mixture, which was set aside, over the top. Decorate the top of the mound with a symbol of an equal-armed cross in the center and a circular border trim using either raisins, almonds, or chocolate chips.

In addition to the staples of the žito and the ritual kolać bread for the dead, I like to offer the popular mixed grilled meats known as *ćevapčići* (see appendix D) and whiskey and beer to my father and brother. They both died under horrific circumstances. I miss them terribly and I visit their graves often at our family plot, where I routinely leave offerings and petition their aid. The dates of their births and the anniversaries of their deaths take on a special ritual focus for me, not just the days set aside as Zadušnice.

As for beloved family dead who are buried in Serbia, whose graves are not physically accessible to me, I honor them on my ancestor altar as well as in Orthodox churches at the candle-burning stations for the dead, which are set on the opposite side of the candle-burning stations for the living. For both groups of people, slender, pure beeswax tapers are burned, one for each person. These simple but sustainably made tapers are usually made on-site by the resident Orthodox monks at the Serbian monasteries near where I live; those tirelessly working men are as well versed in beekeeping as they are in Bible studies, as bees are especially holy creatures in Serbian folk belief.[319]

Serbian Folk Beliefs Surrounding Mitrovdan

The deeply engrained beliefs surrounding Mitrovdan reflect themselves in customs meant to ensure a family's good fortune, materially and spiritually, in what often proved to be lean and trying times in a harsh climate. Outside the home, obligations have to be met and all loose ends tied up

319. Bandić, *Narodna Religija Srba u 100 Pojmova,* 199.

before the start of winter. And so, whatever contracts that may have been signed on Saint George's Day had to have had their business objectives met by the start of Mitrovdan. Whatever dues an individual or family owed anyone had to be paid off; if a person borrowed something from someone, it had to be returned, and so on. Wealthier families who had farmhands or servants working for them had to release them at Mitrovdan so they could tend to their own homes in the long, dark winter. On Mitrovdan itself, it was advisable to lay low and not leave your property at all.[320]

Because, well beyond the carefully demarcated boundaries of your property or the village or town you resided in, things stirred. *Especially in the dark.*

For many Indo-European societies that started out as pastoral ones before the advent of agriculture, a family's or clan's wealth was determined by the amount of livestock they had. In Teutonic lands, this became encoded in the meaning of the Elder Futhark runes: The first rune, *Fehu,* literally means "cattle."[321] A chief goal for pastoral families was (and still is) seeing their livestock successfully through the winter; it can mean the difference between life and death.

For families in Serbia, livestock definitely have to be brought in from pasture either three or seven days before Mitrovdan. Animals couldn't be slaughtered for meat nor sold at market during those few days leading up to the holiday. On the date of Mitrovdan, there were many taboos related to the caring of livestock, especially sheep. They had to be relegated to pens and watched but not really interacted with; they were essentially left alone, which was an act of sympathetic magic. As you leave the sheep alone, it was believed that less benevolent forces will also overlook them. And that's a good thing.

This act of "overlooking" extended into the domestic sphere as well. Taboos were placed on the women's work of carding or spinning wool—those activities couldn't be done on this day. Spindles had to be kept idle

---

320. Bandić, *Narodna Religija Srba u 100 Pojmova,* 291.

321. Paxson, *Taking Up the Runes*, 30. Interestingly enough, the letters *Aleph* in Hebrew and *Alpha* in Greek also denote "cattle."

to prevent drawing unwanted magico-spiritual attention to the flocks.[322] It was a day to observe your flocks, and by doing so you could learn about the severity of the winter weather to come.

Mitrovdan and Weather Divination

According to my father, if the day on November 8 was clear, that meant the winter ahead would be long, dry, and cold. However, if the day was overcast, then it meant the winter would have a lot of snow with huge snowbanks. When it came to predicting the weather based on the behavior of sheep, my dad told me that his father, my Deda Miloš, would note where the sheeps' backs were turned: If they sat in their pens with their backs to the north, then that would indicate the prevalence of southern (milder) winds, which were hoped for. However, if their backs were to the south, then the opposite would hold true—the winter winds would come from the north, heralding brutal cold. My mother adds that her niece's family in the Metohija region of Kosovo would pay keen attention to how their sheep were lying down on the day of Mitrovdan: If they rested with their legs tucked under them, the winter would be horribly bitter. Sheep that lay with their legs splayed out on the ground, looking relaxed, foretold a mild winter.

Sometimes an axe could be used as an additional divination tool, noted my father, along with the color of the sheep. An axe or hatchet could be laid flat on its side in the middle of the pen. Should a white sheep come and actually sit on the blade or the handle, that would foretell a winter heavy with snow. If a black sheep came and sat or lay on it, then the winter would be mild.

Badnjak Veče/Serbian Christmas Eve and the Unclean Days

While the Western world's secular calendar is, of course, Gregorian, Serbia's liturgical calendar follows the older Julian model, which is roughly two weeks behind the Gregorian method of reckoning time. Hence, instead of observing Christmas on December 25, Serbs and other Orthodox Christians who are Julian calendar–observant commemorate Christ's Nativity

322. Bandić, *Narodna Rekigija Srba u 100 Pojmova*, 292.

(or *Božić*) on January 7. What is more remarkable still, from a theological standpoint that showcases the strong Pagan flavor retained in Serbian Dual-Faith Tradition, is that unlike the joyful Twelve Days of Christmas in Western Christendom, the period of time from Christmas Eve to Epiphany is referred to in Serbian as the *Nekršteni Dani*—the "Unclean Days" (Некрштани Дани). During this time, it is thought that all manner of malevolent spirit beings roam the earth, gaining great strength after sundown each night, wreaking havoc and tormenting people with impunity.[323] Merry Christmas, indeed!

How can this be? What about the holy infant Jesus's inherently apotropaic powers against the Forces of Darkness? If he truly is the Son of God, Savior of humanity, and so forth, shouldn't his joyful birth dispel things that go bump in the night—not allow them to roam with impunity?

After all, that's what Western theologians would have one believe. One is thus left to ponder this seemingly discordant, not-very-Christian-affirming phenomenon of the Nativity on January 7 kicking off Twelve Days of Christmas rife with unclean spirits. In a peculiar inversion of standard Christian theology, it is Christ—not the Pagan Powers who preceded him—who becomes spiritually weak and ineffectual at the time of year commemorating his own Nativity, at least for a while. The implications for Western Christians unfamiliar with folk Orthodoxy can be profoundly disturbing: *"God" is* not *omnipotent. "He" can do wondrous things, yes, but there are definite limits to "his" power.* And maybe, just maybe, you've got to give the devils their due.

Liminality, Uncleanliness, and Taboos

That the celebration of Christ's Nativity becomes conflated in Serbian folk religion with the start of a twelve-day period of desperately trying to avoid the attention of evil spirits might make more sense when we examine the concept of "uncleanliness" and look at the wider, magical context of the liminal time of year in which these Unclean Days occur.

Christianity didn't introduce the concept of "clean" or "unclean" spiritual energies. This was known to the Slavic peoples long beforehand, as

323. For example, *vampiri* (vampires), *đavoli* (devils), and *karakonđule* (demonic creatures).

widespread belief in the natural world's manifestations of the Nečistaja Sila (the Unclean Force) attest. Some Slavic scholars postulate that this is the *only* Slavic dualism that matters—the opposition demarcating what is helpful versus harmful to humans, clean or unclean; Pagan and Christian concepts and practices could belong to *either* camp.[324]

The Serbian term *nekršteni* is literally translated as "without having been baptized." That is the Christianized spiritual root, in the Eastern Orthodox mindset, of the problem of uncleanliness. Many (though not all) of these evil spirits said to roam about during the Twelve Days of Christmas are tied to the unclean, presumably restless dead—spirits of people who died lacking the "grace of God" in one of several ways: Either they completed suicide, or they died before baptism, or they died suddenly without receiving the Last Rites from a priest, and so on.

The understanding is that since Jesus himself wasn't baptized until he reached adulthood, he was "unclean" for quite some time himself, and so it only makes sense for evil spirits to have the proverbial upper hand for the symbolic period of twelve days (thought, actually, to be a microcosm for the year) between his Nativity and the Feast of the Epiphany on January 19, which commemorates Jesus's baptism by John the Baptist in the Jordan River.

Spiritual uncleanliness has its correlation in the physical world of manifestation, too. The ancient Greeks taught us that, bequeathing us with the concept of *miasma*. Our understanding of it today in the English language is certainly watered down from its ancient etymology having to do with spiritual pollution wrought by the breaking of taboos.[325] Still, our usage gives us the sense that we are entering dangerous territory and exposing ourselves to unwholesome energies wherever miasma is to be found.

Not surprisingly, in modern Serbian Christmas observances, taboos abound to keep miasma in check. One's main goal in enduring the period from Christmas to Epiphany is to avoid getting the unclean entities' attention. And so, believe it or not, the chief taboo is one directed at clergy,

324. Ivanits, *Russian Folk Belief*, 127.

325. For more on this subject, I highly recommend Walter Burkert's classic tome, *Greek Religion*.

forbidding them to perform the Sacrament of Baptism on individuals–even if the petitioners are on their deathbeds and want to die as Christians! The Waters of Life, a common motif in Slavic folktales, cannot be accessed prior to *Bogoljavljenje*, the commemoration of Jesus's baptism. But there are everyday taboos for regular folk to observe as well, such as:

- Not doing laundry until after the Feast of the Epiphany (January 19).
- Avoiding crying and singing, as these are surefire ways to draw demonic attention to yourself: If you're already crying, the evil spirits will give you more to cry about; if you're exhibiting a carefree, happy attitude, the evil spirits will be sure to change your tune.
- Avoiding arguments, as displays of anger will draw demonic attention to fuel your rage even further to the detriment of yourself and the person or persons with whom you are quarreling.
- Sending children early to bed and ensuring that they adhere to the previous bullet points.
- Doing all domestic chores—especially women's work such as sewing, the carding of wool, spinning wool, etc.—during daylight hours *only*.
- Avoiding unclean places, especially after sunset (any place that carries a death current, like cemeteries and hospitals, but even *literal* unclean places such as garbage dumpsters, landfills, etc.).
- Not going out late at night.[326]

If that last taboo in particular is violated, you're exposing yourself to all sorts of spiritual danger, as the very air in the predawn hours of the Unclean Days are thought to be congested with evil spirits. Late-night wanderers court the hazard of having a malevolent force such as the *karakonđula* (караконџула) attach itself to them. The extrication process can be challenging and may even have to entail an official exorcism ritual.

326. Bandić, *Narodna Religija Srba u 100 Pojmova,* 307.

A Reprieve from Darkness with the Coming of the *Badnjak*/Yule Log

Fortunately, with all this spiritually unclean energy afoot, it *is* possible to find magical protection during Christmas—but in my culture, this comes from the sanctity of the natural world, not from Christian mythos. Further underscoring the pre-Christian nature, sensibilities, and activities of a Serbian Orthodox Christmas is the fact that the terms for "Christmas Eve" and "Christmas" don't reference Christ at all. "Christmas Eve" is *Badnje Veće* (Бадње Веће), which literally translates as "Oak's Evening." And the holy day of the Nativity is known as Božić (Божић; "Little God" or "Young God." The suffix *-ić* is used as a diminutive). We're planted firmly in the bosom of Paganism here, with the Pan-Slavic sacred World Tree of the harvested oak sapling or badnjak serving as the symbolic avatar of the Little God whose birth at or after the Winter Solstice Christmas commemorates more than likely one of the Slavic sky gods, either Svarožić or Perun.

We've learned that the Slavic World Tree is an oak (храст/*hrast* in Serbian; *Quercus cerris*), and it's precisely the wood of a healthy, young, east-facing oak that is ritually cut and welcomed into the house to serve as the Yule log. Traditionally done by the head of the household or oldest male family member, the wood chopping is preceded by prayers and offerings and should take place early in the morning.[327] (Note: The entire tree is not cut down, just a good-sized limb with leaves attached.)

The return of the head of the household with the prized badnjak (бадњак) has a ritualistic element that bears a similarity to Scottish New Year's Day/*Hogmanay* customs associated with greeting the luck-bringing "first footer" into the home: The awaiting family members welcome the good fortune of the greeter at the threshold, and subsequently invite that person inside only to pelt them with coins and walnuts, the food of the dead. In other words, the family welcomes the return of the ancestors with symbolic tokens of the blessings that originate in the ancestors' Underworld: wealth and sustenance. The song that is sung by the family while this cheerful action is taking place is strikingly Pagan and deeply moving:

327. Bandić, *Narodna Religija Srba u 100 Pojmova*, 295.

"Badnjače, Badnjače, Srpski rodžaće, dobro nam došli u našu kuću," which means, "Oak, Oak, cousin to the Serbian people, you are welcome in our house!"

Badnjak can also be obtained at the end of Serbian Christmas Eve Divine Liturgy. This latter kind of badnjak sprig is specially blessed by the clergy and is thought to have healing and apotropaic powers, especially when hung over the entrance to the home. It's a highly prized talisman, one that is revered and kept until next year's Christmas Eve, when it gets ceremonially burned in massive bonfires outside the front steps of Serbian Orthodox churches!

Baba Marta (March 1) and Spring Equinox

In South Slavic folk belief, the month of March is personified as a goddess named Baba Marta (Баба Марта, "Old Woman March"). The erratic weather patterns typical of this month are ascribed to the goddess's seemingly fickle nature: She likes to be an old winter hag one day and a beautiful spring maiden the next, ushering in either snow and cold or balmy temperatures with sunshine, depending on her mood.

My mother taught me, as an adult, to sing the "Baba Marta" children's poem she remembered as a child. It was composed by the beloved Serbian poet Jovan Jovanovich Zmaj (1833–1904). I'll write it in transliterated Serbian first and then translate it into English:

Baba Marta, narod veli
Čas sneg, čas vedrina
Sprolećem se vrlo često
Usput sretne zima!

Baba Marta, the people say
Now blizzard, now clear sky
Springtime very often
Meets winter!

For many Indo-European cultures, the year began with the arrival of spring, and the main deity presiding over the transition from the old year to the new aptly has characteristics of a liminal nature. This divinity can alter the hinges of reality, switching between What Was and What Is Yet to Be. The Kalends of ancient Rome commemorate the arrival of the month of March and the new year by celebrating the Matronalia, a days-long festival honoring several goddesses (the Mothers), chiefly Juno as the Supreme Mother and Bona Dea but also Anna Perenna, the goddess of timekeeping. The Romans honored mortal women as the earthly counterparts of these goddesses.[328]

The Slavic Baba Marta reminds me of tales I have heard from Ireland and Scotland of the Cailleach Bheara/Bheur, the ancient goddess of the land, Hag of Winter, who, when she sees fit, can transform herself into a beautiful spring maiden (Bríd or Brigid), often by rejuvenating herself in a sacred body of water. Doubtlessly, these tales wove their way into Arthurian lore of the late Middle Ages with the recurring "loathly lady" characters like Dame Ragnell in one of Sir Gawain's misadventures, women of power who can transform themselves from frightful crones to seductive young lovers when knights worthy of their help learn the valuable lesson that a woman's greatest desire is to never have her sovereignty forfeited.[329]

Many Slavic cultures retained the folk memory of this kind of a goddess long after Christianity displaced their official worship. East Slavic customs like the burning of the (female) effigies of personified winter (i.e., the goddess Mara/Morana/Marszanna) during the Maslenitsa festival, a carnival-like celebration that precedes the start of the Lenten fasting season, or the March 1 exchange of red and white *martenitsi* figures—worn or hung to invite good luck and health—on Baba Marta's Day in Bulgaria show that the death-dealing winter witch and the life-affirming goddess of new beginnings are ever in their people's hearts.[330]

---

328. Robertson, *Juno Covella*, 1.
329. Anonymous, "The Wedding of Sir Gawain and Dame Ragnell," stanza 70, lines 420–424.
330. Bulgarian National Television, "The Bulgarian Tradition of Martenitsa."

Until the Spring Equinox (variously known as *Velikdan*, *Jare Święto*, or *Vesnin Dan*) or even later, during the days leading up to Easter, Mother Earth was considered to be both asleep and pregnant and it was highly inadvisable to harm her with invasive activities such as digging or ploughing.[331] Once the ground softened after the snows melted, the season would be welcomed by bringing in early-blooming vegetation, especially pliable branches of willow and birch trees, and dyeing hard-boiled eggs with natural dyes and rolling them directly onto the earth, transferring the symbolic power of renewal in hopes for an abundant harvest later in the year.[332]

Also at this time of nascent spring, West Slavs partake in a time-honored custom of dousing pitchers of "untouched" water (meaning that the sun's rays hadn't shone on it) from a well or a spring on single women of childbearing age. Known as *oblévačka* or *śmigus-dyngus*, the "pouring" ritual was performed by young unmarried men who splashed women who crossed their path.[333] In the spirit of equanimity, the women get their turn the following day.

Baba Marta can serve as an archetype for the South Slavic village Cunning Woman, or bajalica, who performs acts of healing magic. Let us now turn our focus to this empowered and valued woman of Slavic village life.

331. Warner, *Russian Myths,* 29.

332. Natural dyes can be obtained from boiled yellow onion skins, red cabbage leaves, and powdered madder root.

333. Cvetković, *Slavic Traditions & Mythology,* 267.

CHAPTER 9
Bajanje (Healing Magic) and the Magic of Plants

Today, unless a modern magical practitioner in a South Slavic country identifies as a Wiccan or as an adherent of a related kind of Neopagan spiritual tradition, it would be very difficult indeed to find a magical practitioner who identifies as a witch, especially among folks belonging to generations older than mine (Gen X). The word *witch* (*veštica* [вештица] in Serbian; *vještica* in Croatian) has had exclusively negative connotations attributed to it over many centuries post-Christianization, so no visitor to the Balkans eager to receive services along the lines of spiritual healing or of having their cards (or coffee cups) read would ever ask village inhabitants, in, say, eastern Serbia about their local renowned "witch."

Which Witch Is Which?

There are a variety of other terms used in lieu of *witch* that are preferred and do not carry negative cultural connotations. These terms can vary by region, and as nouns, they linguistically and grammatically vary not just to reflect gender but also to reflect the type of magical specialization, as it were. In Serbia, Kosovo, Bosnia-Herzegovina, and North Macedonia, a fortune teller who specializes in cartomancy is referred to as the thrower of the cards: *bacačica* (female) or *bacač* (male; both are derived from the Serbian verb *bacaj*, "to throw"). An alternate term is *gatara* for a woman and *gatar* for a man, terms cognate with "divination": *gatanje* (гатање).

Gatanje is the term that encompasses all forms of divination, fortunetelling, soothsaying, and so on. As a phenomenon and practice, it is distinct from the category of performing magical workings, which are divided into the "white" magic subcategory of *bajanje* (бајање), which focuses on healing, and the "black" magic subcategory of *vračanje* (врачање), which can span everything from leveling curses to conjuring spirits for baleful workings, itself a sub-subcategory of black magic known as *madžije* (маџије) or *madžijanje.* A woman who has a reputation as a *vračara* or "sorceress" (a man would be a *vračar)* would be a shunned figure in her rural community.[334]

The Serbian term *bajalica,* literally "enchanter," or North Macedonian *basmara* (басмара) fits the closest definition of the practitioner of magic who, in the English language, would be referred to as a Cunning Woman: She's the resource her villagers turn to for healing spells and to have curses removed. A male charmer or Cunning Man would be called a *bajač* (бајач) or *basmar* (from the Proto-Indo-European root word **bha-* meaning "to speak").[335] The *basma*, or "incantation," is what the healer recites (typically by whispering) during their working, and this is almost exclusively performed on behalf of a client within the spiritual context of folk adaptations of Orthodox Christianity.

In other words, the bajanje workings are examples of the Dual-Faith Tradition and can feature Christian ritual tools repurposed as talismans, such as blessed chunks of freshly baked Eucharistic bread from church, Holy Water, blessed beeswax candles procured from a church, and icons of Orthodox saints in addition to the Pagan staples of the live coals that are used to diagnose the spiritual causes of illness or misfortune, the appropri-

334. Petrović, "Charmers on the Folk Practice of Charming in Serbia," 135.
335. Petrović, "Charmers on the Folk Practice of Charming in Serbia," 135.

ate kinds of fresh or dried herbs, and other *materia magica*, such as amulets derived from animal parts. Truly, as modern Trad Craft witch Roger J. Horne informs us, "Although many Pagans would try to deny it, witchcraft developed into the form we recognize it today alongside Christianity, not before it."[336]

Bajanje: Healing Magic

As Dr. John Miles Foley, director of the Center for Studies in Oral Tradition at Indiana University, explains, "Serbian folk taxonomy distinguishes between *vračanje*... [or] 'black magic,' and *bajanje*, the set of healing charms whose function is to restore a person's or animal's health by dispelling the... agent of the sickness. This latter variety of 'white magic' is practiced widely throughout villages around Šumadija in central Serbia, conventionally and virtually exclusively by postmenopausal women."[337]

The bajalica and her clients share certain *a priori* assumptions for the healing magic to work. Chiefly, there is the belief that modern physicians, no matter their educational backgrounds or expertise from years of practice, lack the necessary emotional intelligence to truly understand the patient's experience of sickness and its impact on the patient's family and wider community.[338] A doctor also cannot sufficiently provide the patient with a satisfactory explanation for the actual, meaning *spiritual*, basis for the sickness, which the bajalica does provide through her ritualized process of diagnosing the magico-spiritual causes of illness and obtaining the materials to effect a cure for the patient.

The worldview shared by the bajalica and her patient allows for citing the Otherworld as the locus of certain illnesses. Recall that the twelfth-century *Primary Chronicle* of the Eastern Slavs stated that the chthonic god Veles was thought to punish oath-breakers with death by plague. A malevolent vračara, eager to harm a target, has the skill sets to access the Unclean Force from within the Otherworld and direct it to her target in this world as a "sending" on one or several malefic "winds," resulting in a specific physical illness, or

336. Horne, *Folk Witchcraft*, 30.

337. Foley, "Spellbound," 102.

338. Petrović, "Charmers on the Folk Practice of Charming in Serbia," 137.

state of spiritual oppression, or even a spate of severe bad luck. The bajalica would also be able to determine if the malevolent magic was sent by urok (урок) or the evil eye, or by evil spirits carrying out the orders of the vračara. Sometimes, the patient inadvertently came into physical contact with the Nečistaja Sila, such as by picking up a cursed object deliberately left behind at a crossroads, thereby unknowingly bringing their affliction upon themselves. The telltale sign for the bajalica that something supernatural and not something medically pathological is the root cause of the patient's malady has to do with the sudden onset of the affliction, as Serbian folk religious historian Sonja Petrović explains: "Such illnesses occur suddenly, mysteriously and incomprehensibly and are treated by charming, whereas illnesses occurring from visible causes (cuts, broken bones, a bullet, etc.) are not charmed away."[339]

As recorded by late-twentieth-century anthropologists doing fieldwork in Serbia's Šumadija region, the basma or incantation banishes the sickness out of the afflicted's body and returns it to the Otherworld. The striking imagery of one such spell, recorded in 1975, to heal a person suffering from the "red wind" envisions the disease being sent away "across the sea," i.e., returning to the Otherworld.[340] That liminal location is characterized by negation. The sights and sounds of "normalcy" in the world of living humans (meowing cats, crowing roosters, etc.) are entirely absent in the Otherworld because it is a Not-Normal Place. Hence, the red wind must be sent back to "where the rooster doesn't crow/where the hen doesn't cackle/where the priest doesn't visit/where the cross isn't carried/so that the ritual bread isn't broken/so that the candles aren't lit."[341]

The recitation, uttered rapidly *sotto voce* and done three times in a row, is accompanied by specific ritual gestures on the bajalica's part—usually sweeping and cutting motions with the *kostura* or ritual knife and a broom to sweep or cut away and disperse the disease from the afflicted individual. The bajalica also has sacred herbs such as sweet basil soaking in a vessel

339. Petrović, "Charmers on the Folk Practice of Charming in Serbia," 137.

340. The "red wind" manifests as a dermatologic and lymphatic infection called erysipelas, or Saint Anthony's Fire, due to its severe, dark red rash.

341. Foley, "Spellbound," 119.

of blessed water, and she uses the herbs to asperge her client's body where needed. Afterward, the water remaining in the container is either poured out in a faraway location where it will not come into contact with anyone else, or the client can take the vessel home with them and continue to wash themselves.[342]

Perhaps most important of all in terms of a shared worldview, the bajalica and her patient share the belief that the bajalica is truly a blessed individual, that she's in command of spiritual healing forces, whether she came to obtain those forces as a "gift from God" *or* from the *vile,* who were believed to bestow their gifts of plant medicine upon certain women.[343] The bajalica's understanding of her own piety, of the sacral nature of her work, and of her sincere belief not just in magical practice, but in behaving with the utmost integrity and discretion with her clients, cements her respectable position in the social hierarchy. As an elder, she truly is seen in her community as a mediator, one step away from being on a par with the ancestors, occupying the liminal space between the world of the dead (Nav) and that of the living (Yav). The allure of her reputation explains why even to this day her services are sought out.[344]

Plant Medicine and Magic

As we've seen, there are two very special periods or tides of power in the summer months that are especially set aside for the ritualistic cultivation of wild herbs that will eventually be used by a bajalica as part of her arsenal of magical healing aids. Those days are Biljini Petak, the Friday that precedes Saint George's Day (May 6), and Ivandan/Ivan Kupala/Kupala Noć, the Feast of Saint John the Baptist that ushers in Midsummer magic (July 7). Depending on the climate where the bajalica may reside in any given South Slavic country, Saint John's Day is the likelier of the two holy days when the desired herbs will have grown to the point that they're ready to be cultivated. The farther away from human habitation the herbs grow, the

342. Đorđević-Belić, "The Motif of Extinguishing Fire with Grass and Water in One Type of Serbian and South Slavic Chanting," 76.

343. Ristić, *Balkan Traditional Witchcraft,* 392.

344. Petrović, "Charmers on the Folk Practice of Charming in Serbia," 140.

more effective they are thought to be in their healing power.[345] Here are some of the wild plants that a bajalica would definitely incorporate in her folk healing rituals:

Saint John's wort *(Hypericum perforatum)* is a plant with red, blood-colored spots on its leaves and red-colored sap, so it may not come as a surprise that various folk names for the plant in most Slavic languages reference the healing power of the plant's "blood," which is the Old Common Slavonic word *krv*. The "blood" has various mythic origins, attributed to either the blood streaming from severed head of John the Baptist, the blood of the crucified Christ, or even the menstrual blood of the Virgin Mary(!): Ukrainian *Hristova kristva*, Belarusian *kryvavets*, Czech *krvavnik*, Russian *Ivanova krov*, and the Serbian *Bogorodičina krva* (Our Lady's blood). We associate Saint John's wort today with antidepressant properties, but in the old Slavic worldview, thanks to the sympathetic magic of correspondences, it's an herb used to stop bleeding, as are other red-colored plants such as **red clover** (*Trifolium pratense*), **sweet briar** (*Rosa rubiginosa*), and **European madder** (*Rubia tinctorum*).[346] For magic, Saint John's wort can be prescribed as a tea to be consumed or as an amulet to be worn by women who believe their barrenness stems from being "overlooked," i.e., having the evil eye thrown at them.[347]

Mugwort (*Artemisia vulgaris*) is a time-honored folk remedy for fever in countries such as Poland, Serbia, Ukraine, and Russia. Mainly consumed as a beverage, it can also be massaged into a sick person's skin when they're feverish and shivering with cold.[348] Dried mugwort leaves are used in spiritual cleansings of spaces and people. It and **wormwood** (*Artemisia absinthium*) serve as magical defense against hostile rusalki; pregnant women in particular should wash themselves with water that has had wormwood sitting in it overnight to protect themselves and their unborn babies.[349] Medicinally, wormwood, bitter as it is, treats stomach problems and digestive illnesses, including ones caused by roundworms.

345. Kolosova, "Name—Text—Ritual," 52.

346. Kolosova, "Name—Text—Ritual," 52.

347. Ristić, *Balkan Traditional Witchcraft,* 219.

348. Kolosova, "Name—Text—Ritual," 50.

349. Ristić, *Balkan Traditional Witchcraft,* 231.

Thorny plants are magically useful in repelling the Unclean Force and are medicinally used to treat a variety of conditions. In Russia's Vologda region, patients suffering from rheumatoid arthritis were gently beaten with fresh **common nettle** (*Urtica dioica*) plants; the leaves were used in infusions to treat fever, the seeds in cough medicine. In Siberia, the roots were used to treat colds and chills and the seeds were pounded and mixed with honey and wine to loosen coughs. In Ukraine, nettle switches were used in the sauna by folks suffering from rheumatic pain. In Bulgaria, women who had collected the first nettles of the growing season were encouraged to whisk themselves with it as an apotropaic gesture to avoid illness for the rest of the year. In lieu of jumping over a bonfire on Saint John's Eve (July 6), people can leap over heaps or bushes of nettles or thistle instead.[350]

To help couples with fertility issues, a bajalica would likely turn to plants whose roots curiously resemble human genitalia, such as the **bog orchid** (*Orchis palustris*), also known by its charming Ukrainian folk name of *liubka* (root word *liub,* "love"), whose knobby, testicle-like roots were thought by the Hutsuls of western Ukraine to treat male impotence, as was the root of the famous **mandrake** (*Mandragora officinarium*).[351] The **spotted orchid** (*Orchis maculata*) is associated with aphrodisiac potions and was also used in love magic: The root is an amulet given to single women to carry on their person to attract a mate and for married women who are quarrelling with their spouses.[352] The tubers of all orchid varieties used in love magic have to be facing each other in order for the magic of sexual attraction and potency to work; orchid specimens with "hands" that point away from each other can be used in malefica to break couples up or cause infertility.[353]

Besides the plants she gathers from the wild, the bajalica makes use of herbs and flowers grown in her own garden. In Serbian lore, the two most commonly used culinary herbs that are almost exclusively used for apotropaic magic and not for culinary use are **sweet basil** (*Ocimum basilicum*) and **rosemary** (*Rosmarinus officinalis*). Basil leaves and sprigs of rosemary are worn, carried, or hung for spiritual protection.

350. Kolosova, "Name—Text—Ritual," 53.

351. Kolosova, "Name—Text—Ritual," 47.

352. Ristić, *Balkan Traditional Witchcraft,* 232.

353. Kolosova, "Name—Text—Ritual," 47.

The folk wisdom is so strong regarding these plants in Serbia that not even the Orthodox Church could eradicate the customs associated with their magical use, so the Church embraced these herbs instead. You can see icons adorned with basil leaves in any Serbian church. In a Serbian wedding ceremony, the happy couple as well as the bride's and groom's parties proudly display the pinned sprigs of rosemary to their special clothing, ensuring the evil eye comes nowhere near them on the couple's special day. Holy Water is made in Serbian churches using sweet basil in addition to the biblically cited herb of healing, **hyssop** (*Hyssopus officinalis*); the stalks of both plants are used as an aspergillum by Orthodox clergy to disperse Holy Water and bless spaces, people, animals, and icons. Sick people are encouraged to drink water in which fresh sweet basil had been soaked overnight.[354]

Hung in the home or carried in the pocket when one is venturing into a forest or other wild space where dangers may lurk, **garlic** (*Allium sativum*) is another treasured ally for spiritual and physical protection. Besides famously repelling vampires in South Slavic lore, garlic can repel various infectious diseases: Numerous clinical studies have proven that garlic possesses antimicrobial and anti-inflammatory properties—its main component, allicin, has been shown to strengthen immune cells—and it has been relied upon over many centuries in Serbian folk medicine as both a preventative and a curative resource.[355]

Many a homespun recipe for shortening a cold or the flu devised by my Nana Milojka had just three ingredients: minced garlic, a heaping tablespoon of honey, and a wee teaspoonful of hot *rakija* to kick a pernicious sore throat or chills. Once when I was nine years old and feeling sick but sent off to school anyway, Nana had me go to school with a washcloth wrapped around my neck and tucked into my school uniform shirt's collar. The cloth had minced garlic bits carefully wrapped inside, and the whole rag was doused in warm rakija before it was tied around my neck! Squinting from the strong odors, I resigned myself to being profoundly embarrassed. Needless to say, it wasn't long at all before I was marched upstairs to the office of my

---

354. Ristić, *Balkan Traditional Witchcraft,* 218.

355. Radovanović, Gavarić, and Aćimović, "Anti-Inflammatory Properties of Plants from Serbian Traditional Medicine," 5.

school's principal, a stern Dominican nun, and I had to give a very detailed explanation on how and why I came to reek of hard booze that morning!

In the same *Allium* genus as garlic, the humble culinary staple of the **onion** (*Allium cepa*) is widely used in Serbian folk medicine. Teas and poultices are made from the bulbs to treat the common cold, asthma, headaches, and arthritis pain. Onion juice is also topically applied to treat insect bites, minor burns, and even frostbite.[356] On the magical end of the healing spectrum, to help cleanse a space of negative vibrations, an onion can be cut into four pieces and left on a small dish of salt in each corner of a room to absorb foul energies. Dispose of the onions and salt (keep and reuse your dishes) on the third day by depositing them into a river far away from your house or by placing them in the center of a four-way crossroads, even one in a graveyard. Do this alone at either noon or midnight.

Color symbolism comes into play with these next few commonly accessible plants whose yellow flowers symbolically evoke the healing energies of the sun. The common **dandelion** (*Taraxacum officinale*), that humble and hardy plant, produces a sap whose milk-white appearance lends itself to medically being given to women post-childbirth to help with lactation. The Serbian folk name is *mlečnjak,* from the root word *mleko* or "milk." The roots can be dried and ground up and roasted to serve as a coffee substitute, and the leaves, which are rich in minerals such as potassium and iron, are added to salads. Since the flowers have a bright yellow color, they can be used in magical workings as a preventative measure against jaundice, along with the common **sunflower** (*Helianthus annus*).[357]

Traditionally gathered in the wild from saline or ruderal ecosystems but now grown on large-scale organic plantations, **chamomile** *(Matricaria chamomilla)* is Serbia's most domestically used and most exported medicinal plant.[358] The herb, called *kamilica* (камилица) in Serbian, has antiseptic and anti-inflammatory medicinal properties, which have been known for centuries. It's considered a panacea herb, with applications in dermatology

356. Radovanović et al., "Anti-Inflammatory Properties of Plants from Serbian Traditional Medicine," 4.

357. Kolosova, "Name—Text—Ritual," 50.

358. Stevanovič, Vrbničanin, and Jevdjovič, "The Weeding of Cultivated Chamomile in Serbia," 149.

(treating skin infections) and treating respiratory system and urinary tract infections. Numerous scientific studies have been done that confirm the efficacy of traditional folk medicine usage.[359] As the chamomile flower is symbolically a miniature representation of the sun, its magical applications have widespread usage in spells calling for well-being, victory over darkness, breakthrough energies, abundance, love, and success.

Another herb with universal usage—culinary, medicinal, and magical—is the familiar Mediterranean **sage** *(Salvia officinalis)*. A proven antiseptic and natural antibiotic, sage leaves could be used fresh, chewed raw to help with gingival issues or toothaches, or applied topically to serve as bandages on cuts. When pressed, the fresh leaves can have their essential oil extracted to be ingested or applied topically. Fresh or dried, the leaves are boiled for tea. Modern Pagans, witches, and magical practitioners of all stripes know sage to be an effective spiritual cleansing agent, and traditional Serbian witch Radomir Ristić concurred that the herb's "primary purpose is fumigation" in sanctifying ritual spaces, even Orthodox Christian ones. He noted, "It is commonly used in amulets, often in combination with other herbs, like basil and wormwood."[360]

Used for food, fiber, and medicine, **flax** *(Linum usitatissimum)* plays an important role among the Slavs, who were thought to have brought it from Greece. By the time of the Kievan Rus', widespread flax cultivation began. A truly versatile plant, flax provides precious linseed oil and its fibers have been used for millennia to produce linen clothing, sail cloths and fishing nets, and other valuable products.[361] Magically, flax seeds are used in money spells and in workings for fertility. Given its extensive history of use in weaving and textile crafts, it would make an appropriate offering for the goddess Mokoša or the Orthodox Saint Friday, Saint Petka Paraskeva.

Divine Feminine energy extends into the South Slavic lore surrounding certain trees as well. The fragrant flowers of the beloved **linden tree** *(Tilia cordata)* are boiled into a tea in Serbian culture to promote reproductive

359. Radovanović et al., "Anti-Inflammatory Properties of Plants from Serbian Traditional Medicine," 1.

360. Ristić, *Balkan Traditional Witchcraft,* 222.

361. Saskatchewan Flax Development Commission, "Early European Flax History."

health in women. The tree is considered sacred, and it's forbidden to cut it down, though a branch may be cut to produce "living fire" by rubbing it against its Divine Masculine counterpart, the oak tree. Linden wood also lends itself well to carving a *kipa* representing a Slavic deity.[362]

One of the great "female" healing trees is the **white willow** *(Salix alba).* Young willow bark, peeled in early spring and administered as a decoction, has been known in Serbia to possess pain-relieving, fever-breaking, and anti-inflammatory properties for centuries: It has been used to treat the common cold, strains of the flu, and rheumatoid arthritis. As ethnobotanist Katarina Radovanović explains, "In the form of oral rinses, a decoction of willow bark is recommended for the treatment of inflammatory conditions of the mucous membranes. Until the synthetic production of salicylic acid was perfected, this plant and related willow species were long used as a raw material from which this acid was obtained. Contemporary research has confirmed the experiences of folk medicine."[363] On a folk magic level, willow branches can be used to gently spank children and livestock to help them grow healthily; wreaths of braided willow branches can be hung in the home to protect against lightning.[364]

Similar in nature and practical application to the willow is the **birch tree** *(Betula pendula),* whose leaves, bark, roots, and sap have been used in teas and poultices to treat conditions as varied as urinary tract infections, rheumatoid arthritis, and eczema.[365] Birch branches are the spiritual cleansing tools of choice in East Slavic steam bath/sauna rituals; as with willow branches, they can be used to flog people and animals to stimulate fecundity. On the Feast of Pentecost as well as Saint John's Day, East Slavic girls weave birch garlands into wreaths and throw them into rivers to observe whether they float or drown, a form of love divination.[366] Brooms

362. Ristić, *Balkan Traditional Witchcraft,* 243.
363. Radovanović et al., "Anti-Inflammatory Properties of Plants from Serbian Traditional Medicine," 8.
364. Ristić, *Balkan Traditional Witchcraft,* 240.
365. Radovanović et al., "Anti-Inflammatory Properties of Plants from Serbian Traditional Medicine," 5.
366. Gilchrist, *Russian Magic,* 154–155.

made from birch branches serve a mundane as well as a magical function when it comes to sweeping spaces.

Birch brooms have another magical use: Serbian girls entreating the *vile* to protect them would hoist their birch brooms into the air to evoke them.[367] The fairy associations with birch are strong in East Slavic lands as well, as food offerings to propitiate the rusalki are left by village girls in rural Russia at the bases of birch trees on Trinity Sunday (seven Sundays after Easter), which is part of Rusal'nalia Week. After festooning the tree's branches, the girls link arms and circle dance (khorovod) around it, singing:

Don't rejoice, oak trees
Not to you the girls are coming
Rejoice, birches! Rejoice, green ones!
To you the girls are coming,
To you they are bringing pies, pastries, omelets,
Dancing about you, little birch,
They are singing songs.[368]

Trees that embody Sacred Masculine energies include **pine** *(Pinus silvestris),* whose wood is made into rods that South Slavic male witches (vračari) use in their magical combats with each other; **juniper** *(Juniperus communis),* a tree so blessed with apotropaic powers that its wood is the time-honored wood of choice among the South Slavs for fashioning stakes to kill vampires; and **hazel** *(Corylus avellana),* the tree of wisdom and understanding, whose nuts and branches feature in folk remedies to promote learning and banish mental illnesses. Additionally, if a parish priest is nowhere to be found when a person is in the mood to confess their sins, the guilt-wracked individual merely has to confide in the nearest hazel tree, a tree so protective of people that it is even thought to be inherently immune to lightning strikes.[369]

---

367. Ristić, *Balkan Traditional Witchcraft,* 239.
368. Gilchrist, *Russian Magic,* 154.
369. Ristić, *Balkan Traditional Witchcraft,* 243.

But by far, the two most celebrated "male" trees are the **oak,** whether the species in question is Turkey oak *(Quercus cerris)* or English oak *(Quercus robur),* and the English **walnut** *(Juglans regia).* As we've noted, the oak is the Pan-Slavic tree par excellence that most closely evokes the mythic cosmology of the World Tree. Oak wood is rubbed with linden wood to make "living fire" for sacred occasions or "live coals" for divination use by a bajalica to determine the spiritual cause of a client's sickness: Three, seven, or nine pieces are placed into a fire until they glow, then they can be carefully extracted and doused in a heatproof bowl or small cauldron that has had spring water or Holy Water from a church poured into it and put to use. It's taboo to cut down an entire oak tree in South Slavic lore, though branches of it are ritually cut by the head of the household on Serbian Christmas Eve and brought into the house, as noted in Chapter 8.

Christmas lore involves oak and walnut magic together, as on Serbian Christmas Eve it's customary to decorate the family's feast table and the saint's corner with leaf-bearing twigs of the badnjak/Christmas oak as well as walnuts. I was told by my parents when I was a child that the walnuts are prosperity symbols, but it's likely they specifically represent the symbolism of material blessings that issue out from the Underworld and are a food item associated with the cult of the dead, making the walnut tree an ambassador of chthonic energies. After all, ancestor magic is at its height during the winter months.[370]

In Serbian folk medicine, walnut leaves are brewed into a tea that's consumed to soothe digestive issues. Topically, the tea can be applied to cleanse and treat irritated skin; walnut has anti-inflammatory and antioxidant properties. My mother has told me that when she was a little girl during the harsh times of World War II, when basic household necessities such as personal care items were hard to come by, she and her sisters were taught to boil walnut husks to make shampoo.

---

370. Ristić, *Balkan Traditional Witchcraft,* 243.

Exercise
Try Healing Spells Using Plants and Trees

The first spell noted below is a fascinating historical curiosity. The subsequent ones are all attested to by my family. My brother Mark was sick in his infancy and my Nana Milojka was horrified to have learned that my mother never poured his first bathwater onto the roots of a plum tree like she was supposed to have done. By way of contrast, I was a healthy, no-fuss baby and Nana said it's because my mother agreed to perform the last spell in this section.

Spell to Treat Jaundice

The following Serbian spell to treat jaundice, as documented by ethnologists in the latter part of the twentieth century, uses sympathetic color correspondences for both the flowers and the colors of thread, with yellow representing sickness (the jaundice) and red representing vibrant health. The patient should take a yellow silk thread and twine it around their neck, while hanging a separate red thread on a healthy **red rose** in their garden. In the morning, the patient removes the yellow thread from their neck and hangs it on the rose, while taking the red thread and twining it around their neck as they say, "Rose, my sister in God, give me your red and take my yellow in its stead!"/*"Ružice, Bogom sestrice, daj mi tvoje rumenilo, a uzmi moje žutilo!"* The disease is thought to transfer itself to the plant, assuming no one else in the household inadvertently touches the yellow thread.[371]

To Get Rid of a Fever

A person suffering from a high fever should take a white onion and then, early the next morning, visit a white **willow tree** *(Salix alba)*. While shaking the tree three times, they should recite, "I'm not shaking away your morning dew; I'm shaking away my fever." After the third recitation, the onion is left at the base of the tree. As the person walks away (without looking back), they declare, "The fever will leave me when this onion sprouts."

371. Kolosova, "Name—Text—Ritual," 53.

Serbian Basil Plant Spell to Promote Health and Well-Being

Take a lock of your own hair or the hair of the target/person you are doing this working for (obviously, with their consent given beforehand) and tie it with a red or white silk thread or length of cotton/natural fiber yarn to a sprig of fresh sweet basil. Place it on your healing altar or tuck it under the target's mattress as a healing amulet.

Spiritual Cleansing with Garlic

Spiritual and physical cleansings and purging of sickness can be done by rubbing a huge garlic bulb all over yourself, done in total silence and solitude exactly at noon, and then tossing the bulb into a river or depositing it at a crossroads. Walk away in silence and don't look back. Your health will improve soon.

Simple Spell to Bless a Newborn Baby

To ensure a newborn baby grows healthy and strong, the water from its first bath must be poured onto the roots of a **plum tree** *(Prunus domestica).*

CHAPTER 10
Vračanje (Witchcraft) and the Magic of the Otherworld

At the beginning of the last chapter, we noted the South Slavic distinction made between magical practitioners known for practicing healing magic, bajanje, versus its opposite, vračanje. A practitioner of vračanje is called a vračara (врачара) in Serbian, if a woman, or a vračar if a man; women are much more prevalent and attested to in the lore. The noun of "witch" is *solely* gendered female in both Serbian (*veštica*) and Croatian (*vještica*, plural *vještice*); the term derives from the Old Common Slavonic *vedeti* (to know; to have secret knowledge) and is cognate with similar words for related kinds of practitioners in East Slavic lands (e.g., Russian *ved'ma* [ведьма], Ukrainian *vedun'ia* [ведунья]).[372]

372. Ryan, *The Bathhouse at Midnight,* 86.

Witchcraft Is for Women in South Slavic Lore

In Serbian folk belief, a witch is usually "born that way" and is destined to become one, inheriting her abilities from her matrilineal line. Signs include being born in a "red shirt" or caul, being born in an "evil hour" or on the eve of a major Church feast day or at the start of the Lenten or Advent fasting periods, having piercing eyes, and, as she gets older, possessing a commanding and loud voice. However, a witch can also be "made," in other words, trained in the magical arts by other witches—almost always older, postmenopausal women, usually relatives of the young witch.[373]

Witches are said to gather at their favorite haunts of crossroads or underneath a walnut or pear tree—the farther away from human habitation, the better. Special dates singled out for gatherings include the first of March (Baba Marta's Day), the solstices and equinoxes, Saint George's Day, and Christmas Eve. As with their counterparts in Western Europe from the Early Modern period onward, South Slavic witches are thought to have traveled to these gatherings in spirit form or via the art of what we now call astral travel, projecting their consciousness out of their bodies and out of their homes—their inert bodies lying calmly in bed next to their unsuspecting spouses all the while—via keyholes, the chimney, or through cracks in the mortar.[374]

A flying ointment utilizing hearth ashes as a major ingredient is something they're thought to rub on themselves beforehand. They rub themselves as well as their magical staffs, iron rods, spindles, or the brooms they may use as flying aids. Should they decide to shape-shift, the most common form to adopt is that of an innocuous butterfly; other forms include a dog or cat, especially ones that are unknown and approach without being called.[375]

The witch's nocturnal business is nefarious and consists of physically attacking people known to her, including the age-old, vampire-like drinking of blood, especially children's blood. She also performs works of malefic magic, such as instructing the winds to send diseases to her enemies, magic that has to be countered by the healing magic of a bajalica, as this remark-

373. Bandić, *Narodna Religija Srba u 100 Pojmova,* 123.

374. Bandić, *Narodna Religija Srba u 100 Pojmova,* 123.

375. Conrad, "Female Spirits Among the South Slavs," 27.

able charm recorded in central Serbia by anthropologists in the year 2006 attests:

The Mother of God goes up the road, down the road.
She meets a sick man and asks, "Why do you wail, sick man?
Why are you yellow-skinned?"
"Mother of God, God's Mother,
I'm yellow from enchantments.
I wail because of black magic."
The Mother of God takes nine shovels,
Then digs the sick man out of the grave.
The Mother of God takes nine brooms,
Then sweeps the sick man clean with them.
Then across nine mountains and nine waters
The Mother of God drives away [the Unclean Force].
The sick man remains clean as clean silver,
Clear as a clear sky,
Pure as mother's milk.[376]

The imagery in this healing spell clearly attests to the fusion of Pagan and Christian elements that compose the Dvoverovanje tradition so associated with the rural populations of Slavic countries. The figure of the Blessed Virgin, one of whose epithets in the Orthodox Church is the *Bogorodica,* the "God-Birther" or "God-Bearer," takes on the qualities of a capable bajalica herself, making use of the magical multiple of three and performing ritual actions that the bajalica is known to do: "bury" the "black magic," "sweep" the afflicted individual clean, and return the magically sent disease state back to its source in the Otherworld, which is located beyond the "nine mountains and nine waters."

Another sinister activity rural South Slavic witches are still known for is stealing the milk from their fellow villagers' cows. A hapless cow's path

---

376. Đorđević-Belić, "The Motif of Extinguishing Fire with Grass and Water in One Type of Serbian and South Slavic Chanting," 72.

to and from barn to pasture can have salt sprinkled on each side, which, with the right incantation, can cause the animal to dry up in three days.[377] An alternate method, which was documented by eyewitnesses in Croatia's Bilogora region in 1948, is for the witch to place a bucket underneath an enchanted rope that is tied to the streetside doors of the barn that contains the bewitched cows inside; by going through the motions of milking, even when she's nowhere near the site, the witch can milk the cows and transfer the liquid into her bucket via the rope. The witnesses in Bilogora reported seeing fresh milk issue from such a rope![378]

A South Slavic witch's true power lies in secrecy. By day, she may be a sweetly smiling neighbor who regularly attends church services. She may be a mother, a widow. But should her activities ever be disclosed, she loses her power. Curiously, if she's ever caught during her nocturnal escapades—if she's shape-shifted into a butterfly, she can be accosted, physically harmed, and threatened with salt—and her foul deeds exposed, she is offered the chance to be reintegrated into society provided that she confesses her sins and promises to "switch teams." In other words, she must agree to give up being a harmful veštica and become a helpful bajalica instead, using her extensive knowledge of plant medicine exclusively for healing physically sick and magically attacked people and animals.[379]

Still, even after her reformation, she may not be fully trusted by her community. Villagers with any remaining doubts would do well to place their brooms upside down by the hearth to prevent the witch from entering their home. And a little prophylactic does wonders: Rubbing raw garlic over one's body before retiring to bed is a widespread South Slavic deterrent to being magically attacked during sleep.[380]

Children in particular are cautioned to steer clear of the known village witch as well as her primordial mythic forebear. For centuries, a way to frighten misbehaving South Slavic children is to threaten them with winding up on the menu of the fearsome, forest-dwelling Baba Roga (Баба

377. Conrad, "Female Spirits Among the South Slavs," 31.

378. Conrad, "Female Spirits Among the South Slavs," 32.

379. Bandić, *Narodna Religija Srba u 100 Pojmova,* 126.

380. Conrad, "Female Spirits Among the South Slavs," 31.

Pora, "Horned Baba"), the archetypal South Slavic witch-o'-the-woods whose curious, telltale physical feature of horns or antlers hearkens back to the iconography of the ancient Velika Šumska Majka, the Great Forest Mother. As the Croatian saying goes, *"Odnjijet će vas Baba Roga!"*/"Baba Roga will take you away!" Baba Roga is clearly mythic kin to the infinitely better-known East Slavic Baba Yaga, who also has a penchant for devouring wayward children who stray too close to her Underworld-bordering hut.

Were There Witch Trials in Slavic Lands?

While persecutions of people, overwhelmingly women, tried and executed on the charges of witchcraft in Western Europe and the American colonies lasted from the fifteenth to the eighteenth centuries (well into the so-called Age of Enlightenment), there isn't anything of such a scale in the Slavic lands of Eastern Europe.[381] There are a variety of reasons for this. South Slavs in the Balkans, as with their Romanian, Albanian, and Greek neighbors, were living under Ottoman rule for nearly five centuries, from the fourteenth to nineteenth centuries. The influence of the Orthodox Church was extremely curtailed during that time, so even if there had hypothetically been widespread accusations of witchcraft in Balkan cities and villages, the resources required to mount the necessary prosecutions and trials simply were not available.[382]

Another reason lies in the fact that, unlike its Roman Catholic and Protestant counterparts in Western Europe from the Early Modern period onward, the Orthodox Church generally lacked what Slavic scholar Linda J. Ivanits calls "a philosophically grounded demonology," which encouraged its clergy and laity to see women in league with the Devil everywhere.[383] Ever since the fourth-century CE Council of Laodicea, the Orthodox Church certainly strongly condemned magic and certain (but not all!) forms of divination—and pointedly prohibited its clergy from engaging in magical practices themselves. However, in East Slavic lands, no amount of canon law or penitential writ ever resulted in a witch-hunting scale even

381. Drury, *Magic and Witchcraft*, 68.

382. Dvornik, *The Slavs*, 234.

383. Ivanits, *Russian Folk Belief*, 90.

remotely near the epidemic proportions in Western Europe.[384] In the late eleventh century, the Metropolitan of Kyiv, Ioann II, issued canonical law condemning the women and men who practice witchcraft, but emphasized that such individuals are *not* to be put to death.[385] In Ukraine and Russia right up through the middle of the nineteenth century, accused witches were likely to face penalties of church penance (exile to a monastery for five or six weeks) or the payment of fines. The lack of severity in doling out punishments is especially striking as just across the western border of Ukraine in Catholic Poland, the Inquisition was well underway in its brutal and systemic extermination of supposed witches (via burning at the stake) well into the 1780s![386]

A third and perhaps most important reason for the lack of large-scale persecutions is also ideological. The folk view of sorcery is not demonological but pantheistic: *Nature is the source of spiritual energies perceived as either benevolent or baleful to human beings.* The dualism is not that of Christian mythos, which squares an omnipotent God against its own creation of an exiled angel named Lucifer. "Christian dualism is absolute rather than complementary," explains Slavic studies scholar Kenneth Johnson. "There is God and there is the Devil, and healing most certainly does not consist of balance or equilibrium between the two."[387]

Non-Catholic Slavic countries offered an alternative worldview, or, if you prefer, dualistic paradigm that is more of a union of complementary opposites. "The more ancient concept of dualism implies an interdependence rather than opposition; the two principles are complementary rather than hostile to each other," clarifies Kenneth Johnson.[388] Opposite but complementary forces reside in nature and in nature's Source in the Otherworld: life force interwoven with death current, forces of *živa* (life) and *zdravlje* (health and well-being) in balance with the *Nečistaja Sila,* the "Unclean Force," in all its many manifestations. "The broad masses attributed the power of the sorcerer or witch not so much to the Devil as to the mysterious

384. Warner, *Russian Myths,* 66.

385. Ryan, *The Bathhouse at Midnight,* 409.

386. Ivanits, *Russian Folk Belief,* 91.

387. Johnson, *Slavic Sorcery,* 31.

388. Johnson, *Slavic Sorcery,* 30.

forces of nature," explains Slavic historian Linda J. Ivanits. "It's best to consider the Devil one of a number of possible unclean forces, and not a grandiose image around which a highly elaborate demonology coalesces."[389]

Tellingly, more than a millennium after the synod that became the Council of Laodicea issued its edicts against magic and the practicing of magic by Orthodox clergy, the Stoglav Council convened in Moscow by Ivan the Terrible in 1551 found it necessary to issue an edict to the city's clergy, prohibiting them, upon pain of excommunication, from accepting the cauls of newborn infants, salt, soap, and other gifts from their parishioners who asked such items to be placed under church altars in order for them to be magically charged![390] The average village priest was himself often suspected of being a wizard of sorts, one who could deal out angelic-sanctioned healing or demonic-tinged baleful magic in equal measure. "In the eyes of a Serbian villager, the priest figured as a special kind of sorcerer, a Christianized sorcerer," explains Serbian ethnologist Dušan Bandić.[391] The topic of male practitioners of magic in Slavic countries is where we turn to next.

East Slavic Sorcerers and the Dark Art of "Spoiling"

The textual evidence from Ukraine, Belarus, and Russia—especially from works, including recorded judicial proceedings, dating from the nineteenth century—makes it abundantly clear that the darker spectrum of magic that falls under the rubric of sorcery was widely believed in by all members of society. And, unlike in Western Europe or even among the South Slavs, where (older, postmenopausal) women were prevalent as practitioners, sorcery was an equal-opportunity playing field in East Slavic lands, with men being just as prevalent as women, perhaps even more so.[392]

We learned about the shaman-like figure of the Pagan priest, or volkhv (волхв), in Kievan Rus'. As with the Druid in Celtic societies, his role had tremendous social significance that included the political, as uprisings

389. Ivanits, *Russian Folk Belief,* 95.

390. Ryan, *The Bathhouse at Midnight,* 409.

391. Bandić, *Narodna Religija Srba u 100 Pojmova,* 133.

392. Ryan, *The Bathhouse at Midnight,* 69–70.

against the religious import of Christianity were led by the volkhvy.[393] From the seventeenth century onward, the terms *volkhv* and *koldun* (колдун) were initially interchangeable, until it became clear that the koldun was perceived in the popular imagination to be solely preoccupied with magical workings of "evil," which were usually accomplished through the direct intervention of nefarious spiritual beings or other manifestations of the Unclean Force.

Like his female counterpart of the *koldun'ia,* he lived alone on the margins of society. He was thought to have been born with a small tail as a visual indicator of his Otherness and his inherent abilities (bushy, wolflike eyebrows and wild eyes were another giveaway), and he could powerfully cast the evil eye to the extent that targets would instantly wither or be driven mad.[394]

His magical aptitude was mostly believed to have been inherited, but it was also believed that any man could choose to become a koldun if he underwent this initiation experience willingly: At midnight, and all the better if it happened to be the night before a major Church feast day, the candidate had to appear at a remote four-way crossroads with only a blessed icon given to him by his parents or grandparents. He then removed his Orthodox cross necklace, took the icon and placed it facedown in the dirt, and stomped on it while renouncing the Christian God and his own mother and father. Lastly, he invited the Unclean Force to take his soul in exchange for the gift of magical powers.

An experienced, mentoring koldun may or may not have been in attendance to furnish the necessary contract to be signed in the candidate's own blood (obtained by cutting his left hand). The widely held belief was that some manifestation of the Unclean Force would appear, either in the form of a man or a black dog or some other animal; additional actions involving somersaults between knives(!) or other wildly acrobatic feats that highlighted upside-downness and liminality (aspects of the Otherworld) might have also been required of the candidate. There are several mid-nineteenth-century Russian accounts of failed pacts wherein the aspiring koldun became so

393. Ryan, *The Bathhouse at Midnight,* 72.

394. Ryan, *The Bathhouse at Midnight,* 72.

frightened by whatever met him at the crossroads that he ran away, subsequently became severely ill, and died soon thereafter.[395]

The koldun was thought to be driven at great lengths to pass on the burden of his dark knowledge before he came to the agonizing death that was destined for him, whether or not the heir was willing to receive such a legacy. One such stratagem of subterfuge involved hiding under the stove, groaning, with one hand stretched out for help. A neighbor or other passerby compassionately wanting to offer aid, unwittingly extending a literal helping hand, would instantly have the koldun's terrible knowledge transferred onto him, while the original koldun's soul would shape-shift into a black animal and scurry off to hell.

The pervasive belief was that the holy Mother Earth could not accept a koldun's corpse, however, and the damned individual was likely to become a vampire or werewolf as a result, especially if he'd failed to pass on his powers before death. In Belarus until the late 1860s, the precaution taken was to exhume the buried corpse of a known koldun, decapitate it and place the head between the legs, rebury the corpse, and then sprinkle the grave with poppy seeds. In Ukraine and Russia during the same time, the remedy was a good old-fashioned staking through the shoulder blades with an aspen stake, the wood of choice for such a dreadful magical implement.[396]

Other terms for various male practitioners of the Dark Arts include *ved'miak, vedun, charovnik* (spell-caster), *otgadchik* (for a diviner), and *znakhar* (literally "one who knows"). This latter term was usually attributed to the more favorably regarded village magical healer, though they were also sometimes suspected of being in league with summoned spirits and possibly trafficking with the Unclean Force.[397]

Every East Slavic village was thought to have had at least one known and respected koldun, who could be hired, for example, to protect the families and guests on a wedding day against the evil eye of rival kolduny or anyone else who wanted to cause misfortune through magical means. Protocol and etiquette required that the koldun be invited to sit at the table of

395. Ivanits, *Russian Folk Belief,* 190–191.

396. Ryan, *The Bathhouse at Midnight,* 73.

397. Ivanits, *Russian Folk Belief,* 85.

honor during the feast, giving him an expansive view of everyone at the reception venue and its entrance.[398]

But perhaps even more feared than the known koldun was the villager with their specific role to play within society (the local blacksmith, the miller) who did their malefic magic on the down-low, causing harm and using subterfuge to disguise their real natures. Even as recently as the Soviet era (mid-1970s) in Belarus, this was considered a serious social problem in rural life. Again, it requires a known koldun to out a secretive one. However, there may be more cooperation than competition among the kolduny today: A koldun interviewed on a Moscow television program in 1989 called for starting something of a trade union with his peers, something which actually has historical precedent from centuries ago.[399]

Whether he's a koldun or a charovnik or a znakhar, the destructive powers attributed to him in East Slavic lore fall under the Russian verb of *portit'* (портить), or "to spoil," as in "to cause to deteriorate." The range of misfortunes attributed to it included crop failure and drought, severe issues with animal husbandry (stillbirths of livestock, milk cows going dry, etc.), epidemic diseases and various illnesses, infertility and impotence, and all manner of familial discord—in short, every aspect of life for people in rural communities.[400]

The most nefarious, death-dealing spells a koldun could inflict entailed the collecting of their target's footprints, hair, snippets of fabric from their clothes, or fingernail parings—what American Hoodoo terms "personal concerns." The more organic the *materia magica,* the better. Those ingredients could be mixed with clay and enchanted and then hung to dry, ideally in a discreet place such as a chimney. As the ingredients dried and withered away, so, too, would the target's life force.

The koldun also could create spoiling by engaging in necromancy, trafficking with the unclean dead in particular. One such invocation, meant to be uttered at the unhallowed places such as crossroads and swamps where the unclean dead used to have their corpses interred, calls them forth with

---

398. Ivanits, *Russian Folk Belief,* 105.
399. Ryan, *The Bathhouse at Midnight,* 78.
400. Ivanits, *Russian Folk Belief,* 103.

the words "arise ye dead, murdered, ye who hanged from trees, wayward ones, unbaptized, and nameless ones."[401]

Villagers certainly ought to have been taught better than to compulsively retrieve seemingly ordinary household objects deposited at unusual places. For example, a late-nineteenth-century report from Russia's Riazan' Province describes the fate of a man who noticed a spoon of butter strangely lying outside of his house. Not suspecting the items had been magically spoiled, he brought the spoon and its contents inside to ask family members about who had done such a thing, placing something so precious and vital to daily cooking at an odd location. Of course, no one from his family had. He immediately became strangely ill and died within the year.[402]

The best defense against a koldun was the insurance policy of behaving courteously and deferentially toward one in the hopes of never giving cause for offense. Failing that, one could resort to the Christian counter-magic available through the ritual gestures of praying aloud and making the Sign of the Cross, wearing an Orthodox cross necklace, consuming Holy Water and asperging afflicted places and people with it, fasting prior to receiving Holy Communion, burning frankincense incense, petitioning the Virgin Mary and the saints for their intercessory aid, or asking for a priest to perform one or a series of blessings and possible exorcisms. Other, decidedly *ballsy,* remedies included robbing the koldun of his power by directly confronting him and cutting his beard, sticking needles into his clothes, or throwing water collected during a thunderstorm right in his face![403] Now *that's* some charged Slavic war water right there!

Performing Magic Today: Some Preliminary Words

The following catalog of a whole host of documented Slavic spells begin with ones I present as historical curiosities *only,* followed by ones I've personally used and whose efficacy I can attest to, including a love spell taught me by the late, wonderful Baba Živka, a sweet elderly Serbian lady who was

401. Ivanits, *Russian Folk Belief,* 104.

402. Ivanits, *Russian Folk Belief,* 104.

403. Ivanits, *Russian Folk Belief,* 105.

one of my parents' closest friends and who mentored me in her cartomancy method using regular playing cards.

If there's one general principle about performing magical workings, the key is to *go about your work unseen.* Highlighted times of day are noon but especially midnight, and work done outdoors in remote places where, ideally, you feel safe enough to be nude and have your hair unbound (if applicable) is best. Astrological timing is not something an average Slav in ages past paid attention to, though moon phases as well as certain days of the year were considered more favorable than others for a given working.[404]

Effective spell-casting not only requires solid intentionality and the ability to direct your will as an operative force in that liminal space where this world meets the Otherworld, the locus of possibility where magic takes place, but the thorough understanding that *your will manifests through your words.* Every culture throughout human history has some kind of lore surrounding the sanctity of speech, utterances, and song. Spells entail vocalizations set into meaningful patterns. As Slavic witch Natasha Helvin explains, "The original meaning of the words *spell* and *hex* was 'speak unto.' Traditionally, you must say spells directly onto the things and objects you are using so that your breath reaches their surface. Essentially, this is a direct transfer of magical power and energy to a material object."[405]

If you're not speaking extempore but using written material, take the time to fully memorize the text well in advance of the chosen date of your working. Few things are more energetically disruptive than having to get out of the ecstatic state magic requires by fumbling for a scrap of paper onto which you've scrabbled your words of power when the moment calls for an eruption of magical force. Worse yet is fumbling for your phone to open an app! Just *don't.* Know your material, inside and out, and truly believe in it—believe in what you're doing and in your own aptitude. Attain a laser-like focus on obtaining your desired result as something that's already happened. The spell should be recited aloud, sometimes for a total of three times to reinforce the magic. Whether you enchant in a quiet tone or thunderously is up to you, likely depending on the nature of the spell and the

404. Ryan, *The Bathhouse at Midnight,* 171.

405. Helvin, *Slavic Witchcraft,* 11.

environment wherein you're performing the working. Above all else, recite your spell clearly and commandingly.

No matter the setting or scenario, the magician must arrive at the location of the magical operation in total silence and walk away from the site of their working or the location where they deposited their *materia magica* and never look back. Return home in total silence—no music playing on portable devices or in the car stereo, nothing.

I would add spiritual aftercare as a vital next step once you're home: Immediately cleanse yourself physically and spiritually, especially if you've done graveyard work. In Serbian culture, even when visiting the graves of our beloved dead, we're considered unclean just from having been in a cemetery. At the very least, we have to wash our hands as soon as we return home and before we do anything else.

I also heartily recommend grounding and centering after you've cleansed yourself by eating a mix of carbohydrates and protein, such as a handful of salted crackers with a small cup of yogurt or a toasted English muffin with a spread of cottage cheese or some avocado as a vegan alternative. It can be light or hearty, but whichever carbs and protein combo you choose, make sure you ingest some salty food.

A Miscellany of Spells

From baleful to healing works, these diverse spells reflect East and South Slavic practices.

Knotted Cord Curse for an Enemy

Take a length of black-dyed woolen yarn or cotton thread and go out to a crossroads at midnight. Tie eight double knots, saying these words at each corresponding knot: (1) "Out onto the road I go"; (2) "Into the open field, I throw"; (3) "I throw into the crossroads"; (4) "I throw between the houses"; (5) "I throw into the gardens"; (6) "I throw into the ocean"; (7) "I throw into the deepest forest"; (8) "I throw into the quaking bog. Accursed spirits, aid me so that *[name of target]* has no peace by day, no sleep at night. May *[name]* know every grief and woe." Leave the knotted cord where the target will likely step on it.[406]

---

406. Adapted from Ryan, *The Bathhouse at Midnight,* 185.

To Create Waters of Death

Obtain from a worker in the funerary industry water that was used to wash a corpse.[407]

Binding Spell for Love

Pluck three strands of your own hair and obtain three strands of your beloved's hair. Throw them into a roaring fire with the words, "Fire binds our flesh, hearts, and minds."[408]

Baba Živka's Spell to See Your Future Spouse

Note: This spell is to be performed on January 18, the eve of Epiphany in the Serbian Orthodox Church.

Obtain a comb, a small pocket-size mirror, and a pair of new, clean socks. This spell is to be performed immediately before retiring to bed for the night; do not get out of bed for any reason or speak to anyone until well after sunrise the next morning. Place the three objects under your pillow. Make the Sign of the Cross and then say out loud, *"Ko je moj sudženi, neka dodže, da se očešlja, da se ogleda, i da mi obuje čarape."* Translation: "To the one who is my destiny, let them come to comb their hair, to look at themselves in the mirror, and to put my socks on for me."

Repeat the gesture of making the Sign of the Cross again, followed by the recitation of the charm. Make the Sign of the Cross again for a third and final time and then recite the charm again for a third and final time. Immediately go to sleep. Upon awakening, it's critical to not even glance at the bedroom window; this is to avoid having the image of the future spouse dissipate beyond all recollection. Therefore, arise and exit your bed in a manner that would have you completely averting your gaze from the window.

For Success in Court

On a breezy day, find a birch tree that's swaying. Cut off an east-facing twig and say, "As with this twig, so too with my opponent's tongue in court!"

---

407. Adapted from Ryan, *The Bathhouse at Midnight,* 185.

408. Adapted from Helvin, *Slavic Witchcraft,* 52.

Take the twig with you and pray for the Most Holy Mother of God to grant you a just judge.[409]

To Bring Rain

Submerge an icon of Saint John the Baptist in water on his summer feast day, July 7.[410]

When Setting Out on a Journey

Once the person leaving is out the door, a family member (ideally the mother or grandmother) tosses a glass of clear, fresh water after the departing individual, stating, "Your path ahead is smooth." My mother did this for me not just when I was traveling but through my grad school years when I had exams! The person leaving must never look back, acknowledge the verbal charm uttered or the spilled water, or return to the home's threshold for any reason. Doing so would negate the spell and cause all manner of obstacles and failure.

Magical Taboos to Observe to Help a Newborn Baby Grow Strong

Before a child turns one year old, it should never be shown a mirror, be lifted above eye level, be spoken to during bathing, or have its hair or fingernails cut.[411]

To Ensure an Abundant Catch of Fish

Upon arriving at your desired fishing hole, remove your hat if you're wearing one, bow thrice, and address the resident *vodeni duh*, stating, "Grandfather! I thank you for your hospitality and offer you some as well—be welcome to my simple feast!" Toss in a round loaf of fresh bread that has a pinch of salt on top and follow by sprinkling in three pinches of quality loose tobacco.[412] Release the first fish that you catch alive and unharmed back into the water as a sign of gratitude.

---

409. Adapted from Ryan, *The Bathhouse at Midnight,* 187.

410. Adapted from Ryan, *The Bathhouse at Midnight,* 196.

411. Adapted from Ryan, *The Bathhouse at Midnight,* 177.

412. Adapted from Ryan, *The Bathhouse at Midnight,* 195.

Money Cinnamon Bath

Brew one cup of cinnamon tea and four cups of parsley tea. Mix them together in an empty gallon, then divide the mixture into five equal servings. One serving will be used in a spiritual bath per day for five days total. For each bath, pray for your financial situation to improve. Don't specify the methods for the needed improvement; let the gods and your ancestors figure that out for you. Fully immerse yourself five times as you soak for six to eight minutes per bath. Air-dry upon exiting the tub; don't towel-dry.[413]

Spell to Reverse Negative Energy

Obtain a coffee cup filled with dirt and a small thin taper of a candle, such as the beeswax ones sold in Orthodox churches, but even a birthday candle will do. Light the taper and watch the flame for a moment. Using swift movements, pluck out the candle and flip it upside down, snuffing out the candle flame in the dirt. Bite out a section of the unlit portion of the candle so the wick is exposed, light it, and place the candle back into the dirt, stating, "As the candle flame is reversed, so, too, do I reverse any workings thrown at me. As the fire died in the dirt, may my enemies' schemes come to nothing." Leave the candle to fully burn down. Once it has, throw the entire cup away with dirt and candle remains at a garbage can far away from your residence.[414]

Apotropaic Plant Magic

On a round piece of linen cloth approximately nine inches in diameter, place one part of each of the following dried herbs: Saint John's wort, rosehip, sweet basil, rosemary, angelica root, geranium, wormwood, yarrow, juniper. Lastly, add one fresh garlic clove. Gather the edges of the cloth and bundle upward, then take a white or red cotton string or piece of yarn and tie the bundle together with these words: "Jarilo rides on his white horse and puts to flight the Unclean Force." Carry the bundle with you on your person, hang it from the rearview mirror of your car, place it under your pillow, or tuck it into your desk drawer at the office.

---

413. Adapted from Mickaharić, *Spiritual Cleansing*, 48.

414. Adapted from Mickaharić, *A Century of Spells*, 12.

PART III
THE WORK

(Посао)

CHAPTER 11
Ritual Tools and Altars

Looking at witchcraft through a South Slavic lens, ritual tools used by country Cunning Folk fall into one of these two groups: (1) everyday tools, kitchen implements in particular, that serve a dual functionality in magical and mundane application; or (2) "virgin" tools that will be set aside solely for magical work from their first usage onward. This latter category includes *materia magica* acquired from the natural world in unusual ways, items that are ritually prepared to serve a specific function.[415]

Suspended Between the Worlds: The Cauldron and Its Chain

In the first group, one will find the nigh-universal witches' tool of the cauldron, but of even greater significance to witches in Serbia, Croatia, and Bosnia is the iron chain that dangles the cauldron over the sacred hearth. Known

415. Ristić, *Balkan Traditional Witchcraft,* 84.

as a *verige* (вериге) or *lonac* (лонац), this chain has tremendous symbolic significance as a mediator between the world of humans and the realms of celestial powers above and chthonic ones below.

Historically, oaths were sworn by family members while grasping this chain. Liars and oath-breakers would evoke divine curses as retribution, not just upon themselves, but their entire families for generations, curses that could never be broken. More intriguingly, offerings to the Judeo-Christian god or to the Slavic gods were and are, to this day, affixed to its sanctified links, everything from chicken feathers and scraps of carded wool that are bound in green thread (apotropaic magic to keep wolves away) to the severed heads of black roosters that were slaughtered at the threshold! Tellingly, the roosters' heads were the only acceptable offerings that were black in color; the belief was that if any other black-colored objects hung upon the verige, family members would quarrel among themselves.[416]

From the verige hangs the cauldron, known as a *kazan* (казан), which for humble country folk serves double duty as the mundane instrument for everyday cooking as well as a magical instrument for preparing herbs and dousing embers gathered from the fires burning below. The hearth fire that cooks the cauldron's ingredients is, of course, itself a sacred entity; ideally, it should originate from a "living fire" made by rubbing sacred twigs of oak and linden together.[417] As we've seen, the hearth is strongly connected to the cult of the ancestors and the lore surrounding the *čuvar kuća*, the serpent-guardian in charge of the family's luck or destiny.

The Witches' Broom

Known as a *metla* (метла), the witches' broom was a handcrafted household item, but made of locally sourced plant fibers and branches that ideally were harvested on the sacred occasion of Ivandan, Saint John's Day (July 7); one of the folk religious epithets of John the Baptist is *Ivan Metlar,* John the Broom-Maker. The bulk of the material is the plant known as Field Broom *(Xeranthemum annuum),* which would be gathered at sunrise on that day by older women who had unbraided their hair and gone nude into the fields.

416. Podunavksi, *Tradicionalno Balkansko Veštičarstvo,* 81.

417. Ristić, *Balkan Traditional Witchcraft,* 86.

Once bound into broom bristles with yarn, the metla would be left to dry in the sun of Saint John's Day and then could be hung over the inside of the door or left standing upright near the door to ward away evil energies. Superstitions in Serbia in both rural and urban areas include never hitting children with brooms for fear of stunting their growth, waving brooms over pregnant women who are past their due dates to help induce labor, never bringing old brooms into new homes, and placing brooms under the beds of the ill to help them recover.[418]

Cunning Men in rural Serbia and elsewhere in the former Yugoslavia were said to use brooms from the threshing floor as magical weapons against other sorcerers; the combat appears to have been astral, but if one villager's threshing floor broom was seized by a rival's, the fertility of the vanquished sorcerer's entire village was at risk of being lost/usurped.[419] The losing sorcerer would likely also have his life in severe danger as a consequence. This loss of a sorcerer's magical power due to the theft of the magical tool applies to all brooms as well as to the ritual staff.

Witches obtained the knowledge of how to craft their brooms by a variety of methods. Some received "downloads" directly from divine forces, while other witches learned by oral tradition as passed down generation to generation from within their families. Brooms made in three-dimensional reality also had their astral plane equivalents that witches could use during deep states of trance, during which they'd astrally project onto their brooms and fly out of the house via the chimney. The chimney was the preferred exit point because if witches chose to exit via windows or doors, their spirit doubles ran the risk of being seen by their fellow villagers.

The broom could also be used in lieu of the ritual staff to demarcate a circle for ritual, as well as perform cleansings from within a cast circle. The broom was thought of as the physical representation of a witch's personal power to drive away all hostile forces. Serbian folk belief upholds that if demons were to try to enter a home but beheld the broom poised near the

418. Ristić, *Balkan Traditional Witchcraft,* 88.
419. Ristić, *Balkan Traditional Witchcraft,* 89.

threshold, they wouldn't dare to enter.[420] Now, as in ages past, this ritual tool is synonymous with witchcraft.

The *Kostura,* a Black-Handled Knife

The kostura (костура, related etymologically to *kostur,* "bones" or "skeletal structure") might be an everyday kitchen utensil, but it is usually an implement that has to be specially made and consecrated only for magical/ritual work. Horn obtained from a black ram was the preferred organic material to make the handle. Ideally, a blacksmith, working without speaking to anyone, would be the one to forge the blade after midnight during a full moon.[421]

The process for consecrating the knife, once assembled, was also a complex affair that astronomically depended upon a total lunar eclipse during a full moon closest to the feast day of Saint Vratolomej/Bartholomew (July 11 in the Julian calendar observed by Orthodox Christians). The kostura would be placed in a type of round baking pan called a *tepsija* (тепсија), itself a ritual tool. Filled with pure spring water that had not been used during the day for any other purpose, the tepsija would be taken outdoors to a running body of water and the reflection of the lunar eclipse would be sought by the witch by positioning the tepsija at just the right angle. Then she would say the following out loud for a total of three times, addressing the moon:

> *Just as you, Divine Light, can never have any demons nor dragons devour you, so too will no disease or harm ever befall the one who carries this knife.*
>
> *Empower it, Moon!*
>
> *Strengthen it, Moon!*
>
> *Consecrate it, Moon!*[422]

The witches then make the Sign of the Cross, remove the knife from the water-filled tepsija, and carry the consecrated knife in their bosoms for a

420. Podunavski, *Tradicionalno Balkansko Veštičarstvo,* 84.

421. Ristić, *Balkan Traditional Witchcraft,* 91.

422. Podunavski, *Tradicionalno Balkansko Veštičarstvo,* 86. The translation is the author's own.

twenty-four-hour period. Once that time passes, the knife can be sheathed onto their belts. It bears their personal signature and no other individual can ever touch it; should that happen, the knife would lose all its magical force and would be totally useless to any subsequent individuals.

The main magical purpose of the kostura is to protect witches during astral travels or shamanic journeys: The knife would be propped up, blade upright, at the threshold of the bedroom, on windowsills, or at the ends of beds to ward the witch in trance.[423]

Sacred Wood: The Staff or *Štap* (штап)

The lengths of these straight sticks of wood may vary (tall rods that double as walking sticks or shorter, arm-length pieces), depending on the individual witch's need. They can be placed in the same general category as wands. What tree the wood is from and how the wood is acquired are what inform the magical uses of *štapovi* (rods).

Dogwood and willow branches could literally be used as whips to drive diseases and fevers out of people, especially children. Oak, hazel, linden, and birch were and are considered the most blessed woods, known for their powers of fertility/virility and apotropaic virtues. Given the sacredness of the oak, it's really a taboo to cut off any branches of it other than during the Christmas Eve festivities that ensure spiritual protection of the household. Yew and black hawthorn are also considered to be formidable magical defenders.[424]

There's a curious way that hazelwood has to be obtained: The tree has to be a strong year-old tree, one that has not yet been pruned. Witches must approach the tree, naked, at midnight, cutting the desired limb or branch swiftly in one movement so as to not protract the pain the tree may experience. This work is carried out in total silence.[425]

The tree with the most sinister reputation in Serbian lore is the walnut tree.[426] It is the one most sought out by witches who work *malefica*. It clearly

423. Podunavski, *Tradicionalno Balkansko Veštičarstvo,* 87.

424. Ristić, *Balkan Traditional Witchcraft,* 96.

425. Ristić, *Balkan Traditional Witchcraft,* 97.

426. Charney and Slapšak, *The Slavic Myths,* 220.

has chthonic associations, as walnuts are a cultic food of Veles; walnuts are also a staple symbol of abundance consumed as an act of sympathetic magic at Christmastime.

The Hatchet

In addition to knives, brooms, and cauldrons suspended from their chains, hatchets (*sekire*/секире) would be the most commonly used everyday objects that had magical applications. Many Serbian ethnologists have elevated the object to the level of a cultural fetish.[427]

In addition to splitting logs for firewood, hatchets are used to fell the sacred wood to obtain the Christmas Eve badnjak or to procure branches and limbs to make rods and wands. Like the sacred blade of the kostura, the hatchet is used for apotropaic magic, slicing away would-be magical attacks against witches and deterring malevolent forces from entering the home. Farmers also use hatchets to disperse hail-carrying storm clouds. Midwives place hatchets under the beds of women in childbirth.[428]

The Mirror and the Copper Dish

Whether of the decorative glass variety adorning walls and sitting atop bedroom dressers or the more rustic, homespun antecedents composed of copper baking dishes filled with spring water, it's clear that mirrors (огледала) and mirror substitutes like the tepsija are primarily used for divination, whether for oneself or on behalf of someone else. Young unmarried women wishing to get a glimpse of their future husbands could take advantage of the magical powers circulating at the holidays of Saint George's Day or Saint Vitus's Day and place small mirrors under their pillows when they go to bed.[429]

An even more striking example of mirror divination for a young unmarried woman to see the face of her future husband entails this ritual documented in eastern Serbia. The young woman in question has to fast on the Friday or series of Fridays before she intends to perform the mirror divina-

427. Podunavski, *Tradicionalno Balkansko Veštičarstvo,* 92.

428. Bandić, *Narodna Religia Srba u 100 Pojmova,* 234.

429. Ristić, *Balkan Traditional Witchcraft,* 102.

tion; then, in the evening just past the new moon date, when the moon is a slender waxing crescent, she'll procure a piece of linen onto which she'll embroider a talisman (sadly, no description of any image or text is given). When the slender moon becomes visible in the early evening of the given Friday, the woman goes out into her garden with either a boy not older than twelve years of age or with a girl who has not yet reached menses. The child is made to wear the embroidered cloth around their throat. The unmarried woman then places a mirror in front of that child and the child will clairvoyantly see and describe the woman's future husband.[430]

Aside from providing images related to the future, a glass mirror or a tepsija filled with spring water (*živa voda* [жива вода] in Serbian, meaning "water of life") or even staring into the waves of a flowing river or creek can also allow the diviner to look into the past. From Montenegro comes this time-honored practice of using a tepsija to help a family that's been robbed identify the thief: The head of the household of the burglarized home places the water-filled tepsija at the threshold of the main entrance. Placed across the diameter of the tepsija is the family sword, onto which a wolf's face has been engraved. A pair of young girls not older than eight years of age, either the daughters in the family or kin or even village neighbors, are brought in and seated on either side of the tepsija. They will be able to describe in detail the thief as they appeared during the moment of robbery.[431]

The principle at work here is that since they serve as portals to the Otherworld, mirrors can reveal what is otherwise hidden from sight in the everyday mundane world. Like any magical tool, they can be used for good or harm. The witch eager to cast the evil eye on someone has merely to position a mirror in such a way as to catch the reflection of the image of their target while uttering a curse; the target's destiny can also be seen by the clairvoyant witch. The act of turning the mirror at the correct angle to see one's surroundings can aid in magical workings of binding or healing an intended target, viewing the vicinity where the target lives if the image of that person is unattainable.

430. Bandić, *Narodna Religija Srba u 100 Pojmova,* 101.

431. Bandić, *Narodna Religija Srba u 100 Pojmova,* 102.

As with many other cultures around the world, there's an old South Slavic belief that when a family is in mourning, the mirrors in the home should either be turned to face the walls or be covered; this needs to happen at the moment of death or immediately after the loved one dies. Failing to take this action could result in a violation of the natural order of things, bringing the dead back to life and killing the remaining family members. The act of covering the mirrors or turning them toward the walls effectively closes the entrance to the Spirit World.[432]

Unlike mirrors, the tepsija are primarily used outdoors, while the light of the waxing crescent moon can be reflected onto the surface of the water. However, my mother tells me her paternal uncle was said to have the gift of clairvoyance, and he used his tepsija in the attic of his house, pouring hot beeswax into the water and divining its shapes. Healing rituals could involve placing the photographs or "personal concerns" (e.g., fingernail clippings, hair, saliva, etc.) of an ill person into a tepsija in combination with appropriate herbs or amulets derived from the natural world (stones, animal teeth or claws, etc.).[433]

Yarn and Thread

A tool with immense practical use in daily life also has tremendous magical significance among the South Slavs: yarn. Its importance is tied to the symbolism associated with its color, with the most popular colors for magical work being white, red, black, and yellow/gold. White yarn or thread would be used exclusively for works of blessing, especially healing magic: Bundles of herbs with the sick person's lock of hair would be wrapped and knotted three times while appropriate incantations or prayers were recited to heal the ill.

Red yarn or red thread is used in love magic—to "bind" couples happily—as well as in workings of fertility or even prosperity magic, though for the latter the yellow/gold yarn or thread could be used as well if it's available. Incantations accompany the tying of knots done thrice, usually with evoca-

432. Bandić, *Narodna Religija Srba u 100 Pojmova,* 102.

433. Ristić, *Balkan Traditional Witchcraft,* 95.

tions of the Holy Trinity. Black yarn or thread is exclusively used in workings of *malefica.*[434]

The *Bič* (Бич): Magical Hemp Whip with Serpent Power

I now present the following Serbian folk magic as an anthropological curiosity *only,* and hope that no one reading this tries to undertake the fashioning of this hemp whip, known as a bič, as it involves cruelty to animals, which I unequivocally abhor. This magical tool falls under the category of something acquired from the natural world in an unusual, rather complicated way.

The witch would first have to gather seeds of wild hemp (*Cannabis sativa*); the stem of the hemp plant is going to form the whip. Here's the cruelty: While out in the wild, the witch needs to find a living snake and then decapitate it with a pure silver coin. The hemp seeds go into the mouth of the snake's severed head, which then gets buried. Over time, the hemp plant will grow and the harvested stem and fibers get woven into a rope that composes the whip. This whip, thought of as the new body for the spirit of the slain snake, can only be used for magical acts such as creating fertility and prosperity magic (whomever is struck becomes fertile/virile, prosperous), driving away or dispersing evil forces, and weather magic (e.g., ending drought, protecting fields against hailstorms, etc.).[435]

Snakes are incredibly powerful animals in the Slavic mythic consciousness. But please, please, please—don't torture and kill an animal to obtain a magical tool! If you like the idea of working magically with a whip, use a riding crop or cat-o'-nine-tails whip readily available from your friendly neighborhood sex toy/adult entertainment boutique instead!

Lesser-Used Tools

These tools fall more under a "nice to have" but not "essential" category. Along with the other ritual blades mentioned earlier, some Serbian witches find having a **sickle (*srp*/срп)** helpful. In addition to the obvious use of harvesting magical herbs with it, a sickle can be used in divination when

434. Podunavski, *Tradicionalno Balkansko Veštičarstvo,* 91.

435. Podunavski, *Tradicionalno Balkansko Veštičarstvo,* 92.

thrown toward the direction of the sun; the direction it lands in can be subject to inspired interpretation. As with other sacred blades, it has an apotropaic magical function and can be carried for spiritual protection.

A **small bell (*zvonac*/звонац)** has the dual function of calling upon deities and protective spirits while driving away evil or Unclean Forces. These bells are very easy to obtain today.

When traveling to perform workings away from their homes, Serbian witches carry their tools in a **bag (*torba*/торба)**, traditionally made out of goat hide or sheepskin or woven wool, but many materials are used today.

A **frame drum (*bubanj*/бубањ)** is used to facilitate the cultivation of trance states, especially among Croatian witches.[436] They are lightweight and nowadays can be made of synthetic skins that won't warp or become distorted when exposed to temperature changes and humid conditions, a fate that will befall an animal-skin frame drum. I highly recommend the frame drums made by an American manufacturer called REMO; you can even paint or decorate the synthetic heads with Slavic motifs.

For practitioners in the Dual-Faith Tradition, it's common to have an array of tools such as medicinal herbs, crosses, icons, bottles of Holy Water, incense (frankincense is preferred), and blessed beeswax tapers from an Orthodox church. In healing spells, magical force (*sila magija*/сила магија) lies in the *materia magica* activated by verbal utterance, especially prayer (*molitva*/молитва).[437]

Exercise
Create a Working Altar

We know that the ancient Slavs worshiped their ancestral gods outdoors, whether on hilltops or in forest clearings or near bodies of water.[438] To be a homeowner with private land on which to create a demarcated Slavic temple space is an incredible privilege, one not made available to many, so definitely make use of the space you have available to you to create at least a working altar, though having an ancestor altar as well would be optimal.

436. Podunavski, *Tradicionalno Balkansko Veštičarstvo,* 94.

437. Ivanits, *Russian Folk Belief,* 224.

438. Gimbutas, *The Slavs,* 157–158.

Assess what your spiritual needs are for having a home altar and work within the realistic limitations of your current living situation. Do you share living space with people who might not be understanding or welcoming of your views? Then perhaps you need to look at creating a portable altar, such as a trunk or even a hard-exterior suitcase into which you can pack your deity images, tools, and ritual supplies when not in use. On the opposite end of the spectrum, do you have the good fortune of being able to demarcate an entire room in your home as sacred space for your Slavic Pagan devotionals and magical workings? If so, you have the freedom to consider the layout of multiple shrines and a permanent working altar: Adapt the saint's corner idea and have an eastern wall laden with shelves that house deity images; place images of chthonic powers like Veles, Mokoš, or Baba Yaga on the floor; erect images of sky beings like Perun or Svetovid on a high promontory; set up a small cauldron with a pillar candle inside it to represent the central fire of Svarožić; and so on.

You're only limited by your imagination. What or who do you resonate with most strongly in terms of the deities and their correspondences (symbols, cultic animals, associated plants, etc.) that can lend valuable insights into crafting an altar that is both personally meaningful and aesthetically pleasing? Remember, this is an area that you're going to choose to use often, so create your altar space in such a way that its energies keep drawing you back in a spirit of wonderment, joy, and vitality. After all, altars "are visual reminders of a spiritual dimension that lies all about us," writes Celtic scholar John Matthews.[439]

Altars constructed with intentionality, where every element is curated to produce an intended effect not just for the deity honored but for *you* as the devotee and witch, reverberate with powerful, positive energy. They emanate a ripple effect that even the most non-magical, uninspired, mundane person can detect and feel invigorated by. That's the hallmark of being in proximity to a well-done, active altar space: *You feel revitalized when you're near it.* It keeps pulling you toward it, and you're refreshed and inspired just standing or sitting in front of it and eyeing every purposeful item you've placed upon it with loving care.

439. Matthews, *The Winter Solstice*, 236.

Be as traditional or as eclectic with the elements you place on your altars as you please. We know from archaeological artifacts like the Zbruch Idol that Svetovid, for example, was depicted as having one of his arms holding a drinking horn, so perhaps an altar to him can feature your divination tools and a drinking horn (with a stand) that you fill with libations of mead or Slavic liqueurs like the Polish honey-based *krupnik* or the Serbo-Croatian plum brandy, šlivovica.

If you don't come from a Slavic heritage, in which family heirlooms like an embroidered *rushnyky* (рушники)[440] or other textiles or objects of cultural significance can be given to you by loved ones, fear not: We live in a wonderful age of global e-commerce, and handmade Slavic artisanal goods—everything from traditional clothing to housewares to linden wood carvings of Slavic goddesses such as Mokoš and Vesna—are thriving on online marketplaces and retailer websites. I like Etsy (I'm certainly biased because I sell my own Polytheist jewelry pieces on that platform) and there are several artists based in Ukraine, Czechia, Poland, and other Slavic countries that sell amazing hand-carved images or idols of Slavic deities as well as replicas of housewares from the days of the early Slavs. Set your budget before you begin your online explorations, as the freewheeling spending can certainly add up! But take heart—with your purchases, you are supporting the livelihoods of unique artists and celebrating the act of sharing Slavic cultures with the world. That's definitely something to cheer with a hearty "*Slava!*"

440. Ukrainian linen scarf. See Madame Pamita's *Baba Yaga's Book of Witchcraft* for more information on that sacred embroidery.

CHAPTER 12

Spiritual Cleansings, Prayer, and Offerings

Healthy relationships begin with the setting of healthy boundaries. Whether we're contending with a demanding boss, an intrusive family member, or a clingy romantic partner, we need to demarcate zones in space, time, and energy that respectfully announce how, when, and where we're off-limits. This is something done in a self-honoring way that respects the relationship dynamic for all parties involved.

When we don't implement healthy boundaries, we seriously risk compromising our emotional, mental, and physical well-being. We've all had experiences in the mundane world where our intuition and even our very bodies were saying *no* to something, but out of fear of abandonment or out of an unhealthy people-pleasing instinct, we begrudgingly go ahead and decide in favor of something or someone against our best interests. We ultimately wind

up paying the price with a lowered immune system at the very least, if not full-blown sickness, a sense of being physically and emotionally drained, or emotions of intense shame and self-loathing—or all of the above!

If healthy boundaries are needed in real-world, mundane daily activities related to our careers, date nights, and bill-paying woes, imagine how much more critically those boundaries are needed in our magical and spiritual work. The occult principles I was taught more than two decades ago in my Chicago Gardnerian coven espouse that human beings engaged in magical (especially theurgic) work give off a certain quality of light in their auric fields. Beings on the astral, etheric, and other planes of existence notice our lights and can become intensely attracted to them, honing in on us like we're beacons in the darkness. If we're not careful and we're not taking the proper precautions and we're not immediately following our workings with some kind of spiritual or psychic cleansing regimen, we could be unwittingly inviting all kinds of energies to mesh with our own. This risk becomes greater when we're intentionally navigating liminal zones like the Otherworld and deliberately trying to engage the beings that dwell in it.

Hence the importance on coming correct—physically clean and energetically pure, with a clean heart—before your gods and spirits prior to doing your working as well as cleansing yourself afterward. Just as visitors must leave their shoes outside the door before entering a Serbian family's home, we must cast away the detritus we've accumulated in our emotional, mental, and etheric bodies in the course of a day before we go about our sacred work.

For some folks, hours or even days of fasting beforehand are the way to go—a way to sharpen mental focus and clarity by curtailing the body's desire for nourishment. This is certainly established practice by laypeople in Orthodox Christianity in the lead up to major holidays, or when a bajalica is preparing to do a major healing work on a client. In conjunction with fasting, many practitioners may choose to forego sexual activities for days leading up to a ritual to better shore up their personal energy reserves. Still others closely monitor what they ingest and steer clear of alcohol, meat, and fish/seafood and eat light meals that eschew animal products, including eggs and dairy. Legumes such as white beans made into a stew (South Slavic *pasulja)* with a piece or two of bread might be the sole meal of the day.

I personally prefer external forms of cleansing that rely on water in the forms of cleansing baths and sprays as well as fire and air via incense. In all cases, I advocate making your own blends instead of buying mass-produced items, though I make an exception to Florida Water and various spiritual colognes that are widely available at *botanicas* or occult/metaphysical supply shops.

Exercise
Make Your Own Exorcism Spray and Incense

In my work as a legally ordained priestess, I've been asked by families in unusually dire circumstances to perform spiritual cleansings of places, such as a home with paranormal activity caused by restless, unwanted spirits, or to perform a mild exorcism on a consenting adult.[441] I've come to rely upon the following ritual tools that aid spiritual cleansings; these are my recipes for my go-to Spiritual Cleansing Spray and Exorcism Incense.

Spiritual Cleansing Spray

I think it's a good idea to have a smaller, travel-size spray bottle mixture (I carry one in my purse) and a larger, industrial-size one for physical spaces. Using whichever spray bottle you think is appropriate for your needs, add the following ingredients:

- 1 part spring water
- 1 part Florida Water
- 1 part Holy Water
- 3 tablespoons sea salt
- 3 small black tourmaline chips or hematite beads
- 1 pinch dried rosemary herb
- 1 pinch dried nettle herb
- 1 pinch dried agrimony herb
- 1 pinch shredded rowan bark

441. It's adapted from the Roman Catholic Church's *Roman Ritual,* of which I have an official Vatican-authorized, English-language copy published in 1962 that was gifted to me in 1998 by a Jesuit priest I once worked with at a Catholic publishing company.

- 1 pinch powdered blackthorn root or leaves
- 1 pinch powdered "lucky hand" root or leaves
- 1 pinch dried rue herb
- 5–7 drops lavender or sage essential oil
- *Optional*: 3 drops blessed olive oil procured from an Eastern Orthodox or a Roman Catholic church

Florida Water, a spiritual cleansing staple in African Diaspora Traditions and American Hoodoo, has no small amount of rubbing alcohol in it, which acts as a preservative. Every *botanica* in the mainland United States carries Florida Water and you may also find it in grocery stores in Latin*x* neighborhoods.

Black tourmaline is a wonderful crystal helper that absorbs negative energy and dissipates it, while iron-rich hematite provides grounding, stability, and protection against evil spirits.

The blessed olive oil is something I personally always like to incorporate and feel very fortunate to have. This oil features prominently in the Roman Catholic Sacrament of the Anointing of the Sick, and Eastern Orthodox churches share it with parishioners during certain liturgical holidays, such as the Feast of the Epiphany. If you can procure some from a priest, by all means do and add it to the mixture of the spray. Really, just three drops will suffice, as the potency is quite effective.

Exorcism Incense

This incense mixture has a dual purpose of banishing harmful spiritual entities that may be in your midst while also marshaling the aid of your helping spirits, guides, and protectors. Obtain a small vial of lavender essential oil. Using a mortar and pestle, finely grind the following ingredients into a powder:

- 1 part frankincense granules
- 1 part benzoin resin (solid)
- 1 part dragon's blood resin (solid)
- 1 large, dried bay leaf
- 3 small pieces dried Solomon's seal root

- 3 small pinches dried rosemary
- 3 small pinches dried angelica root
- 3 small pinches white sage leaves
- 3 small pinches dried rue
- 3 small pinches dried rowan bark
- 3 small pinches dried Saint John's wort
- 3 small pinches dried Dittany of Crete

Once all the dry ingredients are mixed well together, add seven drops of the lavender essential oil. Stir the mixture again and store it in a jar with an airtight seal. Burn it loosely on small charcoal disks to remove unwanted spiritual attachments to people or to expel negative entities from spaces.

Prayer Is the Backbone of a Devotional Life

As folks whom I count as personal friends in the broader American Pagan community know, I did *not* enter into Reconstructionist Polytheism with a seething hatred for the Eastern Orthodox Church. Participation in the faith certainly served as a cultural preservation stratagem by my immigrant Serbian parents. As practices, going to church on Sundays and actively praying at home at our own ancestor shrine and our protecting saint's prayer corner was as Serbian as eating my mom's lovingly prepared *sarma*.

Aside from reinforcing a sense of cultural belonging, the faith of my childhood definitely imprinted upon me two main features that have served as anchors in my subsequent personal religious evolution: (1) devotional piety expressed through four types of prayer (prayers of praise, prayers of gratitude, prayers meant to confer blessings, and intercessory prayers/petitions for divine aid); and (2) the need for sensory stimuli in ritual—especially visual, auditory, and olfactory stimulation. I was immersed in a world where, to the accompaniment of constant, melodious antiphonal chanting in the medieval Pan-Slavic liturgical language known as Old Church Slavonic, hand-carved and -painted wooden icons depicting the Blessed Mother and a panoply of saints and archangels were lovingly fumigated with the smoke of frankincense and ritually adorned with sprigs of fresh basil on holy days of the year.

As a nine-year-old girl, I would keenly observe my deeply devout maternal grandmother, Nana Milojka, following her as she prayed several times a day before various windows in the house, moving from east to south to west. It was quite clear that she was following the course of the sun. One day when I confronted her about this curious devotional practice and she replied that she was, naturally, praying to Jesus Christ, I told her I didn't believe her. Old Church Slavonic linguistic expert that I was, I told her how *I'd heard with my own ears* that the noun of the being she kept addressing in her prayers was the word *sunce* (sun), not *sjin* (son).

Nana cackled at my cleverness and told me they were interchangeable in bestowing their powers of health and vitality. So she would keep praying to whichever one of them took note of her piety and blessed our household. She ended this brief theology lesson by donning her reading glasses once again, pulling out the little tattered hardcover Eastern Orthodox *Book of Hours* from her cardigan sweater pocket so she could resume reading her prayers in front of the appropriate window for the time of day. Her discipline in carrying out these prayers on a daily basis and her joy in praying made a deep impression on my own developing devotional sensibilities.

Pagans who revere at least one deity or abide by the Wiccan duotheism of Goddess and God, and certainly Polytheists who aim to cultivate devotional relationships with *multiple* gods, are people of prayer. Yet **I've often wondered why the centrality of prayer in devotional practice or even in magical workings seems to be curiously lacking as a subject in any Pagan discourse.** *What's the hang-up? Is it just perceived as not cool—something people don't want to admit to doing because acknowledging that they pray to beings external to themselves, whether formally or not, makes them sound weak or incapable of handling their problems? Do people find that prayer is a tainted practice for them because of negative associations acquired from one of the Abrahamic religions of their upbringing?*

Naturally, many people entering "the big Pagan tent" as their new spiritual home can bring a lot of baggage with them from their previous associations with monotheism. One of my goals as an ordained priestess is to get frank discussion out into the open as well as to provide encouragement, raising ourselves to a high-vibrational level by learning from each other's beliefs and practices. Few things elevate my spirit more than witnessing another person's devotional practices, whether those are expressed through carefully planned rituals or spontaneous acts. Even if the deities honored are ones whom I personally do not relate to, my sun sign Virgo heart leaps with joy because **I can feel the *love* behind the act of *service*.**

Christians do not have a monopoly on prayer or worship. "Paganism" and "devotions" are not mutually exclusive concepts. After all, the word *religion* itself derives from the Latin verb meaning "to bind," and whether you interpret that from a Right-Hand Path standpoint of yoking your Self to a Divine Being external to you, or the Left-Hand Path standpoint of the Divine Within, prayer is what fuels that dialogue.[442]

Prayer doesn't require a formal ritual context. Far from it—simple, spontaneous words of gratitude, praise, or requests for divine aid spoken in the moment and from the heart can be deeply moving. And of the four types of prayer noted above (thanksgiving, praise, conferring blessings, petitioning for aid), note that a single prayer can combine complementary purposes, as my following examples do (thanksgiving and petitioning). Feel free to use or adapt the following prayers to a variety of Slavic deities during a whole host of occasions in the course of a day.

Prayer Upon Awakening

Živa, I give you thanks for this day in which your currents of life force energy sustain and empower me. All-seeing Svetovid, bless my mind with clarity. Father Svarog, make good the works of my hands. Swift Jarilo, speed me well and in safety to where my path leads me today. And brave Perun, protect me in all that I do and say, lead me out of harm's way, and instill courage in my heart and a steely resolve to my deeds done in a spirit of integrity and respect toward all whom I encounter on this day. Slava Rodu—Glory to the Kin!

When Beginning Your Workday or Starting a New Creative Endeavor

Holy Svarog, blacksmith at the forge, you who value and appreciate good, hard work, lend me your craftsman's vision and tenacity and the

442. Vocabulary.com, "Religion."

magic of the forge and the smithy to shape this new opportunity to my desires, allowing me to fully exercise my creative gifts in meaningful work. Let the end result meet my own personal standards of excellence and your criteria for solidity and beauty, work that is done well, enduring through time. And so it is!

Prayers Before Meals

How bountiful are the blessings of our holy Earth Mother, Matushka Zeml'ja! Her loving maternal care provides us with our fare. May this food be blessed in her holy name. May our eating of it be a ritual of thanksgiving for all she does for us. Slava, Majka! Hail, Mother!

Holy Powers, holy and highty, holy and immortal, bless this food you have so generously given me. As I eat of it, may I be ever reminded that there is no part of me that is not of you. Slava!

Perun, I give you thanks for the life-giving rains that grew my grains. Father Veles, I thank you for sharing your herds of beasts for my meat. I give thanks for the sanctity of this holy moment, acknowledging as I do the chain of life and death that links us all. Slava Rodu!

When Traveling

Open wide my paths and keep me from peril and spiritual malevolence, mighty Triglav! Slava!

When Studying

Svetovid, I draw you near that my mind absorbs wisdom, expresses thoughts so clear.

When Facing a Painful Medical Procedure

Slava, Perunu! Grant me this boon: help me to courageously endure come what may, and speed me well to healing without delay!

When a Beloved Animal Companion Is Sick or Dying

Otac [Father] Veles, Master of Animals, kindly lend your magic to swiftly heal my beloved [name of pet]. I am in need of your mercy now; relieve my [type of animal] of their pain and help me shoulder the burden of my distress. Empower the veterinary staff to act swiftly, with skilled hands, for the healing of [name of pet]. But if the dreaded time has come for my dear one to cross over into your realm, gently shepherd them to you, I humbly pray, with minimal suffering, and give me the fortitude to endure the dark currents of the grief that will assail me. Holy Shepherd Veles, help us!

To Bless a Newborn Baby

Roženice, come! Enter through the keyhole! Sudženice, attend, you are welcome at our hearth! Weave a favorable destiny for this precious little one, newly welcomed into the world! Come and take your fill of the honey cakes and wine: In sweetness come, and bring sweet blessings for a healthy, prosperous, and long life to baby [name]! And so it is!

At the Conclusion of the (Work) Day

The day's labors done, my well-earned time of rest has begun. Holy Ones, I thank you for seeing me through this day. I thank you for guarding and guiding me in the day's experiences and lessons. See me safely home, where peace and comfort await me, and where I may come before your altars with a thankful heart, bearing offerings. Slava Rodu!

Before Retiring to Bed

To the domovoi of this house and to my ancestors, stand watch in peace through the night. Protect all who dwell here. Return the urok to its sender; let naught but peace prevail. To the land spirits, let peace and harmony always be between us. May your green spaces continue to thrive. To my gods, you who know my heart, if I unwittingly offended you today, forgive me and give me the chance to be a better person tomorrow. Bless me with pleasant dreams and guiding messages as I sleep soundly. Here in the dark, I can rest in the certainty of your love and care, and I give great thanks! Slava!

Formal Prayer

According to Celtic Polytheist, spirit worker, artist, and social justice activist Morpheus Ravenna, a lorica is a formulaic prayer that functions as a type of "poetic spiritual armor" that makes use of verbalized incantation to invoke divine aid; the specificity of protection even catalogs parts of the petitioner's body.[443] Much of the extant literary texts of these prayers from Celtic countries dating from the Middle Ages onward (most notably, the *Carmina Gadelica*) are Christian in theme, but it's certainly possible to adapt the structure of these prayers to any deity or spirit, including your own ancestors.

Exercise
Compose a Formal Prayer Honoring a Slavic Deity

As you develop in your devotion to one or more Slavic deities, research their attributes and spend time communing with them. Ask them to enter your heart. Think of how a prayer you'd like to compose can weave together epithets that praise the deity in question while also directly naming the part of your body you're asking the deity to spiritually protect. My following example is a lorica-style formal protection prayer to Svetovid. Let it inspire you to create a similar prayer.

In Praise of Svetovid

I stand in the light of Svetovid,
Celestial fires of the All-Seeing Lord of Wisdom.
Svetovid's spear skewers the Unclean Force before me,
Making my paths clear to peace.
The lamp of Svetovid rests in my right hand;
The divine right order of Svetovid leads me.
The Eight-Eyed One places his helmet on my head:
Lo, now do I see with divine vision.
Svetovid, Divine Lawgiver, pronouncing judgment,

443. Ravenna, *The Magic of the Otherworld*, 50.

Makes clear my ears to receive his just counsel.
All falsehood flees before me as the Shining One rides out on his warhorse,
His sword of truth held high.
Svetovid strides before me,
Svetovid guards behind me.
He hurls his mace on my right side,
And he lets loose a volley of arrows on my left side.
Svetovid soars above me, a comet of purity arcing across the heavens.
Svetovid races in the Underworld below me,
Illuminating the halls of the blessed dead.
I stand encompassed in the righteous splendor and the perfect protection
Of the god who looks out into the cardinal directions!
I will adore him and serve him always,
As it is right and just.
Slava, Svetovidu!

Prayer and Offerings

"When we come before the Gods, it is wise not to come empty-handed," writes Indo-European Reconstructionist Polytheist Ceisiwr Serith.[444] Accompanying certain types of prayer with offerings is one of the oldest forms of human religious expression. While we may intellectually know that the gods don't need material gifts from us, we know that matter is imbued with Spirit, and in the spirit of reciprocity, we want to give the gods symbolic tokens of the blessings they impart to us every moment of every day. Furthermore, "There is a mystery in the natural dynamic of giving and receiving gifts."[445] What if we think of ourselves as the hosts and the gods are our guests?

444. Serith, *A Book of Pagan Prayer*, 7.
445. Serith, *A Book of Pagan Prayer*, 7.

Exercise
Offer Acorns to Perun on *Perundan*

On either July 20 or August 2—days in the Gregorian and Julian calendar, respectively, that Slavic Native Faith adherents have reclaimed from the Dual-Faith feast days associated with the cult of Saint Ilija—perform this simple devotional offering to Perun outdoors. If you can build a small fire, even in an outdoor grill, all the better. All you need is a sincere heart and a fist full of oak acorns, which, if you're in the Northern Hemisphere, should be falling onto the ground from oak trees at this time of year.

Hold the acorns aloft in your right hand. Approach the fire and say,

> *Slava Perunu! Upholder of justice, mighty one who puts to flight all manifestations of the Unclean Force! Gromovnik! Thunderer! Oh Perun with your fierce axe, I call upon you to let loose the life-giving summer rains, ensuring the continued growth of crops and all plant life from our Moist Mother Earth on this, your sacred day! Spare us from drought and barrenness!*
>
> *I call upon you also to hold me to task in my individual quest to be the best version of myself, not just for my own excellence but for the good of all in the unbroken Circle of Rodu, which endures through all time! Warrior, Healer, Witness of Oaths! Be with me at this holy tide! Slava!*

Toss the handful of oak acorns into the flames, careful to dodge any that may potentially pop.

In the spirit of hospitality, our giving of gifts is only right and just. We must return the gods' generosity. In doing so, we form an unbroken circle of kinship—the fullness of the concept of the Rodu, uniting us with the gods. *Slava!*

In table 2, I've created correspondences for different holy powers—ancestors included—that you may want to keep in mind for devotional rituals.

The first powers noted in the table are the ancestors. Methods of appeasing them and enlisting their aid are where we'll next focus our attention. *Slava!*

Table 2. Offerings to Various Slavic Gods and Spirits

Holy Power	Food	Beverage	Herb/Tree	Other
Ancestors	Žito/kutia (boiled wheat dish); bread/ pogača (round loaf); navy beans; food they enjoyed while alive; portions of your daily meals	Rakija; spring water; black coffee	Rosemary; basil; pussy willow fronds; garlic	Hearth fire; frankincense incense; icon of the Virgin Mary or Saint Michael the Archangel; photos of the deceased (*Note:* Do not display photos that show the dead with the living); wheat sheaves
Domovoi	Bread and salt; butter or heavy whipping cream; eggs	Rakija; beer; spring water	Rowan; juniper; garlic	Hearth fire; amber beads
Vodeni Duh	Pork meat	Rakija; black coffee	Tobacco	Goat or pig skulls offered at a rural, active water mill

Holy Power	Food	Beverage	Herb/Tree	Other
Vile and Great Forest Mother	Buttered bread; heavy whipping cream; wildflower honey	Rakija; white wine; milk	Saint John's wort; daisies; birch and willow branches; ferns; wildflowers	Walnuts; deer antlers; wreaths made of wildflowers
Bannik	N/A	Spring water	Evergreen branches/pine	New soap
Goddess Mokoša	Eggs; bread; pastries; honey; cheeses (cow or sheep's milk)	Red or white wine; spring water; milk; mead	Basil; roses; patchouli; yarrow; birch; wormwood; mugwort; verbena; ferns; garlic; flax; linden flowers and wood; hyssop	Distaff; carded wool; icon of Saint Petka Paraskeva; linen cloth; embroidery supplies
Goddess Vesna	Dyed hardboiled eggs; honey; bread; apples; cheeses (sheep's milk)	Mead; spring water; milk	Flowers that herald the spring season where you live; violets; lady's mantle (*Alchimilla vulgaris*); orchids; dandelions; sweetbriar (*Rosa rubiginosa*); linden flowers and wood	Symbols of larks, cuckoos, rabbits

Holy Power	Food	Beverage	Herb/Tree	Other
Goddess Devana/ Devica	Game meat/ venison	Dark ale; spring water	Cedar; red clover; mugwort; wormwood; broadleaf plantain	Antlers; a bow and arrow or symbolic representation of one
Goddess Mara/ Marszanna	Goat or pork meat; dark (rye) breads	Rakija; dark ale	Blackthorn; yew; nettles; sickleweed/ longleaf (*Falcaria vulgaris*); walnut and willow trees	Handheld scythe; waning moon; symbols of snowflakes; skulls; Russian and Ukrainian folk art depicting the Snow Maiden; swan feathers
God Jarilo/ Jurej	Various produce, corn, legumes; bread; wheat; honey; lamb	Spring water; white wine; mead	Basil; lily of the valley; Saint John's wort; violets; chamomile; blue eryngo (*Eryngium planum*); hyssop	Green Man images; icon of Saint George; white horse images; beeswax candles

Holy Power	Food	Beverage	Herb/Tree	Other
God Veles	Mushrooms; walnuts; dark breads; pork; beef; roast lamb; honey; goat's milk cheese; elderberries, blackberries	Rakija; dark ale; blackberry juice; goat's milk	Walnut wood; hound's tongue (*Cynoglossum officinale*); nettles; hemp; aconite (**Caution: poisonous**, please handle with gloves and do NOT ingest!)	Icon of Saint Blaise or Saint Nicholas; small stringed musical instruments; wolf, bear, cattle/bull symbols; songs, poems; glyph for Veles; coins/currency
God Triglav	Pork; dark (rye) breads	Rakija; dark ale; spring water	Thistle; burdock; wormwood; calendula	Three-headed deity image; images of mountain peaks and/or caves; coins/currency
God Perun	Beef/lamb mix as in Serbian ćevapi (sausages) or *pljeskavice* (patties)	Mead; beer	Oak leaves and acorns; iris; finger anemone (*Pulsatilla patens*); hawthorn; garlic; marshmallow	Icon of Saint Elijah/Ilija; oath ring; Axe of Perun symbol; golden eagle symbol; Gromovnik symbol; six- or eight-petaled rosettes

Holy Power	Food	Beverage	Herb/Tree	Other
God Svetovid/ Vid	Millet, barley, wheat; garlic; produce; beef; honey; bread	Mead	Common eyebright *(Euphrasia officinalis,* a.k.a. *ochanka* [Ukr.], *očnaica, vidac* [Srb.]); agrimony; delphinium; couch grass *(Agropyrum repens)*; scarlet pimpernel *(Anagallis arvensis)*	Four-headed deity image; icon of Saint Vitus; sword; spear; divination tools; white horse images
God Svarog	Ground beef and pork patties (pljeskavice) with minced onions and hot peppers, making it a *ljuto* (hot/ spicy) dish	Rakija; whisky	Wild onion; European madder (*Rubia tinctorum*); Saint John's wort; red trillium	Small blacksmith anvil or tongs; iron nails; railroad spikes; an iron cauldron
God Dajbog/ Dažbog	Walnuts in their shell; oranges; broad beans; pogača (ritual round bread)	Rakija; red wine; mead	Oak; sunflowers; chamomile; sand sedge grass *(Carex arenaria)*	Solar symbols; hearth fire; straw; coins/ currency

Holy Power	Food	Beverage	Herb/Tree	Other
God Rod	Bread and salt; žito/kutia (boiled wheat); pogača	Rakija; spring water; red wine; mead	Poppy; European madder (*Rubia tinctorum*); Mediterranean sage	Snake symbols; hearth fire; coins/currency
The Fates/Roženice/Sudženice	Three honey cakes and three cubes of sugar	Three glasses of red wine and three glasses of spring water	Basil; rosemary; garlic; birch; yarrow	Hearth fire; antique keys; scissors; small hatchets; one gift of gold, such as a ring or necklace

CHAPTER 13
Ancestor Work

In Serbian culture, families keep ancestor altars. Growing up, Mark and I watched our parents perform devotions to our family dead at an antique wooden credenza, which served as our permanent ancestor altar. The surface of the credenza had family-embroidered linen tablecloths on it. My mother would rotate the cloths seasonally or to honor the spirit of a relative who'd made one of the cloths when their death anniversary drew near. Atop the tablecloth would be placed framed photos of our beloved dead (pets included) plus more icons and candlesticks with beeswax candles and incense burners. Additionally, there would be cups of Turkish coffee and glasses of water, dry red wine, or shot glasses filled with šlivovica or whatever the deceased liked to drink when they were alive. When my maternal grandfather's death anniversary or birthday were upon us, my mother sometimes lit cigarettes

and briefly puffed on them and blew the smoke onto the photo of her dead father, as my Deda Bogoljub was a smoker.

I am honored to have had that antique wooden credenza passed down to me, and it still serves as my home ancestor altar. Today, it showcases Serbian cultural objects such as small, handwoven wool rugs *(ćilim)* with distinctively folk magick-y patterns woven into them; wooden canteens used by shepherds; miniature distaffs with carded wool strung on them; wooden spoons with more folk art motifs engraved into them; and literal corn dolls as effigies to honor the people on my father's side of the family especially, folks who were steadfast farmers for generations. I also display framed photographs of both sets of grandparents, my father, my brother, two first cousins, both sets of uncles, and a great uncle who was a World War I veteran. I also include framed photos and other mementoes (collars with their ID tags on them) for beloved animal companions, cats and dogs and even a pair of gerbil sisters that kept me company when I was in graduate school in the mid-to-late '90s.

True to its Dual-Faith nature, my altar also has, commingled with the framed photos, quite the smattering of Eastern Orthodox icons, especially my family's protector, John the Baptist; plus Saint Michael the Archangel, Saint George (Jarilo), Saint Nicholas (Veles), Saint Ilija (Perun), Saint Petka Paraskeva (Mokoša), and Mary of the Three Hands (*Marija Troijce Ruke*), a miracle-working icon. Other icons may be added depending on the season or if it's a given saint's feast day.

I also permanently display a handful of plaster-cast, hand-painted statues depicting Roman Catholic saints; these were made either in Italy or Brazil, and I bought them in shops in New Orleans as well as at the Chicago-based *botanicas* Athenian Candle Company (South Side) and Botánica Lucero (North Side). Standing guard as the tallest of these statues are Saints Cosmas and Damien, the magicians. I also have the Holy Infant of Prague, the Niño de Atocha, Saint Lucia, and San Martín de Porres, a champion of the poor and of animals.

My Nana Milojka, although a devout Orthodox Christian, was very fond of Catholicism also. She was glad my brother Mark and I were educated through the Archdiocese of Chicago's schools because Orthodox and

Catholic Christians share the same beliefs on the Holy Sacraments and have overlapping traditions, especially concerning fervent devotions to the Blessed Mother and the cults of the saints. And "a priest is a priest," Nana used to say. Whether he was Orthodox or Catholic, any readily available priest was someone whom my brother and I were exhorted to regularly confess our sins to in order to stay in her god's good graces. Nana Milojka clearly had a strong influence—way more than my parents, in fact—on my developing sense of piety, and that is one of the things I thank her for when I pray to her.

I think it's important to always offer your ancestors a glass of water, changed daily, and incense, provided that you aren't sensitive to smoke. Granules of frankincense and rose incense are what I burn for my dead per Serbian tradition, but any scent you think your dead would appreciate would work just fine as an offering. Perhaps you'd also like to consider adding a small vase of flowers, a small bell or ceremonial rattle to shake when you're about to pray (to get the deceased's attention), and some of their personal effects if they can fit in the space. For example, my maternal grandfather, Deda Bogoljub, was an engineer for the Yugoslav railway system, and he kept a fantastic post-WWII pocket watch on his person all the time; I now have that watch placed next to his photo. And my maternal uncle Milan was a pipe tobacco smoker, so I offer him an antique pipe through which I periodically blow tobacco smoke onto his framed photo. He preferred cognac over šlivovica, so I have a small shot glass with some Crown Royal in it placed next to his pipe.

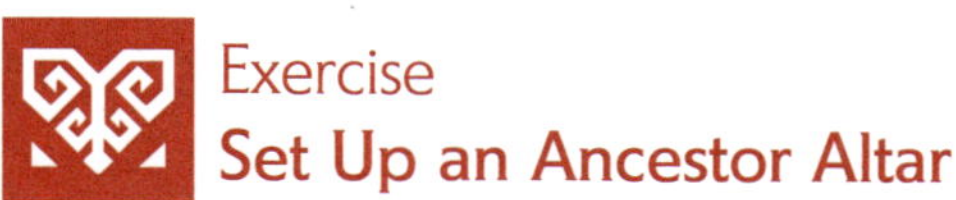

Exercise
Set Up an Ancestor Altar

An ancestor altar can be placed as close to the floor (or on the floor) or as elevated physically as you like. While it's a challenge to keep every object atop the altar dust free, a good cleaning once a month (I time mine to coincide with the dark of the moon phase) should suffice. *Your ancestors are your first line of spiritual aid because they have a vested interest in seeing you, their descendant, happy and thriving in life.* Don't disrespect them by letting their altar space accrue dust bunnies, wilted flowers, moldy food, or general untidiness.

You can have a lot of highly significant mementoes displayed without it looking too cluttered, or you can also have an aesthetic that is minimalist to the core, displaying hardly any objects. I have a Polish American friend whose practices are heavily mediated by the Zen Buddhist influences of her late husband, and her ancestor altar is a shelf with a white silk cloth and a white orchid placed atop it. That's it. It is beautiful and elegant in its simplicity, without drawing attention to itself as an ancestor altar.

Do what works for you and what you think is best. If you're really not sure where to begin, I'd suggest a flat surface with a white cloth (ideally 100 percent cotton) laid atop it. A clean glass of water and a single candle, even an LED battery–operated one if fire safety is a concern, are good-to-have basics and cosmically represent the balance of Elemental water with fire.

Beginning an Ancestor Devotional Practice

Once your altar is ready, announce to your beloved dead that you wish to cultivate a devotional relationship with them. Invite them into your life and into the space that you have demarcated for them. Let them know that you are grateful, as their descendant, for the gift of life. As Croatian Native Faith believer, musician, and artist Dražen Markotić Vega explains, "I honor my ancestors very much. I even sing about them in my Neopagan band Su'Vid because without them there would be no 'me' either. They paved the way for my steps and still, I know, follow me."[446]

In a spirit of coming full circle, also let them know that you hope to live a good life and pave the way for those who will come after you. After all, the goal is that someday you, in turn, will be an attentive ancestor to your future descendants' petitions for your aid. This simple, short prayer expresses these ideas. It may be just the thing to recite before your altar as you begin your day:

Hail, beloved Ancestors!
You are never forgotten.

446. Dražen Markotić Vega, interview with the author, October 30, 2024. The English translation is the author's own.

Blood of my blood,
You inspire me each day.
May my thoughts, words, and deeds
Ever honor you!
Slava!

What if you're adopted? I like to think you have the blessing of not one, but two sets of families you can invoke in your prayers of petition and thanksgiving. You can alter the third line in the prayer, "blood of my blood," to something along the lines of "Ancestors forged to me by ties stronger than blood," "Ancestors of spirit," etc. The love is real; therefore, the bonds of kinship are just as real and as binding as familial bonds composed of shared DNA.

Since you're dealing with family, ancestor devotionals can be very informal, devoid of the ceremonial overtones we tend to associate with full-blown Pagan "ritual." Talk to your beloved dead as you would to living friends. Share your joys with them. Let them help you process your burdens. Ask for their counsel—invite them to visit you in your dreams and impart messages that you will remember upon awakening. Ask for their help, especially for protection. As the late medieval historian and linguist Claude Lecouteux once wrote, "If they were good dead who died under normal circumstances and not before their time, they take a place among the ancestors and were reputed to watch over the clan and the family, in accordance with certain rites that testified to the fundamental concept of *Do ut des*, 'I give so that you give.' In exchange for oblations and sacrifices, the dead granted favor and protection."[447]

What About Problematic Ancestors?

This is a very valid question that more people in Pagan communities should be asking. Stepping back in objective consideration, there's certainly a spectrum of what constitutes "problematic," of course. On the milder end, every family has its share of folks who, whether living or dead, aren't thought of fondly and are gossiped about by other relatives or community

447. Lecouteux, *The Return of the Dead,* 181.

members, whether it's because the proverbial black sheep strayed from the expectations set before them (especially if those expectations were culturally prescribed) or they otherwise caused a perceived sense of shame that rippled across space and time and impacted other family members. A legacy of a bad reputation associated with a deceased ne'er-do-well can be hard to overcome, especially in smaller, tight-knit communities where people know each other's business. But that legacy doesn't necessarily serve as a deal-breaker for you as the living descendant when moving about in social circles. Perceptions can change over time.

Then we have the more severe end of the spectrum. This encompasses unquestionably reprehensible—if not egregiously criminal, then certainly morally bankrupt—behavior committed by the truly problematic dead: individuals who may have been abusive, exploitative, and unjust. These problematic dead can serve as the initial prime mover domino whose fall ripples into future family dynamics marked by generational trauma or the onset of a family curse. What then? What do we do when we know we are faced with troublesome dead in our family who did inexcusable things when they were alive and left behind a damning legacy?

There are two approaches. The first approach itself can be twofold: Either cut off all energetic ties by (a) never, ever mentioning or acknowledging the problematic dead, thereby rendering them *personae non grata*, leaving them to work out their karma on their own in the afterlife; or (b) performing a cord-cutting ritual that severs you from their energetic imprint or their legacy, ensuring that the spiritual repercussions of their past behavior don't adversely impact you. Let's look at this latter approach in more detail.

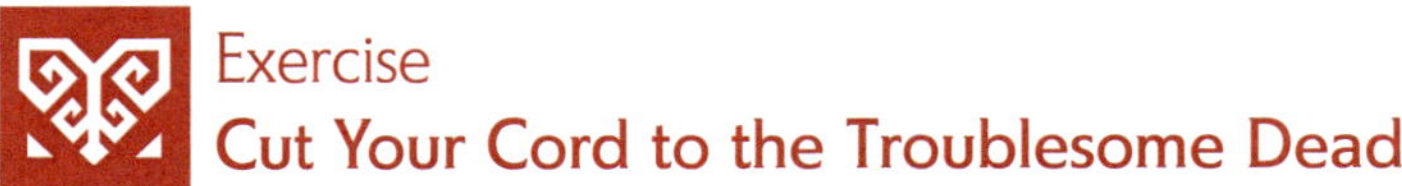

Exercise
Cut Your Cord to the Troublesome Dead

This banishing spell seals the dead to their fate and seals up your energetic fields to become invulnerable to that person's spiritual pollution. Here's what you'll need:

- Dried herbs: 1 part agrimony, 1 part nettles, and a large, dried aspen leaf
- A mortar and pestle
- A plastic bag
- Spool of black cotton cord or yarn or black silk thread
- A pair of scissors
- Exorcism Spray (see Chapter 12) in a portable spray bottle

Perform this at midnight, either on a Monday into Tuesday or a Friday into Saturday. It is best if the lunar timing coincides with the waning moon phase leading up to the dark of the moon.

Take the dried aspen leaf and the agrimony and nettles, mix them, and finely grind them together with a mortar and pestle. Store the powdery mixture in a small plastic bag that can be sealed or another kind of small, sealed container—even a former prescription medicine plastic container that has been washed out (and had its label removed) will work—and set it aside.

Go to a four-way crossroads away from your house, where both your privacy and your safety can be ensured. I make use of intersecting gravel-lined footpaths and trails at my local forest preserves, but you may want to even use a rural cemetery or graveyard (the latter is affixed to a church) or alleyways or other unfrequented intersections for more urban environments. Just be mindful of closed-circuit cameras affixed to lamp posts or surrounding buildings! Note that this is a location you are not to ever visit again after this working is completed, so make sure you're selecting a site that in no way interfaces with the places you frequent on a regular basis.

At midnight, take the spool of black thread or yarn. As you are about to cut an approximate twelve-inch length off with the scissors, say aloud:

> *"Powers of Fate, the Mothers who make their decrees in darkness, implacable Sudženice, hear me. I,* [state your name], *am kin no more to* [state name of problematic dead]. *I hereby sever* [cut off length of thread] *all ties at every level between this person, their urok, the heinous actions they committed*

> *when they were alive and the consequences of those actions, which have rippled out across time and space, and me and my destiny. Let* [name of problematic dead] *be bound by your power, now and forever* [tie first knot close to one end of the thread]. *The urok of* [name of dead] *is carried away by the lame wolf to beyond the nine kingdoms* [tie second knot in the middle of the cut thread]. *The legacy of* [name the dead] *binds him/her/them* [tie third and final knot at opposite end from first] *to their Spirit World journey and not me. From this place, before the new day dawns, I walk from here clean and free. Istina! And so it is!"*

Drop the knotted thread/cord onto the ground, stating, *"Majka Mokoša takes care of this for me. Amin!"*

Step over the cord and take three additional steps so that it is well behind you. Do not turn around and look at it. Remove the Exorcism Spray bottle and vigorously spritz the nape of your neck, the undersoles of your shoes, your crown, your forehead, the backs of your calf muscles, and the nape of your neck again. Silently, without speaking to anyone, return home. Be sure to do a full spiritual cleansing of yourself afterward and go eat something nourishing that will help ground you. Talk to no one until after you've fully attained a grounded, centered state of being. However, it's best if you can just immediately retire to bed after cleansing yourself and eating a quick bite.

Working to Elevate the Problematic Dead

A second way of dealing with problematic family dead requires a great deal of maturity and a strong spiritual anchor. The goal is to emotionally and spiritually hold a space of hoping that the problematic dead, if they lived generations or even centuries ago, will have had their experience of contending with their karma, perhaps making them eligible for evolving past their sins.

From my own decades of experience as a spirit worker, I will attest that the post-death state is not a static one; no one is just sitting around in "Heaven," indolently plucking harp strings for eternity. There is constant movement; the dead have journeys that they undertake in stages, and they have to progress in their journeys from the bewildering, hazard-laden state of the newly dead to the stable, collectivized group state if they are to ultimately reach the sanctified status of ancestors. It's not a blessing that's automatically conferred upon them once they die. This is where the efforts of the living in "providing proper sacralization rites" with remembrances, prayers, and offerings are crucially needed.[448]

Doing work to help elevate the problematic dead can be tremendously challenging for the living descendant. It can be a hazard to interact with such dead; they likely are far more draining than the benevolent dead, causing physical symptoms of sickness ranging from migraine-type headaches to fatigue during the day and insomnia when it's time to sleep.

The living will have to set nonnegotiable boundaries around where and how they do workings to help elevate these troublesome dead. Personally, I would not have them represented in any way on my ancestor altar, not even with a single lit candle. I would relegate all prayers and offerings either to a four-way crossroads far away from the home or inside an Orthodox or a Catholic church where candles are lit in memory of the deceased. Let the clergy of those Christian denominations perform Requiem Masses (the Catholic understanding would deem the problematic person to perhaps be in Purgatory) and deal with the dead themselves based on their creed of forgiveness of the truly repentant. Call upon your gods, guides, and guardians to serve as mediators between you and the problematic dead, curtailing your energetic imprint so you don't get enmeshed with the spiritual pollution or miasma of this problematic dead person. And step up your spiritual hygiene regimen; revisit some of the techniques mentioned in the previous chapter and make them daily habits.

---

448. Ravenna, *The Magic of the Otherworld,* 165.

CHAPTER 14
A Rite of Spring

Slavic Native Faith overlaps with Traditional Witchcraft with the emphasis placed on bioregionalism, which affects the timing of seasonal rituals first and foremost. It's wise to leverage the energy currents of the climate and seasonal changes that are specific to your area at a given time of year instead of relying upon a fixed system of calendar dates, whose listed events may not reflect the conditions of your bioregion at all.[449] For example, the sacred time of the Spring Equinox is an astronomically determined phenomenon that gets assigned to a calendar date every year, but its arrival in the part of the world where you live does not guarantee that the seasonal shift from winter to spring has actually occurred yet.

For me in Chicago, where winter tends to (annoyingly) linger well past the date assigned to Spring Equinox in a given year, a celebration of the earth's awakening

449. Kelden, *The Crooked Path*, 141–142.

and the emergence of vegetation can very well be premature if the actual seasonal conditions on the ground still reflect snow and below-freezing temperatures. As Kelden, the Minnesota-based Traditional Witch, reminds us, "If you're attempting to apply a fixed system of seasonal celebrations but it doesn't match what's happening in your local landscape, how well are you actually connecting to the natural world?"[450]

So I choose to wait for the bioregional markers besides lengthening daylight that inform me that spring has arrived: Has the river in my backyard begun to thaw to the extent that I can hear the water trickle once again? Are the winds of Stribog bringing in pleasantly warm air gusts? Do I hear the delightful trilling of sandhill cranes flying overhead, or the raucous chirps and warbles of red-winged blackbirds, newly arrived at my bird feeders? Have my beloved electric-yellow daffodils begun to bravely protrude from the cold ground? If I can answer yes to those questions, then I know it's time for me to perform the following ritual, which honors the Slavic Earth Mother goddess *(Mater Sira Zemlija)* and the goddess of spring, Vesna.

This rite is written below for a solitary practitioner, but it can be easily adapted for group format by assigning speaking roles and ritual actions to different participants. Ideally, this rite should be performed outdoors on privately held land, where a small fire in an appropriately contained and safe space can be built. If an in-ground or above-ground firepit isn't available, a portable charcoal grill can suffice. If no outdoor fire is possible, at the very least, have a candle in a glass windproof container. Other supplies include the following:

- A small bowl filled with spring water, into which fresh sprigs of sweet or holy basil and rosemary are submerged on one end
- Woven basket containing red-dyed hardboiled eggs (one for each celebrant)[451]
- Handheld gardening tools such as mini spades

---

450. Kelden, *The Crooked Path*, 174.

451. This dye is readily available in Greek grocery stores or online from suppliers like Amazon. In a pinch, you can substitute the 1-ounce bottle of McCormick Red Food Coloring.

- A chalice filled with whole milk
- Flowers (ideally native plants) for decorating the ground and/or altar spaces or potted ferns
- Pogača[452]
- A chalice filled with mead or sweet white wine (Riesling, Moscato, etc.)[453]
- Images/statues depicting Vesna or figurines of animals such as rabbits, geese, cuckoos, larks, or frogs/toads
- *Optional:* incense to burn

The Rite

Ritually process to your location, singing an improvised melody with these words: *"Slava Rodu, Slava Rodu, Glory to my Gods and Kin! Gods of old, may you behold my love for you. My rite begins!"*

Breathe mindfully and hold the intention of serving as a vessel of peace, energy that ripples out through all the worlds. Say, *"Mir svima!/Peace to all!"*

Light the ritual fire (in the designated pit or your candle), stating, *"Out of love for humanity, the gods blessed us with fire, the life-giving sun in miniature. Welcome, Svarožić! I hail also our great Earth Mother and the fire in her belly that birthed this world into being. For the many blessings of fire, I give thanks. Slava Rodu!"*

If others are present, they may echo, *"Slava Rodu!"*

Retrieve the bowl with the sprigs of basil and rosemary in it. Take both sprigs and flick the spring water onto your forehead, chest, and feet, saying, *"From the pools of the Otherworld, palaces of ancestral memory, I am blessed by the gods with this pure water. I put to flight the Unclean Force and welcome the Waters of Life within me and around me. May these waters bring healing and bounty to this and all lands. Slava!"*

If physical ability levels permit, kneel with hands touching the ground, or genuflect on the ground with one hand covering the heart and the other

452. See the Appendix D recipe or obtain a similar round loaf at your local bakery.

453. As a nonalcoholic alternative, serve white grape juice.

touching the earth. Say, "*Stara Majka, Old Mother! Awaken* [kneel and lightly tap forehead on the ground], *awaken* [tap], *awaken* [tap]*!*"

Now rise and stretch your arms high overhead.

"Slava, Naša Blaga Zemlija![454] *Behold, the chains of winter are broken and Mara has descended to her palace beyond the thrice nine mountains! Oh, Mother Earth, awaken! Awaken to the heartfelt prayers and the songs of celebration I, your child, offer to you at this sacred time of the quickening of spring! I am here to honor you but also ask your forgiveness for the times my deeds did not align with the love that I profess for you. Mati Sira Zemlija, I am here to uphold the sacred bonds between us: Witness well my words and hold me accountable to my deeds so that I can joyfully receive with open arms the fullness of the promise that our beloved Vesna brings! Slava Rodu!"*

Take a dyed red egg from the basket and one of the small gardening tools. Announce out loud before Mother Earth as your witness what you will promise to do in the growing season ahead to better the state of the planet. Then dig a small hole. Say, *"Živa za živa!"/"Life for life!"* and bury the egg. The egg is thus a symbolic sacrifice that carries your message deep into the receptive womb of Mother Earth.

Next, retrieve the offering of the milk-filled chalice. Say, *"Behold, the milk of the Mother who sustains all is given back with love unto her, for it is right to nurture her in return for her manifold blessings. Slava!"*

Pour the milk onto a designated spot on the ground or into a libation bowl, if indoors. Next, take some of the flowers from the altar, turn toward the east, and loudly and distinctly recite this prayer to Vesna:

> *"Hail, Vesna!*
> *Goddess of Growing Things,*
> *Glowing in gladness!*
> *Rosy-cheeked Lady of the Dawn,*
> *You illuminate my heart with your wisdom:*
> *'Life cannot be thwarted!'*

---

454. Translation: "Glory to Our Blessed Land/Earth!" The phrase is pronounced as *SLAH'-vuh NAH'-shuh BLAH'-gah ZEM'-lee-yuh.*

Hail, Doda: Bringer of Life-Bringing Rains,
May this land flower under your guiding hand!
Hail, Živa, Mother of All Living Things,
Bless me and my family,
Two- and four-legged kin alike.
Bless the rivers and the fields, the savannahs and the trees,[455]
And the animals who shelter in them.
Bless my neighbors and communities and encircle us all
In your garlands of joy and beauty.
You who break the chains of death
And bring healing and wholeness where you tread,
I honor you,
I give you my undying thanks and praise!
Slava, Vesna!"

If others are present, each takes their turn addressing Vesna and offering their prayers of thanks or petitions. If applicable, the group can bestow their blessings in Vesna's name upon anyone who is pregnant or who wishes to conceive a child.

Next, raise the round pogača loaf of bread, turning it clockwise and saying, "*Kolo, kolo, the circle spins round; to my fate I am bound. Slava!*" Tear off a piece by hand (this bread is never to be cut with a knife) and eat it in silence. The leftover bread is returned to the altar.

Now retrieve the chalice with white wine/mead or fruit juice. Raising the chalice aloft, declare: "*Slava Rodu! Blessed are the gods and blessed am I, for their blood flows through my veins. As I drink of this libation, may I be ever mindful that there is no part of me that is not of them. Slava!*"

Drink a hearty gulp, and if applicable, pass the chalice around to others clockwise. The remainder of the chalice's contents are poured onto the

455. Tailor this line to reflect the features of the landscape where you live or where this ritual is being held. I practice in my oak- and maple-surrounded backyard, which has a river running through it, and which is bordered by oak savannahs and small family farms.

ground with these words: *"Holy Powers, may peace always be between us. Slava Rodu!"*

Then say, *"I carry in my heart my promise to the Earth Mother. May I live in my daily actions my eternal love for her. May Vesna's bountiful blessings be ever with me! Istina!"*

Now safely extinguish the fire, stating, *"Though this flame is extinguished, I know in truth that the Living Sacred Fire ever burns above, below, and within me. Slava!"*

Now say: *"As I entered this hallowed place in song, so may I return to the Realm of Yav the same way."*

If others are present, link hands and process out of the ritual space. If you're alone, clap your hands and improvise a melody to the following: *"Slava Rodu, Slava Rodu, with my gods I firmly stand! Glory to my Slavic Kin; I serve them with my heart and hands!"*

The procession complete, declare, *"Mir svima!/Peace to all!"* If this was a group ritual, now would be a great time for a group hug.

Potluck feasting afterward is a lovely way to continue to celebrate, especially if ethnic Slavic music can be played on portable devices with Bluetooth-enabled speakers. There are thousands of artists from throughout the Slavic world reflecting a variety of musical genres to choose from. For ritual purposes, group or private devotionals, I am fond of playing a specific Serbian folk album of instrumental music from 2005 called *Etno Instrumentali*, a compilation of various artists.[456] If your feet are coordinated and you're game for quite the cardio workout with others, you may want to give group circle or kolo dancing a try. Its high-speed songs set to a challenging tempo of 128 beats per minute make for memorable mania in performance!

---

456. It's available for free on YouTube at https://www.youtube.com/playlist?list=OLAK5uy_mjNCPbHU5ip30wIS1M53OhXSZAk-jgFdg. The first two tracks, which I think are lovely and haunting, lend themselves exceptionally well to devotional rituals.

CHAPTER 15
Kupalo Observance

Kupalo is rooted in the energies of the Summer Solstice and the folk religious festivals attached to it in Dual-Faith Tradition. It marks the liminal state not just between the sun's zenith of power and the start of its decline, but the pause in the agricultural cycle between the spring work of seed sowing and driving animals out to pasture and the preparations for the harvest season. However removed our modern selves may be from the rigors of food production, the metaphors are there for contemplating: *What are the solstice points, or points of pause, in your journey around the sun to commemorate? How do you feel about where you stand in the halfway marker of the year, between the goals that you've accomplished and what remains to be done before the year is out? What are the promises of your harvests to be reaped?*

As you meditate on your answers or journal about them in preparation for this ritual, think also on the kind of plant magic you want to incorporate, especially for the making of the crown for your head. This crown will be offered to the rusalki, so think of a local river or other flowing body of water where you can ceremonially offer it. Traditionally, wild herbs like wormwood, mullein, and, of course, Saint John's wort, to name a few, are sought, plucked, and woven into personal wreaths. If these are not available where you live, which indigenous plants, including native grasses, can you use? In the past, I've woven wreaths composed of roadside-growing common chicory *(Cichorium intybus),* Queen Anne's lace *(Daucus carota),* common daisies *(Bellis perennis),* fronds of lady fern (*Athyrium filix-femina*), and varieties of coneflowers *(Echinacea paradoxa, Echinacea purpura),* with young willow *(Salix alba)* fronds serving as a flexible base into which the wildflowers' stems can be tucked.

Traditionally in Serbia, rituals on Ivandan/St. John's Day have a start time that is well in advance of noon: The symbolic correspondences depend on the energies of the sun still climbing toward the zenith of its power, not declining in its potency from the afternoon onward. The ritual text below includes activities for daytime, starting at sunrise.

Supplies to consider should include the following:

- Altar cloth or whole blanket of linen or wool
- Potted fern plant
- A small bowl filled with spring water, into which fresh sprigs of sweet or holy basil and rosemary are submerged on one end
- *If indoors:* a medium-sized offering bowl plus a candle in a fireproof container, such as a beeswax votive in a glass jar, plus lighter
- *If outdoors:* items needed for the safe building of a small fire, from pea gravel for the base to firewood, kindling, and a starter[457]
- Handheld musical instruments (e.g., tambourines, rattles, frame drums)
- Solar symbols, e.g., a kolovrat painted on a wooden panel or cardboard

457. Also consider a lightweight, kitchen-sized fire extinguisher or fire blanket for safety.

- Sheaves of grain or a small pouch with barley seeds
- A handmade wildflower wreath
- Generous amounts of dried rose petals (1 cup = 8 ounces or 227 grams) in appropriately sized container or paper bag
- A chalice filled with pure spring water
- A chalice filled with mead, krupnik, or another honey-based alcoholic beverage[458]
- Pogača or a similar round loaf from your local bakery
- *Optional:* small cast-iron cauldron/skillets to transfer "live coals" from the fire, plus a set of tongs
- *Optional:* Eastern Orthodox icon of Saint John the Baptist

The Rite

The altar should be on the ground, its materials scattered around it. It should be near the safely demarcated area where the bonfire is going to be lit.

Retrieve the bowl with the sprigs of basil and rosemary in it. Take both sprigs and flick the spring water onto your forehead, chest, and feet, saying, *"At this time of Kupalo, may I awaken in wonder to the magic of the vodeni duhovi, in joy to the songs of the rusalki. I put to flight the Unclean Force and welcome the Waters of Life within me and around me. May they bring bounty to this and all lands. Slava!"*

If others are present, they may echo: *"Slava!"*

Stretch your arms upward and focus on drawing down the currents of solar power into you. When you feel invigorated, say, *"The kolovrat turns and I answer the ancestral call! May the portal to the Otherworld open! By the light of the fiery fern, by the fires of joy and passion in my heart, and by the fires built as a community in Rodu to honor the God Who Gives, may I be blessed at this time of Kupalo! Slava Rodu!"*

If others are present, they may echo: *"Slava Rodu!"*

If you're indoors, light your candle. If you're outdoors, go to where the already-assembled bonfire pit awaits, logs and kindling in place. If using

458. As a nonalcoholic alternative, serve any variety of fruit juice.

the living fire method of rubbing the dried and peeled "male" oak or hazel twig with the "female" linden tree twig to build the fire, raise energy with this chant: *"The living fire I seek from thee, Father Oak [or Hazel] and Mother Linden tree!"*

Cheer the developing fire. Turn and face east. With arms upraised, say, *"Hail, Bright Maiden at the Gates of Dawn! Zorija Utrenaja,*[459] *I greet you with great gladness in my heart! Open the gates, I humbly pray, and let our beloved Dajbog ride out on this Kupalo day! I stand ready to receive the blessings the Heavens pour forth upon the Old Believers today!"*

Retrieve the musical instruments to joyfully welcome the unfolding sunrise. Then go to the altar and raise high the painted wooden kolovrat or other solar symbols and say, *"Glory and honor to the giver of gladness, resplendent Dažbog astride his white steed! Father who courses the Heavens, the one who doles out blessings from the celestial Realm of Prav, I honor you on this holy day! Thank you for your blessings of health, abundance, and peace! Guide me well as I venture forward into the season of the harvest, and may you shield me from all evil, lack, disease, and despair! Slava Dajbogu!"*

If others are present, they may echo: *"Slava Dajbogu!"* Return the solar symbol to where it had been before.

Next, retrieve the sheaves of grain or pouch with barley from the ground. As before, hold your dominant hand high before the fire and say, *"The sultry season moves along at its steady pace to the rhythm of marching hooves, guided by the young and steady hands of grain-giving Jarilo. Fair one, lover of life, come! Join me at this sacred time of Kupalo! Golden Bridegroom, be with me and bless all lovers! Stoke well my fires of desire, Beloved Youth! You who are the bringer of peace and plenty, I ask that you help me reap my golden harvests when the time draws nigh! With grace, may I pause to reflect on your green glory that grows and swells beneath the solstice sky! Slava, Jarilu!"*

Toss the grains onto the ground. If you're indoors, pour the grains into the offering bowl, which will be poured outside afterward. Next, dance clockwise around the fire or the candle flame; feel the joy of this day and mute any inner criticism that may arise about inspired movement. Hopefully, if an outdoor fire is used, it will be at a level where its flames are com-

459. Pronounced *ZŌR'-ee-yah oot-ren-EYE'-uh.*

fortably low enough to be jumped over. Exclaim a one-word intention such as "*Love!*" or "*Abundance!*" or "*Health!*" The same can be done with the candle inside.

Next, process to a selected body of water, taking along the flower wreath and the container with dried rose petals. If you're indoors, face either west or north. Address the water spirits with these or similar words:

"Rusalki! Vodeni duhovi! I bring you greetings this Kupalo day!
From the edge of the forest, I've come
To summon a love so sweet, a honeyed love,
Whose face I kiss to greet,
A handsome/beautiful, honeyed love!"

Toss your wreath in the water along with a generous handful of the dried rose petals. The water spirits thus honored, if you wish, feel free to jump in the water and ritually bathe yourself, setting your magical intentions for purification, healing, and so on. If this is being done indoors, hold aloft your wreath and vow to the rusalki that you will bestow this gift to them outdoors by sunset.

Return to the altar site. Retrieve the chalice of water, the chalice of mead, and the round loaf of bread. Pour out the chalice with spring water and say, "*Holy Mother Earth, I offer back unto you a symbolic token of the Waters of Life you generously give all. Know that I ever hold you in my heart with love and thankfulness. Slava!*"

Now pour out the chalice of mead, saying, "*Mokoša, may you taste of the sweetness in my words of praise for you at this time of Kupalo and always. Let peace and harmony always be between us. Slava!*"

Now raise the round loaf of bread, turning it clockwise and saying, "*Kolo, kolo, the circle spins round; to my fate I am bound. Slava!*" Tear off a piece and eat it in silence. The leftover bread is returned to the altar; it will later be broken apart into small pieces and left behind as an offering to the land spirits with the words, "*Guardians of this place, I thank you for your presence. Eat and know there are mortals like me who wish for peace and harmony between us. Slava!*"

Think of the gods you called upon to attend and say, *"I do not dismiss the Kin I have called upon; instead, I shall be mindful of their magic in my daily life. Slava!"*

Go extinguish the fire's remnants, stating, *"Though this flame is extinguished, I know that the Living Sacred Fire ever burns above, below, and within me. Istina!"*

Glowing coals of embers are what likely remain of the fire. Any celebrants can take embers home with them in small cast-iron skillets or cauldrons. These embers serve as powerful apotropaic talismans that should ideally be kept at the hearth, or one's chief altar dedicated to the Slavic Powers, or their ancestor altar.

CHAPTER 16
An Autumn Equinox Rite for Mokoša

We certainly cannot say for certain how, if at all, the pre-Christian Slavic peoples commemorated the seasonal markers of the equinoxes and solstices. What we do have as a resource is a treasure trove of thriving folk religious customs practiced today, which are rich in tradition and localized to each Slavic community in the Old World, to help inspire us to devise new ways of creating meaningful ritual celebrations. For example, among the country folk in my parents' homeland of Serbia, Autumn Equinox marks the end of the harvest season and thus the end of field work. Folks' attention can focus on the indoor necessities of canning and preserving various fruits and vegetables for vital winter reserves of food.

Mythically, the abundance harvested from the fields could not be possible without the sacrifice of grain-growing Jarilo. The myth recounting his sacred marriage to Mara takes a darker, Fate-full turn at the time of the Autumn Equinox. This is when he is captured and imprisoned in the Underworld by either an angry, vindictive Veles (as a way to punish Perun) or Mara herself, now coming into the fullness of her power as goddess of death and winter's darkness. She claims his life force—but not without having him spill his seed beforehand, of course!

The wealth of the grain seed is one of Veles's well-kept treasures in the Underworld; fittingly, Veles is the most-cited deity in connection with modern Slavic harvesting customs that plait the last sheaf of reaped grain into an elaborate corn dolly that is universally known in the Slavic world as "Veles's beard." Ethnologists have recorded the custom, extant well into the twentieth century, in South and East Slavic rural communities of the anthropomorphizing of the pillar in the threshing house by its seasonal adornment in post-harvest rituals with the Veles's beard corn dolly, pointing to the possibility that this pillar may be connected to the idols of the gods that were carved out of long wooden poles/tree trunks by pre-Christian Slavs.[460] The undeniable metaphor extracted here for spiritual contemplation is that the Underworld is the source for all material blessings that sustain living mortals in *this* world.

So that there's abundance to celebrate at the Autumn Equinox, there is the meaning of reaped harvests in our lives to give thanks for, and these valid causes for celebration offset the more somber themes at this time of year of encroaching literal darkness and death, the imminent arrival of winter.

The ritual below is meant to be performed outdoors, if possible, as a small fire is once again called for, with an altar on the ground dedicated to Mokoša. Ritual color clothing can be all white, white with red accents, or earthy colors reflective of autumn. Items needed for this ritual are as follows:

- Altar cloth of natural fiber, ideally linen or handwoven wool
- *If outdoors:* items needed for the safe building of a small fire, from pea gravel for the base to firewood, kindling, and a starter[461]

460. Cvetković, *Slavic Traditions & Mythology,* 326.
461. Also consider a lightweight, kitchen-sized fire extinguisher or fire blanket for safety.

- *If indoors:* a medium-sized offering bowl plus a candle in a fireproof container, such as a beeswax votive in a glass jar, plus lighter
- A small bowl filled with spring water, into which fresh sprigs of sweet or holy basil and rosemary are submerged on one end
- Decorative wheat sheaves, if available (try craft stores)
- A small pouch into which a handful of barley will be placed
- A chalice filled with milk that has a dollop of honey added to it
- A small bowl or dish with unsalted sunflower seeds in the shell
- A drinking horn, chalice, or large vessel filled with rakija or a nonalcoholic alternative such as sparkling apple cider
- Pogača or a round loaf from your local bakery
- A cornucopia filled with fresh apples and nuts
- Skeins of yarn, embroidery hoops, knitting needles, handheld distaffs, or bundles of carded wool, etc.
- Images/statuary depicting Mokoša or an icon of Saint Petka Paraskeva

The Rite

Go to the firepit (or candle) and light the fire, stating: *"Slava Svarožić! For the many blessings of fire, I give thanks."*

Retrieve the bowl with the sprigs of basil and rosemary in it. Take both sprigs and flick the spring water onto your forehead, chest, and feet, saying, *"From the pools of the Otherworld, palaces of ancestral memory, I am blessed by the gods with this pure water. I put to flight the Unclean Force and welcome the Waters of Life within me and around me. For the bounty brought to this and all lands, I give thanks. Slava!"*

Pause and reflect on what the concept of the harvest means to you, at what you're grateful for having accomplished in the year thus far.

"Slava, Rodu! The harvest has now ended, and I thank the gods for the various fruits of my labor that provide my life with abundance. At this time of purification and preparation, I take stock of myself just as with my provisions for the coming winter. May all that is baleful be winnowed away! This is a time of lamentation as well, as sacrifice is the price to be paid for love. Farewell, Jarilo,

who now treads his solitary way into the Hidden Lands of Nav. I join him in awaiting the descent of the long night of winter that ultimately will herald the morning of spring."

Take the sheaves of wheat and pouch with barley and lay them on the ground. If indoors, place them into a suitably sized offering bowl that will be emptied outdoors for wildlife to eat afterward.

Continue: *"Yet I do not weep, for death and life stand ever in balance—the gaping grave and the cornucopia of abundance. In life is death and in death, life. This is the gods' word-bond, now and ever! Slava!"*

Take the chalice with honey-laden milk from the altar. Raise it high and say,

> *"Slava, Majka Mokoša!*
> *Beloved Mother of Fullness,*
> *Accept, I pray, this token of nurturance:*
> *For as you nourish me with your love and grace,*
> *So too do I wish to nourish you in return,*
> *Out of love and sacred reciprocity.*
> *Guide well my hands in meaningful work in the coming winter season.*
> *Bless me with fortitude to endure any trials that may come my way.*
> *For my full pantry, for the food on my table,*
> *For the joy that comes from the blessed providence of the gods,*
> *I give my heartfelt thanks! Mother Mokoš, I praise you!"*

Pour out the offering, either onto the ground or into the libation bowl. Continue: *"Slava Mokošu!"*

Approach the bowl of sunflower seeds on the altar and say, *"For* [name a blessing received or an accomplishment], *I give thanks. I have harvested the seeds of rebirth."* Eat the seeds.

Raise high in your dominant hand the chalice with rakija or an alternate beverage. Say, *"Slava to the good seasons that have gone and the good ones to come! I stand ready to welcome and give thanks for unknown blessings already on their way!"*

Take three hearty gulps and pour the remaining content onto the ground or in the offering bowl with these words: *"From the gods, through earth, to me; from me, through the earth, back unto the gods. The Circle of Rodu! Slava!"*

Raise the round loaf of pogača, turning it clockwise and saying, *"Kolo, kolo, the circle spins round; to my fate I am bound. Slava!"* Tear off a piece and eat it in silence. The leftover bread is returned to the altar.

Spend a few moments contemplating that the season of the ancestors draws near, and that Mara and Veles encourage the living to think on hospitality as the bridge between the living and the dead. Say:

"The harvest over and winter drawing near, I am mindful of Veles's and Mara's deepening magic in the dark, and their manifold, unseen gifts that sustain life when the land lies barren and fallow. Powers of the encroaching darkness, grant me your counsel in my dreams. I welcome my ancestors to visit me and warm their hands at my hearth. I share my bounty with kin of fur and feather, as well as with the spirits of this land. May peace and harmony always be between us! Slava Rodu!"

Rip the uneaten portions of the ritual bread and scatter them about the ground or deposit them into the offering bowl, whose contents will be spilled outdoors after the ritual. Safely extinguish what remains of the sacred fire, stating, *"Though this flame is extinguished, I know in truth that the Living Sacred Fire ever burns above, below, and within me. Slava!"*

Seasonally appropriate foods to eat in a post-ritual feast include borscht soup (made of beets) and stuffed cabbage rolls known as sarma among Serbs and Bosnians. Enjoy these and other hearty foods that keep the chill of autumn at bay.

CHAPTER 17
Ancestor Devotional on Veles's Night

The following ritual has a few dates on which you can choose to perform it, alone or with a group, whether in late October (26 to coincide with the Polish Dziady ancestors' festival or on the 31), or between November 8 and 11 (dates bookended by the feasts of Saint Demetrios and Saint Martin, respectively), or on February 11.

If celebrating outdoors, weather permitting, a graveside picnic where your family dead are buried is traditional. If being graveside isn't an option but you can still celebrate outdoors in mild weather, you have the option of a picnic table at an outdoor park or renting out a covered shelter at your local forest preserve. These covered shelters, besides offering abundant and free parking spaces, usually have amenities such as a charcoal grill and clean drinking water.

If you choose to hold this festival indoors, the following ritual lends itself very well to the main activity consisting of a communal potluck dinner whose dining table is adjacent to a group ancestor altar. At the table, one chair should be deliberately left empty for the dead to come and visit at will and partake of the food set out on a plate for them. This spirit plate should have a sampling of everyone's food at the meal. If it's just you or your family/household at home celebrating, either eat before your ancestor altar or temporarily move your ancestor altar to where you typically dine.

If this ritual is being performed by a group aiming to honor the combined beloved dead of multiple families, let everyone contribute to the altar's assembly and decoration, from altar cloths, deity images, cut flowers, and various offerings, to framed photos of or mementoes that belonged to the beloved dead whose passing occurred more than a year ago. This is an important distinction to make because those who have recently died have some time to go before they can be elevated to/welcomed into the ranks of ancestorhood.[462]

Besides the practical necessities of plates, cutlery, cups, and the food and libations that your dead enjoyed consuming while they were alive, items that you may wish to have on hand for this ritual include the following:

- Altar cloth or cloths
- Framed photos or mementoes of the beloved dead
- *If indoors:* a bowl large enough to accommodate the libations and other offerings
- Vases with cut flowers[463]
- A small bowl filled with spring water into which fresh sprigs of sweet or holy basil and rosemary are submerged on one end
- *For the ancestor altar:* 1, 3, 7, or 9 clear glass drinking glasses filled with just water

---

462. Cvetković, *Slavic Traditions & Mythology,* 332.

463. They can be white for the symbolic correspondence with death. Or, choose flowers the dead loved during their lifetimes.

- Two baskets of walnuts in their shells (and one cracking device): one goes on the ancestor altar; the second is for the feast of the living
- Container with honey and its ladle on the ancestor altar
- Slices of rye or pumpernickel bread on the ancestor altar
- Small dish of barley or shelled wheat on the ancestor altar
- A chalice or drinking horn filled with dry red wine (syrah, merlot, cabernet sauvignon, etc.)[464]
- Candles, whether they're small and easily arrangeable tealights, battery-operated LED candles, traditional beeswax tapers, or votives[465]
- A covered candle, lantern, or large LED battery–operated candle to represent the balefire
- Suggested offerings to Veles: dark ales, rakija; pork meat, especially cured; game meat/venison; dried herbs of nettle, burdock, wormwood; votive offerings of appropriate animal figurines; amber beads or stringed amber necklaces
- Statues or other images depicting Veles
- Figurines of chthonic animals such as wolves, bears, serpents, or pigs or ethically sourced materia magica such as fur, bones, teeth, etc.
- Small padlock with key (it should be locked when the rite begins)
- Incense, especially myrrh incense, which is attributed to the folk religious cult of Saint Demetrios in the Greek Orthodox Church
- *Optional:* small Orthodox icon of Saint Demetrios (for Mitrovdan on November 8) or prayer card or glass saint's candle depicting the image of Saint Martin of Tours (a.k.a. San Martin Caballero on Spanish-language labels), if the date of November 11 is chosen for the ritual
- *Optional:* tarot deck or other divination tools should the celebrants wish to ask the ancestors for any messages

---

464. As a nonalcoholic alternative, serve grape juice, apple cider, blackberry juice, or pomegranate juice.
465. Ensure that they sit on fireproof dishes that can easily catch any wax drippings.

Ritual celebrants can choose to wear all black, all white, or, if they have such clothing, their Slavic outfits that feature folk embroidery.

The Rite

Process to the designated ritual space, be it at a dining table or on the ground of a loved one's grave, holding hands and singing, "*Slava Rodu, Slava Rodu! Glory to our dead so dear! In death and life, we fear no strife, for we know our gods are here!*"

All celebrants circle once around the space. Before they settle upon the ground or take their seats, they simultaneously cry out, "*Mir svima!/Peace to all!*"

If the ritual is taking place on a loved one's grave, the eldest person present in relation to the deceased speaks the subsequent introduction. If this is a group of friends celebrating this occasion at a location other than a cemetery, any one of the celebrants can step forward and speak the words of welcome:

> *"At this powerful seasonal current that ushers us into the bosom of winter, the dark half of the year, we gather to celebrate the lives of our beloved dead, to hallow their memories. We also come together to nourish and sustain ourselves in our grief and sadness by sharing in community—our Circle of Rodu—memories and stories of our departed loved ones, keeping them alive in our hearts. Večnaja Pamjat!"*[466]
>
> All: "*Večnaja Pamjat!*"

The celebrant continues.

> *"And above all we honor the Holy Powers who reign in this season that looks like barrenness in our world—bare trees, bleak skies, and encroaching darkness—but in the Otherworld we know our Elder Kin gleam and shimmer with a vibrant golden light, their life force energy and the source of their blessings*

466. Translated to "Memory Eternal," a refrain that is sung in liturgies for the dead in South Slavic countries. It's pronounced *VETCH'-naya PAHM'-yat*, rhyming with *not*.

for us, hinting at the treasures of life to emerge in our world once winter's spell is locked up again. Truly, life dwells in death just as death dwells in life. Let us attend to this Mystery with receptive minds and grateful, humble hearts. Slava!"

All: *"Slava!"*

Light or switch on the balefire substitute candle, which can be placed either in the middle of the dining table, at the head of the deceased if at a grave, or on the communal ancestor altar. Say:

"Svarožić, Son of the Sun, shine brightly upon our beloved dead. Illuminate their pathways in the mirroring world of Nav that they may journey well, especially those whom we invite to warm their hands at our hearth. Guide them. So, too, do we ask that you shine brightly within us: Grant us courage and health, physical and mental. Dispel all despair before its clouds have a chance to manacle our minds. Be resplendent even as the sparks from Svarog's forge grow dim at the waning of the year. For your light, we give thanks! Slava Rodu!"

All: *"Slava!"*

Another celebrant goes to retrieve the bowl with the sprigs of basil and rosemary in it. Taking both sprigs as an aspergillum, the celebrant lightly flecks the spring water onto every celebrant's forehead, saying,

"From the pools of the Otherworld, palaces of ancestral memory, we are blessed by the gods with this pure water. We put to flight the Unclean Force and welcome the Waters of Life within us and around us. Slava!"

All: *"Slava!"*

Take up the padlock and key and unlock it while solemnly stating:

"Mara's season of death is upon us. Winter streams forth into our world. We will all know the blackest depths of her Mysteries in due time, as our beloved dead have. Slava Marenu!"

All: *"Slava Marenu!"*

And now with offerings in hand, speak this invocation to Veles:

"Dolazi, Gospodar Vukova! Come to us, Lord of the Wolves! United as a pack, we stand ready to receive the blessings of our foremothers and our forefathers! Oh, Naša Deda Veles, Shepherd of the Dead, steadily guide them hither from the Thrice-Nine Kingdom! By [name any materia magica, especially animal parts], *your kin, your Rodu, call out to you! At this start of winter, in this season of the dead, we invite you to join us, O Seat of Ancestors! We offer you* [name offerings] *and wish for your thirst to be slaked with this* [name libation]. *Be with us, Grandfather! Slava Velesu!"*

All: *"Slava Velesu!"*

The attention now turns to the setting for the meal, be it dining table, picnic table, or on the ground at a grave. The spirit plate is passed around so that everyone who contributed to the potluck meal can add a dollop of their food contribution to the plate. Once it's full, it can go either to the ancestor altar or on the grave of the deceased. Once the plate is left at its location, everyone stands in salute and exclaims,

"For all our dead! Slava Rodu!"

Everyone then sits down to eat and takes turns talking about the person or people they wish to honor. They may choose to speak while seated at the table or go to the ancestor altar and light a candle before the framed photo of their beloved dead as they regale the company with a cherished memory or story of their loved one. Either way, it's an ideal time to pass around the drinking horn or communal goblet with the red wine or dark ale or fruit juice and take a sip before sharing a memory of the beloved dead. When the respective celebrant has finished speaking, everyone exclaims, *"Slava Rodu!"* and on to the next person, and so on. If the meal is being shared in honor of a specific dead person at their grave by their living relatives or descendants plus family friends, everyone can take turns sharing their favorite memory of the deceased. After each story or anecdote is told, the group should exclaim,

> *"Slava,* [name of the deceased]*!"*

With the meal completed, and once everyone has had their turn to honor a loved one, everyone can vote on whether they'd like to engage in a divination to see what messages the dead convey. This can be as simple as a single-card draw from a tarot deck that is passed around, or the group can appoint a "seer" who is in charge of doing a more comprehensive session, such as a more thoroughly developed tarot spread or rune reading or what have you. It would be lovely if there could be documentation of some sort and the results and interpretations shared with everyone afterward via email or a group chat via text, but it's not necessary. The impact will be felt emotionally in the moment, and that's what matters.

Once everyone's had the sense that things are truly winding down, if the ritual was held indoors, it's time for the proper disposal of the contents of the offering bowl at an outdoor location. A celebrant can go alone or have the whole group accompany them as they pour forth the bowl's contents into the ground while saying,

> *"From the gods, through earth, to us; from us, through the earth, back unto the gods. For this is right and just. Slava Rodu!"*
>
> All: *"Slava Rodu!"*

The celebrant who invoked Veles stands up and says:

> *"My kin, may we remain receptive to Father Veles's compassion as Shepherd of our dead, knowing they are well-cared-for in his charge. May Veles continue to inspire us to weave new stories that will settle like cozy blankets over us, our memories of our beloved dead warming our hearts despite the cold and darkness to come. Istina!"*
>
> All: *"Istina!"*

The celebrant who first spoke at the ritual's outset asks everyone to stand in a circle and join hands. They then say,

> *"As we entered this space singing as one family in spirit, may we part the same way. Join with me and may our steps and hearts be light as we sing."*

All link hands and sing the following as they process out of the space, either in single file or as a horizontal line.

> *"Slava Rodu, Slava Rodu! Life and Death, the cycle goes! Glory to our hallowed dead; Memory Eternal and sweet repose!"*

The procession complete, everyone cries out,

> *"Mir svima!/Peace to all!"*

Group hugs will more than likely be the heartiest, most ribcage squeezing of all in comparison to the other ritual occasions noted in this book. *Slava!*

Conclusion

Writing this book has been nothing short of a profound, spiritually contextualized exercise in cultural ambassadorship. I truly felt the weight of the responsibility in doing right by my Serbian family dead and by my ancestral gods—and doing right by the histories and legacies of *all* Slavic peoples—at every stage of this book's development process.

From my Serbian Dual-Faith folk ways upbringing to my academic research begun in earnest nearly twenty years ago to the rituals my fellow Polytheists of Slavic heritage and I perform together here and now in the United States, far from our parents' homelands, I have experienced an incredible sense of honor in presenting what I've learned, lived, and continue to live to anyone reading this book. All these paths born of a shared Slavic Pagan past—whether we choose to call those paths Native Faith, or Old Belief, or Slavic Pagan, or Dual-Faith—are living traditions, vibrantly adapting themselves to the needs and hopes of the people enacting them today, no matter where in the world they live. We Slavs are a resilient people, and so are our deeply ingrained beliefs and treasured practices.

It may be strange for me as a contemporary Slavic Polytheistic witch and priestess to conclude this book by quoting the Bible, but I hope anyone who has truly enjoyed reading this book and who has grown from the act of engaging with it will take to heart the injunction from Paul to "stand fast and hold to the traditions which ye have been taught" (2 Thessalonians 2:15, King James Version). As human beings on a fragile planet facing an uncertain future, we couldn't ask for a better anchor in life.

Slava!

APPENDIX A

Serbian Cyrillic Alphabet and Pronunciation Guide

Српски (Serbian)	English Phonetics	Hrvatski (Croatian)/ Latin Equivalents
А а	father	A a
Б б	beer	B b
В в	very	V v
Г г	great	G g
Д д	day	D d
Ђ ђ	ginger, joy	Đ đ, Dj dj
Е е	left, trek	E e
Ж ж	leisure, treasure	Ž ž, Zh zh
З з	zoo	Z z

Српски (Serbian)	English Phonetics	Hrvatski (Croatian)/ Latin Equivalents
И и	me, heal, indeed	I i
J j	yellow, yes	J j
К к	kindness, campy	K k
Л л	lion	L l
Љ љ	million (Spanish *llorona*)	Lj lj
М м	memory	M m
Н н	no	N n
Њ њ	onion (Spanish ñ)	Nj nj
О о	door	O o
П п	present	P p
Р р	reality	R r
С с	snake	S s
Т т	tip	T t
Ћ ћ	sandwich	Ć ć, Ch ch
У у	rule, moon	U u
Ф ф	fall, phosphorescence	F f
Х х	help (Hebrew *challah*)	H h
Ц ц	Tsar, lots	C c

Српски (Serbian)	English Phonetics	Hrvatski (Croatian)/ Latin Equivalents
Ч ч	Chernobyl, chalk	Č č, Ch ch
Џ џ	George, Jack, journey	Dž dž, Dzh dzh
Ш ш	she, ensure	Š š, Sh sh

APPENDIX B
Glossary

The following terms from Serbian and other Slavic languages are rendered in the Latin-derived alphabet instead of Cyrillic. They include pronunciations based on phonemes tailored to folks whose main language is English.

Amin *[AH'-meen]:* Old Church Slavonic "Amen."

Baba *[BAH'-bah]:* Pan-Slavic singular noun, plural *babe [BAH'-beh]* for "Granny," "Old Woman."

Baba Roga *[BAH'-bah RŌE'-gah]:* Serbo-Croatian mythic witch figure of "Horned Baba." South Slavic equivalent of ***Baba Yaga*** *[YAH'-gah]* of the East Slavs.

badnjak *[BAHD'-nyak]:* Serbian Yule log. A sacred, east-growing limb of oak that's been ritually harvested for either Native Faith celebrations of the Winter Solstice/***Koleda*** or Dual-Faith and Serbian Orthodox celebrations of Christmas Eve, which is called ***Badnje Veće***.

Badnje Veće *[BAHD'-nyeh VEH'-cheh]:* "Eve of the Oak." Serbian Christmas Eve.

Badnji Dan *[BAHD'-nyee DAHN']:* The "Day of the Oak," the diurnal portion of Serbian Christmas Eve, which is rife with ritual activity surrounding the welcoming of the ***badnjak*** into the home.

bajalica *[BAH'-yah-leet-sah]:* Serbian Cunning Woman who specializes in healing. Plural: *bajalice [BAH'-yah-leet-seh].*

bania *[BAH'-nyah]:* East Slavic term for "bathhouse."

bannik *[BAH'-neek]:* The dangerous spirit of the bathhouse.

basma *[BAHS'-mah]:* Macedonian, "incantation." A male enchanter is a *basmar.*

Beograd *[BAY'-oh-grad]:* Serbia's capital city, Anglicized as "Belgrade."

bič *[BEACH]:* Ritual tool made of hemp fibers that grow from a ritually decapitated viper's head.

Bielo/Byelobog *[BEE'-yel-oh-bōg]:* "The White God." Widely considered a theonym for Slavic gods such as Dažbog and Svetovid, not a separate deity.

Biljini Petak *[BEEL'-yee-nee PET'-ahk]:* The "Wild Herb-Gathering Friday" that occurs the Friday before Saint George's Day (May 6).

blaga *[BLAH'-gah]:* Adjective, "blessed," "full of goodness." Term that precedes the name Marija and can refer to the Virgin Mary or Mary Magdalene *(Blaga Marija).*

Bogoljavljenje *[BŌG'-oh-lyav-lyeh-neh]:* "God Calls Out," Serbian term for the Feast of the Epiphany, January 19, which ends the period of the "Unclean Days."

Božić *[BŌW'-zheech]:* "Little God," the Serbian term for Christmas day.

bubanj *[BOO'-bahn-yeh]:* Drum, typically a round frame drum with an animal skin.

Černo/Chernobog *[CHEHR'-no-bōg]:* "The Black God." Theonym for chthonic gods such as Triglav. Cosmic foil to ***Bielobog***.

ćevapčići *[CHEH'-vahp-chee-chee]:* South Slavic grilled skinless sausages, made of combined ground pork, lamb, and beef with onions and garlic powder.

čuvar kućama *[CHOO'-vahr KOOCH'-ah-mah]:* Serbian phrase denoting the spiritual "watcher of the house." This is either the snake that resides by the hearth in village homes and is thought to be the guardian of the family, or it is the talismanic red-dyed Easter egg set in the saint's corner of a Serbian home.

Dajbog/Dažbog *[DYE'-bōg/DAHZH'-bōg]:* The Slavic "God Who Gives," associated with the life-giving powers of the sun as well as chthonic blessings from the Underworld.

đavoli *["J" as in "jam"—JAHV'-ōh-lee]:* Plural, "devils, imps." Singular: *đavo.*

Deda *[DEAD'-uh]:* "Grandpa," "Old Man." Complement of ***Baba.***

Devana *[DEH'-vah-nah]:* Slavic goddess of the wilderness and Lady of the Beasts. Huntress and virgin. Also known as *Devica [DEH'-vee-tsah]* in Serbian, which means "Maiden" and is applied to the constellation of Virgo as well.

Dodole *[DOE'-doe-leh]:* Spring goddess who brings rain in Serbian folklore. All-female ritual performers conduct ceremonies to evoke her and end droughts in villages.

domovoi *[DOME'-oh-voy]:* House spirit, addressed as "Grandfather."

družina *[drew-ZHEE'-nah]:* "Community," multigenerational Slavic households.

Drvo Svijeta *[DUR'-vōh SVEE'-yet-ah]:* Croatian term for the Pan-Slavic "World Tree" of Native Faith/Slavic Pagan cosmology.

Đurđevdan *[soft "g"—JOOR'-jev-dahn]:* "Saint George's Day," celebrated May 6 in the Julian calendar and April 23 in the Gregorian. Saint George inherited ***Jarilo's*** traits.

Dvoverovanje *[DVŌ'-ver-oh-VAHN'-yeh]:* "Dual Faith," Pagan beliefs and practices with an Eastern Orthodox Christian overlay. Slavic folk religion. Folk Orthodoxy.

gatanje *[GOT'-ahn-yeh]:* Serbian term for "divination." A woman who practices it is called a *gatara*; a man, a *gatar.*

Gromovnik *[GRŌM'-ōhv-neek]:* "The Thunderer," an epithet of ***Perun's*** and ***Saint Ilija's.***

Ilija *[EEL'-eeh-yah]:* Saint Elijah. His cult absorbed many of ***Perun's*** aspects.

istina *[EAST'-ee-nah]:* Serbian word for "truth."

Jariljdan *[yahr-EEL'-dahn]:* Croatian, "Jarilo's Day"/"Saint George's Day" (April 23).

Jarilo *[YAR'-ee-lōh]:* Youthful Slavic god of vegetation, crops. Consort of ***Mara*** in South Slavic folk songs. Son of ***Perun*** and ***Mokoša.***

kajmak *[KAI'-mahk]:* Type of clotted cream popular in Serbia and Bosnia.

karakonđule *[kahr-ah-KŌHN'-jou-leh]:* A type of evil spirit in Serbian lore thought to be especially active during the ***Nekrštani Dani.*** It is active after sunset and loves to leap onto unwary travelers' backs and drive them to exhaustion, even death.

kazan *[KAHZ'-ahn]:* Ritual and mundane cooking tool of the cauldron.

khorovod *[HŌR'-oh-vōde]:* East Slavic style of circle dance, etymologically derived from *Khors,* a sun god. The South Slavic equivalent is the ***kolo*** dance.

kikimora *[KEY'-key-mō-ra]:* Female equivalent of ***domovoi***. See ***šišimora***.

kipa *[KEY'-pah]:* A god-pole, wooden carved effigy depicting a Slavic deity that is inserted into the ground.

kolać *[KŌH'-lahtch]:* An elaborate round bread loaf typically served at a ***Slava***.

koldun'ia *[kohl-DOON'-ee-yah]:* East Slavic term for "witch," "sorceress."

Koleda/Koliada *[KOHL'-ed-uh / KOHL'-ee-yad-ah]:* Yuletide period, stretching from Winter Solstice's astronomical observance through to Orthodox Epiphany, January 19.

kolo *[KŌ'-low]:* Serbo-Croatian for "wheel." A fast-paced circle dance performed in honor of the sun's movement and the cycles of time. Root of ***kolovrat.***

kolovrat *[KŌ'-low-vraht]:* A Pan-Slavic term for the most recognizable symbol in ***Rodnovery***—the wheel whose eight spokes emanating from a central hub may or may not terminate into little arms. A symbol for the spinning cycles of time.

kostura/kustura *[COST'-ooh-rah/KOOST'-ooh-rah]:* Ritual tool of black-handled knife. Etymologically related to *kosti,* "bones."

krupnik *[KROOP'-neek]:* Vodka-based liqueur with honey, popular in Poland.

kućnih duhova *[KOOCH'-nyeeh DOO'-hō-vah]:* "House spirit," Serbian *domovoi.*

kukavica *[KOOK'-ah-veet-sah]:* "Cuckoo bird," from the Serbian root verb *kuka,* "to mourn."

Kupalo *[KOOP'-ah-lōw]:* Summer Solstice festival associated with Saint John's Day. From the Common Slavic root verb *kupati,* "to bathe."

Lazareva Subota *[LAHZ'-ah-ray-vah SOO'-bōw-tah]:* "Lazarus Saturday," the day preceding Palm Sunday wherein much folk magic is practiced by women called ***Lazarice*** to evoke the fertility of the land. The day is also called ***Vrbica.***

Lazarice *[LAHZ'-ah-ree-tseh]:* All-female mummers' and ritual troupe that blesses Serbian villagers' homes and fields the Saturday before Palm Sunday.

leshnik/leshy *[LESH'-neek/LESH'-ee]:* Spirit of the forest. Plural: *lešnići, leshii.*

lonac *[LŌW-nahts]:* Sacred chain that suspends the cauldron over the hearth fire. Also called the ***verige.***

madžije *[MAHD-zhee-yeh]:* Serbian word for "magic," connotes black magic.

majka *[MY'-kuh]:* Serbo-Croatian word for "mother."

Mara *[MAH'-rah—trill the "r"]:* Slavic sovereign goddess of the land, winter, darkness, and death. South Slavic folk songs pair her with ***Jarilo.***

Martenitsi *[MAR'-ten-eet-see]:* Bulgarian figurines made of intertwined red and white yarn, given as gifts on Baba Marta's Day (March 1).

Maslenitsa *[mahs-LEN'-eet-sah]:* East Slavic carnival-like celebration that marks the end of winter and the start of the Lenten fasting season. Effigies of ***Mara*** are ceremonially burned or drowned to summon spring.

Mati Sira Zemlija *[MAH'-tee SEE'-rah ZEM'-lee-yah]:* "Moist Mother Earth."

međed gradio *[MEJ'—"j" as in "jam"—ed GRAH'-dee-oh]:* "Bear-built."

medved *[MED'-ved]:* "The knower of honey," euphemism for the noun *bear.*

metla: Witches' magical tool of a broom.

Mir svima *[MEER' SVEE'-mah]:* An Old Church Slavonic phrase meaning "Peace to all."

Mokoša *[MŌ'-kōh-sha]:* Slavic goddess of the earth, weaving, childbirth, and destiny.

molitva *[MŌH'-leet-vuh]:* "Prayer." Spoken aloud in Dual-Faith Tradition.

Nav *[NAHV]:* The Underworld, Veles's domain. Bottom third of the World Tree.

Nečistaja Sila *[NEH'-chee-stah-yah SEE'-lah]:* The "Unclean Force," root of all manner of manifestations of negative spiritual and physical energy. An ontological reality rooted in nature, not Christian mythology.

Nekrštani Dani *[NEK'-ir-shtan-ee DAHN'-ee]:* "The Unclean/Unbaptized Days," or period stretching from Serbian Christmas (January 7) to Epiphany (January 19). The Unclean Force and its mélange of dangerous spiritual entities run amok at this time. See also ***đavoli, karakonđule,*** and ***vampiri.***

Ognjena Marija *[ŌG'-nyen-ah MAHR'-ee-yah—hard "g"]:* "Fiery Mary," destructive female folk saint associated with the heat of summer. May be a Christianized female consort of the thunder god, ***Perun.*** Feast day is July 30. Also called ***Sveta Marina.***

onaj stari *[ŌH'-nai STAH'-ree]:* "That old man," a Croatian euphemism for the ***vodenjak.***

otac *[ŌH'-tahts]:* Serbo-Croatian word for "father." See also ***Tata.***

ovinnik *[OH'-ven-neek]:* Dangerous spirit of the threshing barn.

padalice *[PAHD'-ah-leet-seh]:* Young women naturally gifted with mediumship abilities who perform the communal ***rusalje*** spirit communication ritual on Pentecost. Their ritual trance states are facilitated and warded by women called *Kraljice [KRAL'-yeet-seh],* "Queens," and men called *Kraljevi [KRAL'-yev-ee],* "Kings."

Perun *[PEH'-roon]:* Sky, thunder, and cosmic order–upholding god of the Slavs.

pogača *[PŌ'-gah-tchah]:* A simple round loaf of homemade bread. A larger, more elaborate *pogača* becomes a ***kolać.***

polevoi *[PŌ'-leh-voi]:* Plural, spirits of the fields in East Slavic lore. Derived from *polje [POLE'-yeh],* "field."

poludnica *[PŌ'-lewd-neet-sah]:* A dangerous female spirit of the fields who attacks laborers if they don't rest at high noon. Derived from the Serbo-Croatian verb *poluditi,* "to go mad."

Prav *[PRAHV]:* "Divine Law." The upper third of the World Tree, abode of the gods.

promaja *[PRO'-my-yah]:* A draft or current of air that carries baleful energies and is thought to make folks physically ill. A manifestation of the Unclean Force.

rakija *[ROCK'-ee-yah]:* South Slavic plum brandy that's been heated and infused with caramelized sugar. A staple South Slavic adult beverage.

Rod *[ROAD]:* The eponymous Slavic creator god whose name is at the very heart of ***Rodnovery***/Slavic Native Faith. Also "clan," "kin," "ancestry." Depending on a sentence's grammatical structure, can have the genitive case ending of *Rodu.*

roditi *[RŌW'-dee-tee]:* Common Slavic verb, "to give birth." Etymologically related to creator god ***Rod*** and the goddesses of Fate, the ***Roženice.***

Rodnovery/Rodnovjerje *[RŌD'-no-very/RŌD'-no-vyeer-yeh]:* Noun, the term (English, then Croatian) for Slavic Native Faith, believers in ***Rod.***

Roženice *[RŌW'-zhen-eet-seh]:* Goddesses of Destiny, three in number. The Fates.

rusalje *[ROOS'-ahl-yeh]:* Serbian mass-participant mediumship ritual performed outdoors in nature on Pentecost/Holy Trinity Sunday. The medium is a ***padalica.***

rusalki *[ROOS'-ahl-key]:* Class of dangerous female water spirits. Singular: *rusalka.*

rushnyky *[roosh-NEE'-kee]:* Ukrainian embroidered scarf used in folk magic.

sarma *[rhymes with "karma"]:* South Slavic food of stuffed pickled cabbage leaves.

sekire *[SEH'-kee-reh]:* Magical tool of a hatchet. Also the weapon of ***Perun.***

sila magija *[SEE'-lah MAHG'-ee-yah (hard "g")]:* Serbian phrase of "magical force."

Simargl *[see-MAR'-gūl (hard "g")]:* East Slavic griffin-shaped deity of Persian origin.

šipak *[SHEE'-pahk]:* The apotropaic gesture of the "fig sign." Curl the right hand into a fist and insert the thumb between the index and middle fingers.

šišimora *[SHE'-she-mo-ra]:* Female house spirit in South and East Slavic lore. Also called ***kikimora.***

Slava *[SLAH'-vah]:* "Glory." In Serbian culture, it's the feast day (or three-day feast) of a family's or clan's protecting saint. Also known as a *Krsna* (Baptismal) *Slava.*

šlivovica *[SHLEE'-vōh-vee-tsah]:* Serbia's national drink, a brandy made with fermented plums. When heated, it becomes ***rakija.***

sreča *[SRETCH'-ah]:* "Good fortune." Its opposite is ***zlo*** or ***šteta.***

srp *[SERP—trill the "r"]:* Small sickle, a handheld magical tool.

štap *[SHTOP]:* Wooden magical ritual staff.

šteta *[SHTET'-ah]:* Bad luck that results in material/financial losses.

Stribog *[STREE'-bōg]:* Slavic god of the winds.

sudbine *[SUED'-bee-neh]:* Destiny, fate.

suditi *[SUE'-dee-tee]:* Verb, "to judge." Root of goddesses of fate, the *Suđenice [SUED-jen-eet-seh].*

šuma *[SHOE'-mah]:* "Forest."

Šumadija *[SHOE'-mahd-ee-yah]:* "Of the forest." Derived from the densely wooded region of the same name in central Serbia. There, the forest spirit is called *šumnik [SHOOM'-neek] instead of* ***leshnik.***

Svarog *[SVAH'-rogue]:* Slavic sky/sun and creator god, often envisioned as a divine blacksmith. Father of ***Svarožić.***

Svarožić *[SVAHR'-oh-zheech]:* "Little Svarog," "Svarog Junior." God of "young" winter sun post-Solstice and god of fire. See ***Božić.***

Sveta Marina *[SVET'-ah MAHR'-ee-nah]:* "Saint Marina," e.g., ***Ognjena Marija.***

Svetovid *[SVEH'-tow-veed]:* Polycephalic god of four heads/faces, which look out into the cardinal directions. God of war, divination, and abundance. High god of the West Slavs. Also known as *Svetovit, Świętowita, Svantevit, Sviatovyd, Su'Vid,* or just *Vid.*

Tata *[TUH'-tuh]:* Serbo-Croatian term of endearment that means "Daddy."

tepsija *[TEHP'-see-yah]:* Divinatory tool of a round shallow baking dish.

Tetka *[TET'-kuh]:* "Auntie." Euphemism for "bear" (the animal) in Serbia and Bosnia.

torba *[TŌR'-buh—trill the "r"]:* Handknit woolen bag used as a magical tool.

Triglav *[TREE'-glahv—trill the "r"]:* Polycephalic chthonic god with three heads/faces.

Trojan *[TRŌW'-yahn]:* "Thrice." An epithet of triple-headed Triglav's.

urok *[OOH'-rawk—trill the "r"—with the "a" like the English "chalk"]:* "The Evil Eye." It is a manifestation of the ***Nečistaja Sila*** and has sentience, its own will, and agency.

vampiri *[VAHM'-pee-ree]:* Plural, "vampires." Belief in them is still widespread in rural Serbia. Thought to be corporeal revenants that return to attack family members.

Večnaja Pamjat *[VECH'-na-yah PAHM'-yaht]:* "Memory Eternal." Refrain sung to bless the dead during an Orthodox *parastos* ceremony during the Days of the Dead as clergy intone names of the deceased.

Veles *[VEH'-less]:* Complex Slavic god of the Underworld and the human dead, magic, music, livestock, and wild beasts. Also known as Volos *[VŌH'-lōs].*

velika *[VEL'-eek-ah]:* "Great" (feminine genitive case); used as adjective in title of a divine female being, such as the ***Velika Šumska Majka*** or Saint Marina as a *Velika Mučenica,* "Great Martyr."

Velika Šumska Majka *[VEL'-eek-ah SHOOM'-skah MY'-kuh]:* "Great Forest Mother" of Serbian lore, perhaps a Fairy Queen. She is depicted horned.

Velikdan *[VEL'-eek-dahn]:* "Spring Equinox" in Serbian Rodnovery. Also known as *Vesnin Dan [VES'-neen DAHN'].* Polish: *Jaro Święto [YAHR'-ōh SVEE'-yet-tōh].*

venac *[VEN'-ahts]:* "Wreath." Specifically, this is a small wreath woven out of newly harvested local grasses that are strewn in Serbian churches on Pentecost Sunday. Each *venac* is woven during a special segment in the Divine Liturgy when the officiating bishop thrice evokes the Holy Trinity. A *venac* is a highly prized Dual-Faith talisman.

verige *[VEH'-ree-geh, hard "g"]:* Sacred chain that suspends the cauldron over the hearth fire. See ***lonac.***

Vesna *[VES'-nah]:* Slavic goddess of spring. See ***Živa.***

veštica/vještica *[VESH'-tee-tsuh/VEE'-yesh-tee-tsuh]:* Respective Serbian and Croatian terms for "witch." Plural would be *veštice/vještice.*

***vetar** [VET'-ahr]:* "Wind."

Vidovčica Trava** [VEE'-dōve-chee-tsah TRAH'-vah]:* "Grasses of the god Vid, or Svetovid," i.e., the varieties of pimpernel used for divination on ***Vidovdan.

***Vidovdan** [VEE'-dōve-dahn]:* June 15 or June 28, depending on whether the Gregorian or Julian calendar is used. Commemoration of the historic Battle of Kosovo in 1389 now widely used in South Slavic folk magic as a day for divination, magical spells for eye health, and so on. A feast day of the god Svetovid for modern South Slavic Native Faith believers.

vile** [VEE'-lay]:* Plural, "fairy women." Singular: vila *[VEE'-lah].* South Slavic folklore imagines them as tall, slender, pale, and beautiful, dressed in all white. Their hair is unbound/unbraided, a sign of magical power. Not kindly disposed toward humans, nevertheless they can impart their herb magic to ***bajalice/Cunning Women.

***vodenjak** [VŌH'-den-yahk]:* Male water spirit. Also known as *vodeni duh [VŌH-den-ee DOOH'].*

***volkhv** [VŌHL'-hff—the "h" is very guttural like Hebrew "ch"]:* Slavic Pagan priest or "sorcerer" in Russian and Ukrainian. Etymologically related to "wolf."

***vračanje** [VRAH'-cha-nyeh]:* "Witchcraft," *malefica.*

***vračar(a)** [VRAH'-char-(uh)]:* Male/female practitioner of magic, sorcerer/sorceress.

***Vračari** [VRAH'-char-ee]:* "Magicians," epithet applied to Saints Kozma and Damijan (Cosmas and Damian) and the name of their feast day on July 14 and November 14.

Vrbica** [VER'-bee-tsuh]:* "Pussy Willow's Day," or ***Lazareva Subota. At the conclusion of Divine Liturgy that morning in Serbian Orthodox Churches, parishioners receive blessed pussy willow stalks to take home as fertility amulets.

***vuk** [VOOK]:* "Wolf." Plural: *vukovi [VOOK'-oh-vee].* Popular name for Serbian men.

***Yav** [YAHV]:* The world of living humans, middle third of the World Tree.

***Zadušnice** [ZAH'-doosh-neet-seh]:* Serbian Days (plural) of the Dead. Singular: Zadušnica.

***Zaduszki** [ZAH'-doosh-key]:* Polish All Souls' Day, either October 26 or 31.

zemlija** [ZEM'-lee-yuh]:* Earth, the ground beneath us. Deified as ***Mati Sira Zemlija, "Moist Mother Earth."

***žito** [ZHEE'-tōw]:* Boiled wheat dish, a staple ritual food to the dead. East Slavs call it ***koljivo** [KŌHL'-yee-vō].*

Živa** [ZHEE'-vah]:* Slavic spring or Mother Goddess whose name means "Life." Sometimes equated with ***Vesna—her epithet—or regarded as a separate being.

***Živa Voda** [ZHEE'-vah VŌ'-dah]:* Sacred water, usually from a natural spring. It can also refer to church-blessed Holy Water.

***zlo** [rhymes with "slow"]:* "Bad luck," "trouble," "affliction."

***zmaj** [ZMY, rhymes with "rye"]:* "Dragon."

***zmija** [ZMEE'-yah]:* "Snake."

***znakhar** [ZNAH'-hai]:* Literally "one who knows." East Slavic term for "sorcerer." Synonymous with ***koldun** [KŌHL'-doon].*

***zvonac** [ZVŌN'-ahts]:* Handheld small bell.

APPENDIX C
Slavic Native Faith Resources (Groups, Musicians/Artists)

By no means a comprehensive tally, the individuals and organizations related to Slavic Native Faith that I list below have been personally vetted. I've organized them by country and have listed them alphabetically.

Croatia (*Hrvatska*)

This former Yugoslav republic became an independent country in 1991 and joined the European Union in 2013. While the majority of its citizens regard themselves as faithful Roman Catholics, Croatia is home to a bourgeoning Slavic Native Faith movement, which, from my observation, has the most tacit cultural support of its government compared to all other South Slavic nations.

Dražen Markotić Vega

Croatian Rodnover and artist specializing in beautifully detailed woodcraft and pyrography creations of interest to Slavic Native Faith believers. A talented musician, Dražen is also the lead singer for the Croatian Pagan folk metal band **Su'Vid.** Croatian is his preferred language, so keep that in mind for communicating with him on social media.

Location: Zagreb

Wood Tattoo (his pyrography art business): https://www.facebook.com/profile.php?id=100063077658899

FB: @Su'Vid

Savez Hrvatskih Rodnovjeraca/Association of Croatian Rodnovers

This federation is to be commended for its denunciation of nationalism. Their website, which has an English translation, offers a wealth of information on Slavic Native Faith in general as well as on Croatian folk ways in particular.

Location: Zagreb

Website: https://rodnovjerje.com.hr/

Perunova Svetinja/Perun's Shrine

This group of dedicated Croatian Rodnovers reestablished a gorgeous public shrine to the god Perun on the Istrian peninsula of Croatia on July 2, 2013. Email communications require knowledge of Croatian or language translation services.

Location: Učka

FB: @Perunova Svetinja—Udruga za promicanje stare slavenske kulture

YouTube: @perunovasvetinja4547

Contact: perunovasvetinja@hotmail.com, kontakt@perunovasvetinja.hr

Poland (*Polska*)

Since the dissolution of the Soviet Union in 1991, Poland has seen exponential growth in the Slavic Native Faith community. This nation of West Slavs is home to the oldest legally recognized Slavic Native Faith religious organization in the world; in the spring of 2025, it celebrated its thirtieth anniversary. Public monuments to the nation's Pagan past are common, especially in parks in and around the lovely medieval city of Kraków.

Maryo Hnoss, Hnoss Silver Craft (Slavic & Viking Art and Jewelry)

Maryo is a very gifted silversmith dedicated to his craft and his commitment to the Slavic gods. He is also a medieval reenactor and musician in a Slavic Pagan folk band, **Volhv Ridnovir.** To communicate with him, knowledge of Polish is required, so make the most of language translation technologies.

Location: Białystok

Website: https://hnoss.pl/

YouTube: @maryohnoss7755

FB: https://www.facebook.com/Hnoss.silvercraft

Email: vendolowicz@gmail.com

Rodzimy Kościół Polski/Native Polish Church

The oldest continuously running Slavic Native Faith organization. Polish communication expected.

Location: Warsaw

Website: https://rkp.org.pl/

Serbia (*Србија*)

Located in the heart of the Balkans, my parents' homeland of Serbia has a population of less than 10 million people with Eastern Orthodox Christianity as the dominant religion. Nevertheless, organized Slavic Native Faith groups are growing and can found in urban centers such as Beograd and Novi Sad. Those cities are anchors of a robust publishing industry that is producing increasingly popular Serbian-language (Cyrillic alphabet) books on indigenous folklore, witchcraft, and Slavic mythology and Native Faith.

Српска родноверна жупа "Луг Велеса"/Serbian Rodnover Community "Lug Velesa" ("Valley of Veles")

It pleases me to see generations younger than mine taking their Slavic Native Faith seriously, and that's exactly the kinds of committed and visionary young folks you'll find in Lug Velesa. They produce wonderful short animated videos on YouTube (with English subtitles) on the deities of the Slavic pantheon as well as on Serbian folk customs. Cofounder Dušan Božić can be reached via the email address below, but please use a Serbian translation service if you're not proficient in the language.

Location: Novi Sad

Instagram: @lugvelesa

FB: https://www.facebook.com/SRZlugvelesa

YouTube: @LugVelesa

Email: lugvelesa@gmail.com

Slovenia (*Slovenija*)

As with neighboring Croatia, the small alpine country of Slovenia, which has a population of fewer than three million people, established its independence from Yugoslavia in 1991. Picturesque and laden with natural wonders such as Triglav National Park and Lake Bled, Slovenia is a Rodnover's paradise.

Društvo Slovenci Staroverci/"The Association of Old Believers"

Slovenia's esteemed Native Faith organization hosts many cultural events in the capital city of Ljubljana throughout the year. Follow their robust calendar of events on their website, which is also offered in English, Polish, and Russian translations.

Location: Ljubljana

Website: https://staroverci.si/

Email: drustvo.staroverci@gmail.com

Native Faith Group "Veles" and Their "Svarunica" Online Portal

This Slovenian Native Faith group is named after the Slavic God of the Underworld, Wild and Domestic Beasts, Magic, and Music. Their online portal is delightful and addictive!

Location: Ljubljana

Website: https://svarunica.com/

FB: https://www.facebook.com/svarunica

United States

It's very difficult to ascertain the number of Slavic Native Faith adherents in the United States, but this book is proof that interest is certainly growing. Hopefully future census efforts that quantify what are called "new religious movements" will be able to parse out Slavic Paganism specifically. Time will tell!

Perun Mountain

This is a publisher of English-language Rodnovery texts, including works translated from Slavic languages. Their goal is to promote Slavic cultures in the English-speaking world. They host an online directory of resources.

Location: Gorham, New Hampshire

Mailing Address: PO Box 110, Gorham, New Hampshire, United States

Website: perunmountain.com

English-Language Slavic Native Faith Resources Directory:
https://slavicnativefaith.com/resources/

Email: Contact@SlavicNativeFaith.com

Słowiańska Polonia/Slavic Polish Diaspora

This is a Slavic Native Faith religious organization located in Chicago's northwest side, catering primarily but not exclusively to the Polish immigrant community and Polish-American citizens. They hold public rituals in Chicago-area forest preserves (Cook County).

Location: Chicago, Illinois

FB: https://www.facebook.com/profile.php?id=100069317501511&sk=about

Fundraising Efforts for Building a Slavic Native Faith Temple in Poland: https://zrzutka.pl/en/pk98ej

APPENDIX D

My Family's Recipes of Classic Serbian Foods

Enjoy these staple Serbian foods, whose recipes are collected from my family; I've added vegetarian and vegan substitutes for the meaty dishes when possible. These items can serve as devotional offerings or as courses for post-ritual potluck feasting. Measurements given are in US format as well as continental European metric.

Pogača (Round Bread)

This is a classic round leavened bread with a spongy texture that makes it ideal for dipping in soups or stews or just enjoying on its own. This is vegetarian or vegan, depending on what you use to grease the baking pan.

What you'll need

- 2½ teaspoons/15 grams dry active yeast
- 1½ teaspoons/6.25 grams granulated sugar
- Small bowl

- 1¼ cups/270 milliliters lukewarm water
- 2 cups/450 grams nonbleached, all-purpose flour
- 1½ teaspoons/6.25 grams sea salt
- Medium-sized mixing bowl
- 4 tablespoons/59 milliliters olive oil
- Cling wrap
- Vegetable shortening (Crisco in the United States) for a vegan version or butter for a vegetarian version when it comes to greasing the pan
- Round baking pan that measures 11 inches/28 centimeters wide and 2 inches/5 centimeters tall
- 2 clean kitchen towels
- Aluminum foil

Procedure

Crumble the dry yeast and sugar into the small bowl with lukewarm water. Mix until it dissolves well. Add the flour and salt to the medium bowl and stir them briefly. Add the contents of the small bowl to the bowl with flour and gently mix. Once you see that roughly half the water has been absorbed, add the olive oil and stir well until mixed.

Scoop out the dough mix onto a lightly floured surface, such as a countertop or large cutting board. Knead carefully—it will be very sticky, but resist the urge to add more flour—for 3 to 5 minutes. Cover the dough with lightly dusted cling wrap and let it rest for 15 minutes.

Grease the baking pan and lightly coat it with flour. Dust your hands as well as the dough prior to transferring it to the pan. Flatten and stretch the dough to cover the entire diameter. Cover the baking pan with a damp kitchen towel and let the dough rise for 20 minutes. While you wait, preheat the oven to 500°F/260°C. Aerate the dough by poking small holes across its surface with a fork.

Cover the pan with foil, ensuring that the edges are squeezed down against the sides, sealing the dough. Bake for 20 minutes. Remove the foil, reduce the temperature to 425°F/218°C, and bake for another 15 minutes. Remove from the pan and sprinkle lightly with cold water. Wrap bread in a clean towel to cool off for 15 minutes.

Serve warm. The pogača can retain its soft texture for 1 to 2 days if it's kept in a sealed bag.

Ćevapčići (Small Skinless Sausages)

Also known as ćevapi (plural), this traditional grilled meat street food is beloved throughout the former Yugoslavia and is increasingly becoming a hit with carnivorous American tourists to countries like Croatia, Bosnia-Herzegovina, and Serbia. The Croatian and Serbian versions use a mixture of beef, pork, and lamb in their ćevapi, but in Muslim-dominant Bosnia, where pork is shunned, chefs use a beef, onions, and peppers mixture.

My father was an excellent cook, and grilled Serbian-style meats were his specialty; he made his ćevapčići extra spicy and heavy on the minced garlic. Before I became a vegetarian as a teen, I loved eating this food more than anything.

What you'll need

- 2 large white onions
- 1 large mixing bowl
- 4 garlic cloves
- 1½ teaspoons/14 grams baking soda
- 2 teaspoons/12 grams salt
- Pinch of black pepper
- 1 tablespoon/9 grams hot paprika
- 1 teaspoon/6 grams smoked paprika
- 2 pairs of latex gloves
- 1 pound/500 grams ground beef (15–20% fat)
- 1 pound/500 grams ground pork (15–20% fat)
- 1 pound/500 grams ground lamb
- Spatula or wooden spoon
- Cling wrap
- Grill for cooking, preferably an outdoor charcoal one, with supplies
- 2 ceramic plates
- 1 set of grilling tongs

Procedure

Finely chop one of the white onions and add it to the large bowl. Set the other onion aside. Mince the garlic and add it to the bowl. Mix in the baking soda and all the dried spices, stirring well to coat the onion and garlic pieces.

Put on the pair of gloves and on a separate clean/disinfected surface such as a large cutting board or countertop space, thoroughly mix by hand the beef, pork, and lamb, then transfer the solid lump into the mixing bowl. Remove gloves and immediately clean and disinfect the surface where the meat was mixed.

Using a wooden spoon or spatula, mix the meat with the onions, garlic, spices, and baking soda. Stir well. Tear off plastic cling wrap and cover the bowl, then chill it in the refrigerator for a minimum of an hour, but ideally at least three hours. Remove the bowl from the fridge and prepare the outdoor grill for cooking.

Don the second pair of latex gloves. Scoop out a meatball-sized portion of the mixture from the bowl and flatten it into a patty in your hands before shaping it into a little sausage, approximately the length of your middle finger and the width of your thumb. Repeat these steps until all the meat has been fashioned into the ćevapčići shape; place all the newly made sausages onto one of the ceramic plates.

Remove and toss out the gloves. Using your tongs, place as many ćevapi as will fit on your grill's surface. Grill each one's surface for about two minutes, turning them to cook evenly. The meat should brown evenly and show grill marks. Cut in half to ensure it's not too pink in the middle.

Grilled ćevapi should be placed on the unused ceramic plate. Chop the second white onion and serve as a simple side dish with the meat. Ćevapi sandwiches can be easily made by cutting open a slice of store-bought pita bread, or else the meat is paired with a simple piece of bread like a torn-off chunk of pogača or a thinner version known as *lepinja*.

Sarma (Stuffed Pickled Cabbage Leaves)

Another staple food of the western Balkans but even parts of Austria and Hungary (which have large populations of Slavs from the former Yugoslavia), sarma can be tailored to be carnivore-centric or vegan (*posno*), especially during the Lenten fasting season.

A hardcore baba or deda in the *selo* (rural village) harvests their own cabbage heads and then pickles them, a time-consuming endeavor. For modern convenience's sake, I advocate buying jars of pickled cabbage leaves/whole sauerkraut, not shredded. In the United States, grocery stores with Eastern European fare carry these pickled cabbage leaves; I use the Polish brand of Cracovia.

The carnivore version of this dish uses both minced meat (typically, ground beef) and a smoked ham hock. The vegan version can use soy crumbles or just have the rice and shredded carrots, which are already present as part of the filling.

What you'll need

- 1 tablespoon/15 milliliters olive oil
- A large skillet
- Cabbage leaves, about 20
- 2 large white onions, finely chopped
- 2 medium carrots, peeled and minced
- ½ tablespoon/8 grams black pepper
- 1 tablespoon/9 grams salt
- ½ tablespoon/8 grams paprika
- *Meaty version:* ½ pound/300 grams smoked ham hock, cut into small squares
- 2 pounds/1 kilogram ground beef, ground pork, or both; *vegan substitute (optional):* an entire bag of frozen soy crumbles (in the United States, Morningstar, Gardein, and Boca brands work best)
- 1 tablespoon/9 grams Vegeta seasoning
- 1 cup/185 grams cooked white rice (short grain)
- A large stock pot or Dutch oven—not too tall so it fits in your oven
- ⅓ cup/80 milliliters olive oil
- ½ tablespoon/8 grams brown sugar
- 3 bay leaves
- Large ceramic or stoneware plate

Procedure

Using medium heat, add the tablespoon of olive oil to the large skillet and toss in the chopped onions, minced carrots, black pepper, salt, and paprika. Sauté until the onions are browned. If this is the carnivore version with ham hock cubes, mix those in as well. Fry for about 5 minutes before adding the ground meat and then the Vegeta seasoning. If this is the vegan version that uses soy crumbles, now is the time to toss those crumbles in and mix well. Add a little more oil if necessary, but sparingly, as the crumbles will produce their own water. Cook for an additional 10 minutes.

Remove the skillet from heat and add the cup of cooked white rice. Mix thoroughly and set aside. Take the cabbage leaves and rinse them off, one by one, gently in warm water to remove excess brine. If the central stems of any of the leaves are too thick, gently thin them with a knife or even a vegetable peeler to ensure the leaves can be folded over.

Preheat your oven to 350°F/177°C.

On a large plate, splay out a single cabbage leaf. Scoop out a heaping tablespoon of the skillet's contents onto the leaf, then roll the leaf so the meat/soy/rice and carrot mixture is tucked in nicely and the overall piece looks like a plump little pillow. It should not be able to unwrap/come undone. Repeat this process until all of your mixture has been used up. Once each sarma has been folded, place it on the bottom of the stockpot/Dutch oven, on whose bottom is the coating of a third of a cup of oil.

Stack the sarma "pillows" tightly against each other in the stock pot. Once one layer is done, the carnivore version calls for adding the remainder of the smoked meat/ham hock. Then add the next layer of sarma, and so on. If you have any remaining cabbage leaves, add them as a top layer, then add just enough water to cover all the sarma. Add the brown sugar and the bay leaves and gently stir the water; don't damage the sarma.

Transfer the pot on top of your burner and use high heat to get the contents to boil (monitor to add water if necessary). Once it's begun to boil, remove it from the heat. Transfer the pot to the oven and bake for approximately 90 minutes. Sarma is best served hot with a hefty chunk of pogača bread.

Bibliography

Anonymous. *The Tale of Igor's Campaign.* Late 12th century CE. Translated by J. A. V. Haney and Eric Dahl. 1992. https://faculty.washington.edu/dwaugh/rus/texts/igortxt2.htm.

Anonymous. "The Wedding of Sir Gawain and Dame Ragnell." Circa 1450. Accessed November 13, 2024. https://chaucer.fas.harvard.edu/pages/wedding-sir-gawain-and-dame-ragnell.

ArgonNights. Reply to "What Are Some of the Biggest Misconceptions That People Tend to Have About Slavic Paganism?" Reddit, July 14, 2024. https://www.reddit.com/r/Rodnovery/comments/1e3190a/what_are_some_of_the_biggest_misconceptions_that/.

Artisson, Robin. *The Witching Way of the Hollow Hill: The Gramarye of the Folk Who Dwell Below the Mound.* Pendraig Publishing, 2009.

Bandić, Dušan. *Narodna Religija Srba U 100 Pojmova. [Serbian Folk Religious Beliefs as Surveyed Through 100 Concepts.]* Beograd: Nolit, 2004.

Barford, P. M. *The Early Slavs.* Cornell University Press, 2001.

The Bible. King James Version (1611). Accessed November 3, 2024. https://www.kingjamesbibleonline.org/Ephesians-2-1_2-2/.

Bulgakov, Sergius Fr. *The Orthodox Church.* Translated by Lydia Kesich. Saint Vladimir's Seminary Press, 1988.

Bulgarian National Television. "The Bulgarian Tradition of Martenitsa." March 1, 2018. https://bnt.bg/news/the-bulgarian-tradition-of-martenitsa-179851news.html.

Catholic.org. "Saint Vitus." Accessed November 14, 2024. https://www.catholic.org/saints/saint.php?saint_id=140.

Charney, Noah, and Svetlana Slapšak. *The Slavic Myths.* Thames & Hudson, 2023.

Conrad, Joseph. "Female Spirits Among the South Slavs." *Folklorica: Journal of the Slavic, East European, and Eurasian Folklore Association* 5, no. 2 (2000): 27–34.

Conrad, Joseph. "Male Mythological Beings Among the South Slavs." *Folklorica: Journal of the Slavic, East European, and Eurasian Folklore Association* 6, no. 1 (2001): 3–9.

Culture.PL. "The Polish Halloween: All You Need to Know About Dziady." Accessed September 12, 2024. https://culture.pl/en/article/the-polish-halloween-all-you-need-to-know-about-dziady.

Cvetković, Stefan. *Slavic Traditions & Mythology.* Independently published, 2021.

Dashu, Max. "The Old Goddess." *The Secret History of the Witches*, 2000. https://www.suppressedhistories.net/secrethistory/oldgoddess.html.

De La Torre, Miguel A. *Santería: The Beliefs and Rituals of a Growing Religion in America.* William B. Eerdmans Publishing Company, 2004.

Dobrin, Isabel. "Dia de Los Muertos Comes to Life Across the Mexican Diaspora." NPR, November 2, 2017. https://www.npr.org/2017/11/02/561527322/mexicos-celebrated-d-a-de-los-muertos-evolves-in-the-u-s.

Đorđević-Belić, Smiljana. "The Motif of Extinguishing Fire with Grass and Water in One Type of Serbian and South Slavic Chanting." In *Plants and*

Herbs in Traditional Serbian Culture. Edited by Zoja Karanović and Jasmina Dražić. Belgrade: University Library Svetozar Marković, 2016.

Drapelova, Pavla G. "Procopius on the Religion of the Early Slavs: Comparison with Other Barbarians." *Studia Ceranea* 11 (2021): 177–200. https://doi.org/10.18778/2084-140X.11.09.

Drury, Nevill. *Magic and Witchcraft: From Shamanism to the Technopagans.* Thames & Hudson, 2003.

Dvornik, Francis. *The Slavs: Their Early History and Civilization.* American Academy of Arts and Sciences, 1956.

Estés, Clarissa Pinkola. *Women Who Run with the Wolves: Myths and Stories of the Wild Woman Archetype.* Ballantine Books, 1992.

Federal Bureau of Investigation. "Hate Crime in the United States Incident Analysis." Crime Data Explorer, September 23, 2024. https://cde.ucr.cjis.gov/LATEST/webapp/#/pages/explorer/crime/hate-crime.

Foley, John Miles. "Spellbound: The Serbian Tradition of Magical Charms." *The Singer of Tales in Performance.* Edited by John Miles Foley. Indiana University Press, 1995.

Frazer, Sir James. *The Golden Bough.* Macmillan, 1922. https://xtf.lib.virginia.edu/xtf/view?docId=modern_english/uvaGenText/tei/FraGold.xml;chunk.id=d28;toc.depth=1;toc.id=;brand=default;query=Brigit#1.

Gajić, Nenad. Словенска митологија. *[Slovenska Mitologija (Slavic Mythology).]* Beograd: Laguna, 2011.

Gilchrist, Cherry. *Russian Magic: Living Folk Traditions of an Enchanted Landscape.* Quest Books, 2009.

Gill, N. S. "Spirits of the Dead: Who Were Roman Lares, Larvae, Lemures, and Manes?" ThoughtCo., January 17, 2020. Accessed August 9, 2024. https://www.thoughtco.com/lares-larvae-lemures-manes-roman-ghosts-112671.

Gimbutas, Marija. *The Slavs.* Praeger Publishers, 1971.

Hall, Alaric. "Calling the Shots: The Old English Remedy *Gif hors ofscoten sie* and Anglo-Saxon 'Elf-Shot.'" *Neuphilologische Mitteilungen: Bulletin of the Modern Language Society* 106, no. 2 (2005): 195–209. https://www.academia.edu/821500/Calling_the_Shots_The_Old_English_Remedy_Gif_hors_ofscoten_sie_and_Anglo_Saxon_Elf_Shot_?auto=download.

Hance, Jeremy. "Stuff of Fairy Tales: Stepping into Europe's Last Old-Growth Forest." July 9, 2014. https://news.mongabay.com/2014/07/stuff-of-fairy-tales-stepping-into-europes-last-old-growth-forest/.

Hayden, Michael Edison. "Disinfo Covers for White Supremacy After Buffalo Attack." May 17, 2022. https://www.splcenter.org/hatewatch/2022/05/17/disinfo-covers-white-supremacy-after-buffalo-attack.

Helvin, Natasha. *Slavic Witchcraft: Old World Conjuring, Spells & Folklore.* Destiny Books, 2019.

Horne, Roger J. *Folk Witchcraft: A Guide to the Lore, Land, and the Familiar Spirit for the Solitary Practitioner.* Moon Over the Mountain, 2019.

Ivakhiv, Adrian. "The Revival of Ukrainian Native Faith." *Modern Paganism in World Cultures: Comparative Perspectives.* Edited by Michael Strimska. ABC-CLIO Religion in Contemporary Cultures Series. ABC-CLIO, 2005.

Ivanits, Linda J. *Russian Folk Belief.* M. E. Sharpe, 1989.

Johnson, Kenneth. *North Star Road: Shamanism, Witchcraft & the Otherworld Journey.* Llewellyn Publications, 1996.

Johnson, Kenneth. *Slavic Sorcery: Shamanic Journey of Initiation.* Llewellyn Publications, 1998.

Jones, Prudence, and Nigel Pennick. *A History of Pagan Europe.* Routledge, 1995.

Kelden. *The Crooked Path: An Introduction to Traditional Witchcraft.* Llewellyn Publications, 2020.

Kolosova, V. B. "Name—Text—Ritual: The Role of Plant Characteristics in Slavic Folk Medicine." *Folklorica* 10, no. 2 (2005): 44–61. https://journals.ku.edu/folklorica/article/view/3762/3601.

Lecouteux, Claude. *The Return of the Dead: Ghosts, Ancestors, and the Transparent Veil of the Pagan Mind.* Translated by Jon E. Graham. Inner Traditions, 1996.

Marjanić, Suzana. "Dragon and Hero or How to Kill a Dragon—On the Example of the Legends of Međimurje About the Grabancijaš and the Dragon." *Studia Mythologica Slavica* 13 (2010): 127–150. http://sms.zrc-sazu.si/pdf/13/SMS_13_09_Marjanic.pdf.

Matthews, John. *The Quest for the Green Man.* Quest Books/Theosophical Publishing House, 2001.

Matthews, John. *The Winter Solstice: The Sacred Traditions of Christmas.* Quest Books/Theosophical Publishing House, 2001.

Mickaharić, Draja. *Spiritual Cleansing: A Handbook of Psychic Protection.* Weiser Books, 1982.

Mickaharić, Draja. *A Century of Spells.* Weiser Books, 1988.

Mountain, Perun. *Discovering Rodnovery: A Beginner's Guide to Slavic Native Faith.* Perun Mountain, 2023.

Pacyga, Dominic A. "Slavic Chicago." December 1, 2011. https://www.historians.org/perspectives-article/slavic-chicago/.

Pamita, Madame. *Baba Yaga's Book of Witchcraft: Slavic Magic from the Witch of the Woods.* Llewellyn Publications, 2022.

Paxson, Diana. *Taking Up the Runes: A Complete Guide to Using the Runes in Spells, Rituals, Divination, and Magic.* Weiser Books, 2005.

Penczak, Christopher. *Feast of the Morrighan: A Grimoire for the Dark Lady of the Emerald Isle.* Copper Cauldron Publishing, 2012.

Petrović, Sonja. "Charmers on the Folk Practice of Charming in Serbia." *Incantatio: An International Journal on Charms, Charmers and Charming* 7 (2018): 131–159. https://ojs.folklore.ee/incantatio/issue/view/issue7/7.

Podunavski, Radomir. *Tradicionalno Balkansko Veštičarstvo.* Beograd: Esotheria, 2007.

Radovanović K., N. Gavarić, M. Aćimović. "Anti-Inflammatory Properties of Plants from Serbian Traditional Medicine." *Life* (Basel, Switzerland) 13, no. 874 (2023): 1–17. https://doi.org/10.3390/life13040874.

Ravenna, Morpheus. *The Magic of the Otherworld: Modern Sorcery from the Wellspring of Celtic Traditions.* Llewellyn Publications, 2023.

RavenWolf, Silver. *Halloween.* Llewellyn Publications, 1999.

Republic of Serbia, Ministry of Environment and Spatial Planning. "Fourth National Report on the United Nations Convention on Biological Diversity." 2010. https://www.cbd.int/doc/world/rs/rs-nr-04-en.pdf.

Ristić, Radomir. *Balkan Traditional Witchcraft.* Translated by Michael C. Carter, Jr. Pendraig Publishing, 2009.

Ristić, Radomir. *Witchcraft and Sorcery of the Balkans.* Three Hands Press, 2015.

Robertson, Lawrence D. *Juno Covella: Perpetual Calendar of the Fellowship of Isis.* 1999. http://www.fellowshipofisis.com/jc/jcmar.pdf.

Ryan, W. F. *The Bathhouse at Midnight: An Historical Survey of Magic and Divination in Russia.* Sutton Publishing, 1999.

Rybakov, Boris Aleksandrovich. "Pagan Rites and Celebrations of the 11th–13th Centuries." *Paganism of Ancient Rus': Part III, Dual Faith: 11th–13th Centuries.* https://bibliotekar.ru/rusYazRusi/25.htm.

Saint Demetrios Greek Orthodox Church (Camarillo, CA). "Saint Demetrios Feast Day Celebration." Accessed September 12, 2024. https://www.saintdem.org/events/st-demetrios-feast-day-celebration.

Saskatchewan Flax Development Commission. "Early European Flax History." Accessed July 16, 2024. https://www.saskflax.com/industry/history.php.

Saveza Hrvatski Rodnovjeraca. [The Federation of Croatian Rodnovers.] "Hrvatsko Rodnovjerje." ["Croatian Rodnovery."] Accessed October 27, 2024. https://rodnovjerje.com.hr/index.php/hrvatsko-rodnovjerje/.

Šavli, Jožko. "Triglav and Svetovit." *Carantha—History of Slovenia.* August 3, 2010. http://www.carantha.net/the_vends.

Serith, Ceisiwr. *A Book of Pagan Prayer.* Weiser Books, 2002.

Slowianska Polonia. "Poles Promoting Slavic Culture." June 11, 2024. https://www.facebook.com/profile.php?id=100069317501511.

Sobolewski, Adrian. "Roots Revival: How Slavic Native Faith Returned to Poland." Culture.PL Series: Spirituality. Accessed October 21, 2024. https://culture.pl/en/article/roots-revival-how-slavic-faith-returned-to-poland.

Souli, Sarah. "Greece's Old Gods Are Ready for Your Sacrifice." *The Outline,* January 4, 2018. Accessed October 27, 2024. https://theoutline.com/post/2843/hellenism-legalized-greece.

Stefanović, Vladimir. "Serbian Christmas Traditions." Accessed November 17, 2024. https://www.crkvenikalendar.com/tradicija/bozic_en.php.

Stevanovič Z. D., S. Vrbničanin, and R. Jevdjovič. "Weeding of Cultivated Chamomile in Serbia." *Acta Horticulturae* 749, no. 15 (2007): 149–155. https://doi.org/10.17660/ActaHortic.2007.749.15.

Strimska, Michael. "Modern Paganism in World Cultures: Comparative Perspectives." *Modern Paganism in World Cultures: Comparative Perspectives.* Edited by Michael Strimska. ABC-CLIO Religion in Contemporary Cultures Series. ABC-CLIO, 2005.

Svarica. *"Postavlanje Kipa Perunu (Udruga Perunova Svetinja)."* July 2, 2013. https://www.youtube.com/watch?v=B4PthWGm8MI.

Vocabulary.com. "Religion." Accessed November 3, 2024. https://www.vocabulary.com/dictionary/religion.

Volosovo Gorod. "Volosovo Gorod." Accessed November 3, 2024. https://volosovo-gorod.ru/.

Vukov, Dragana, et al. "Habitat and Plant Species Diversity Along the River Danube in Serbia. International Association for Danube Research." Conference in Vienna held September 4–8, 2006, entitled Interfacing the Past and the Future of Ecology and Water Management in a Large European River.

Warner, Elizabeth. *Russian Myths.* British Museum Press, 2002.

Zaroff, Roman. "Measurement of Time by the Ancient Slavs." *Studia Mythologica Slavica* 19 (2016): 9–39.

Zaroff, Roman. "Organised Pagan Cult in Kievan Rus': The Invention of Foreign Elite or Evolution of Local Tradition?" 1995. http://www.ibiblio.org/sergei/Zaroff.

Zhao, Ruby. "Qing Ming 2025." China Highlights, April 24, 2024. https://www.chinahighlights.com/festivals/qingming-festival.htm.

Znayenko, Myroslava T. "On the Concept of Chernobog and Bielobog in Slavic Mythology." *Acta Slavic Iaponica 2* (1994): 177–185. https://eprints.lib.hokudai.ac.jp/dspace/bitstream/2115/8061/1/KJ00000034018.pdf.

Index

© Todd Fedler—Fedler Studio

About the Author

Anna Urošević Applegate is a Chicago native, born and raised, and first-generation Serbian American who was raised in the Dual-Faith Tradition/Serbian folk Orthodox Christianity. She was taught to believe in the Spirit World and the beneficent intervention of her ancestors in daily life from a very early age. A modern Polytheist, she tends to roll out a welcome mat to chthonic deities in particular, and Veles (Велес) is her most beloved of her ancestral gods.

Grateful to be raised in a city with such a robust Pagan scene, Anna became active in the Chicago Fellowship of Isis (FOI) community in 2002 and received her legal ordination as a Priestess in 2012. A certified Death Midwife and experienced spirit worker, Anna is the founder of the FOI-chartered *Iseum of the Rekhet Akhu*, a teaching temple whose mission is to highlight the interrelatedness of the communities of the living and the dead and to cultivate transfigured spirits (*Akhu*) within the living through the Egyptian tradition of temple ritual magic. Anna is also an initiate in the West African traditional religion of Ifá.

Anna holds an M.A. in English from Loyola University Chicago and has formerly taught literature and writing courses at the undergraduate level. A dedicated *Muertista* since 2013, Anna is the author of the devotional prayer book *In Praise of the Lady of Power: An English-Language Booklet of Prayers Dedicated to La Santa Muerte* (Nemetona Press, 2024). She enjoys traveling about the country and presenting workshops and rituals at various Pagan festivals. She shares her home with two goofy rescue dogs, six slinky rescue cats, and her beautiful sunset albino corn snake, Brimo, who serves as the Serbian *čuvar kuća*, or "watcher of the house." Anna is passionate about fostering inclusive Rodnovery. Visit her website at CircleofRodu.com to learn more.

To Write to the Author

If you wish to contact the author or would like more information about this book, please write to the author in care of Llewellyn Worldwide Ltd. and we will forward your request. Both the author and the publisher appreciate hearing from you and learning of your enjoyment of this book and how it has helped you. Llewellyn Worldwide Ltd. cannot guarantee that every letter written to the author can be answered, but all will be forwarded. Please write to:

Anna Urošević Applegate
℅ Llewellyn Worldwide
2143 Wooddale Drive
Woodbury, MN 55125-2989

Please enclose a self-addressed stamped envelope for reply, or $1.00 to cover costs. If outside the U.S.A., enclose an international postal reply coupon.

Many of Llewellyn's authors have websites with additional information and resources. For more information, please visit our website at https://www.llewellyn.com.